Although John Ruskin is widely considered to have produced some of the greatest prose in English, there has been no extended study of how he learned to write or of the language with which he represents his learning. This book begins with the prodigiously inventive child who looks ahead to what he will achieve, and ends with the adult who looks to his past for proof that he has never been inventive. Far from a simple about-face, Ruskin's self-denial is a culmination and extension of the art that he mastered in youth, and it is one of the most remarkable acts of self-representation in all of Victorian prose. Drawing on Ruskin's own sources as well as on recent directions in critical theory, Professor Emerson reveals the effects of early literary, familial, sexual, and social experiences on the shaping of a major writer's identity.

RUSKIN: THE GENESIS OF INVENTION

RUSKIN

THE GENESIS
OF INVENTION

SHEILA EMERSON

CAMBRIDGE
UNIVERSITY PRESS

Published by the Press Syndicate of the University of Cambridge
The Pitt Building, Trumpington Street, Cambridge CB2 1RP
40 West 20th Street, New York, NY 10011-4211, USA
10 Stamford Road, Oakleigh, Melbourne 3166, Australia

First published 1993

Printed in Great Britain at the University Press, Cambridge

A catalogue record for this book is available from the British Library

Library of Congress cataloguing in publication data
Emerson, Sheila.
Ruskin : the genesis of invention / Sheila Emerson.
p.   cm.
Includes bibliographical references and index.
ISBN 0-521-41807-0
1. Ruskin, John, 1819–1900 – Criticism and interpretation.
I. Title
PR5264.E46   1993
828'.809 – dc20   92-45708 CIP

ISBN 0 521 41807 0 hardback

FOR

SASHA PARNESS

CONTENTS

List of Illustrations   xi
Acknowledgments   xiii

INTRODUCTION   1

PART ONE · LOOKING AHEAD   17

1   Interrelations (1823–29)   19
2   Laws of Motion (1829–33)   35
3   Disciplines (1833–35)   68
4   Leading Lines (1830–36)   103

PART TWO · LOOKING BACK   129

5   Separations (1829–49)   133
6   Unlawful Motions (1843–80)   187
7   The Gender of Invention (1871–84)   207
8   The Invention of Genesis (1885–89)   229

Notes   239
Index   265

ILLUSTRATIONS

Frontispiece

James Northcote, *John Ruskin*, 1822. Oil on canvas. On permanent loan at Brantwood. (Reproduced by courtesy of the National Portrait Gallery, London.)

T. A. and J. Green, *John Ruskin*, c. 1885. Platinum print. (Reproduced by courtesy of the National Portrait Gallery, London.)

Between pages 128 *and* 129

1   John Ruskin, *harrys new road*, 1826–27 (*Works*, 35.54)
2   John Ruskin, *harrys river*, 1826–27, in "Harry and Lucy, Poems, etc." (The Beinecke Rare Book and Manuscript Library, Yale University)
3   John Ruskin, *My First tree! from nature*, 1831 (The Education Trust Ltd., The Ruskin Galleries, Bembridge School, Isle of Wight)
4   John Ruskin, "The Puppet Show, or Amusing Characters for Children," 1828–29 (autograph manuscript, The Pierpont Morgan Library, New York , MA 3451)
5   John Ruskin, letter to his father, 31 December 1828 (*Works*, 2.facing 264)
6   John Ruskin, title page of *Iteriad; or Three Weeks Among the Lakes*, 1831 (The Beinecke Rare Book and Manuscript Library, Yale University)
7   John Ruskin, finis page of *Iteriad; or Three Weeks Among the Lakes*, 1832 (The Beinecke Rare Book and Manuscript Library, Yale University)

8 Sir Charles Lyell, *Principles of Geology*, 1830–33, 3 vols., 3.78–79 (The British Library)

9 Sir Charles Lyell, *Principles of Geology*, 1830–33, 3 vols., 3.80–81 (The British Library)

10 Sir Charles Lyell, *Principles of Geology*, 1830–33, 3 vols., 3.90–91 (The British Library)

11 John Ruskin, *Early Geology*, 1830s (The Princeton University Libraries)

12 John Ruskin, *Early Geology*, 1830s (The Princeton University Libraries)

13 John Ruskin, *Traceries from Caen, Bayeux, Rouen, and Beauvais*, 1849 (*Works*, 8.facing 88)

14 Lily Severn's "picture writing," 1884 (*Works*, 29.facing 508)

Pages from Ruskin's *Works* were photographed by the British Library.

ACKNOWLEDGMENTS

It is a pleasure to think of the help I have received over the years. The music of Kyung Wha Chung has been a changeful and sustained inspiration. William Keach has given me the inestimable gift of his love and understanding. The profundity and variety of George Levine have been an education to me. In differently powerful ways, Mary Trump and Margaret Homans have altered my sense of the past and the future.

I first encountered Ruskin in the shape of The Genius of John Ruskin. By the happiest of chances many years later, I encountered in person the imaginative perception which has made the work of John Rosenberg so important to so many people; I am deeply grateful for his criticism of my manuscript. Barry Qualls has been protean in his generosity, especially in the generosity with which he has concealed how very much he has done. The support of Kevin Taylor and Andrew Brown of Cambridge University Press has been an encouragement all along the way. For their kindness, their thoughtfulness and advice, I am also indebted to Elizabeth Ammons, Lee Edelman, Carol Flynn, Kathi Inman, Anne Janowitz, John Kucich, George Landow, Peggy Phelan, Christopher Ricks, Paul Sawyer, Elaine Showalter, and Rob Slapikoff. My parents gave me the thirty-nine volumes of Cook and Wedderburn. Their love and that of my sisters has brought me joy in the midst of even my grimmest compositions since high school.

This book owes most to Sasha Parness. She made me want to write it; she made me think of what to write now.

A Tufts University Mellon Grant enabled me to work on this book in the spring of 1988; my thanks to the Committee on Faculty Research Awards for their timely support. I am grateful for permission to quote and reproduce materials in the collections of the Beinecke Rare Book and Manuscript Library, Yale University; the British Library; The Education Trust Ltd., The Ruskin Galleries, Bembridge School, Isle of Wight; the National Portrait Gallery, London; The Pierpont Morgan Library, New York; Princeton University Libraries. James Dearden of The Ruskin Galleries has been particularly helpful. All of Chapter 1 and part of Chapter 2 appeared in a somewhat different form in *Modern Critical Views: John Ruskin* (1986). A number of passages in Part Two were differently arranged in *Chaos and Order: Complex Dynamics in Literature and Science*, ed. N. Katherine Hayles (1991); I am grateful to the University of Chicago Press for permission to reprint.

INTRODUCTION

This book began with a desire to hold in one place a series of recollections about becoming an artist and a series of childhood works in which art itself begins. My impulse to bring these things together did not start with my readings of Ruskin, but was quickened by his eagerness to provoke it. To my questions about the relationship between an artist's reminiscences and juvenilia, or about what this relationship in one artist's life has to say about another's, the well-known works of Ruskin answered with a profusion of evidence that age and youth are always consonant in the greatest careers, and that such consonance is always exemplary. Yet as I tried to move back and forth between Ruskin's conclusions and his own first writings, I was held up by language that registers drastic differences between them. These differences have become the pivot on which my argument turns. It is they, more than any claims of continuity, that have brought me to the conviction that in precise and distinctive ways, Ruskin learned what he later taught – whether or not about himself, whether or not about art – from how he learned to write.

What makes this book unlike others about Ruskin is its concentration not only on how he learned to write but more specifically on the language with which he represents his learning. The course of my chapters is in this sense chronological, cleaving not necessarily to the sequence of his training or to the order in which signal emphases first appeared in his prose, but to the order in which they gained the prominence of self-conscious predilections. The result is a narrative each of whose two parts moves from works that appeared early in Ruskin's life to those that came later. But in the first part my emphasis is on Ruskin's beginnings as a writer; the second part ranges more equally over early, middle, and later works, then concentrates attention near and at the end of Ruskin's career. The first part starts with the prodigiously inventive child who looks ahead to what he will achieve; the second part ends with the adult who looks to his past for proof that he is not and has never been inventive. Far from being a simple about-face, Ruskin's reinvention of his genesis is a culmination and extension of the art that he mastered in youth. His very attempts to prove that his prose is not creative – that it is instead the most uninventively truthful of criticisms – are among the most remarkable acts of creation in all of Victorian prose. And they are as vital to the history of discriminations between critical and creative writing in the twentieth century as they were in the nineteenth.[1]

It is a premise of this book that the forces which made Ruskin a critic have been valuably attended to by others, as have the social and cultural conditions which made it complicated for any Victorian writer of non-fiction to identify him or herself as an artist. In considering the complexities of Ruskin's identity I have given most space to his early writing, because it has not received the attention it deserves for its own merits, or for what it discloses about the formation of prose that is as varied and powerful as any in English. And this formation itself reveals the extent to which it was the very experience of writing which shaped and was the basis of the works by which Ruskin is known. His first prose and poetry provide at least as much information about this experience as survives in the juvenilia of any other nineteenth-century writer – or possibly of anyone in any period – who grew up to write as much about children as Ruskin did. What therefore needs stressing is not only the relationship between Ruskin's accounts of the formation of artists and the accounts that he left of his own, but also the relationship between both of them and what he actually produced as a boy. These cross-references are predictably and unpredictably complicated by the fact that he never outgrew the influence of the ways in which things had mattered to him as a child. The subtlety and self-consciousness of this influence are easily lost in apothegms isolated from his young adulthood. If it is "a fact more universally acknowledged than enforced or acted upon, that all great painters . . . have been great only in their rendering of what they had seen and felt from early childhood" (3.229),[2] that may be because the spectator still imagines too collective or generic a childhood in Modern Painters I, or returns to some "fact . . . universally acknowledged" rather than to the child's painting of it. But the search for Ruskin's beginnings brings us face to face with renderings of how he learned to render what he saw and felt as a child. Two large volumes in the Library Edition, several more published later – plus boxes of loose and bound sheets of manuscripts at The Ruskin Galleries, Yale, Princeton, The Morgan Library and elsewhere – are extraordinary resources for anyone interested in the acquisition of linguistic skills in the early nineteenth century, and in the development of a child prodigy into an adult with a public career. Ruskin's letters, diaries, travelogues, poems, plays, and stories tend to corroborate his claims that he was schooled by Rousseau, William Wordsworth, Scott, Byron, and Percy Shelley; they much more pointedly show why and how he recreated that schooling for others. And it is Ruskin's early works that make most intelligible what will be his own enormously influential ideas about childhood, education, and artistic invention.

It is partly because these ideas appear in works which are familiar that the second part of the book is shorter than the first. I have been able to move more quickly where others have taken their time. But the differences in length are more directly a consequence of my determination to follow a wide-ranging and detailed reading of his early writing with a precise concentration on salient emphases that emerge. Of course it would have been impossible to keep these emphases in focus had I attempted to write about his later works with anything like the continuous attention I give to the dozens of pieces of Ruskin's juvenilia. But the attempt was unnecessary in any case. For a continuous reading of his later works showed me that it is just where the adult Ruskin reflects on elements of the writing process, or on his early experiments with it, that the emphases I pursued were most tellingly involved. It is not that all other passages are immaterial; on the contrary, they are the material out of which Ruskin makes the designs of his writing about writing. It is this interdependency that obviates the risk of losing Ruskin's designs in the details on which I focus in much of this book, or his details in the designs on which I focus in the rest. Design is the composition of details.

Behind my changes in focus are principles – that two objects at different distances cannot be seen distinctly at the same time; that the closest look can no more render everything visible than the longest range can rub traces of anything out; that abstraction is not separation from matter but a seizing upon the essential elements of it – which readers will recognize as Ruskin's. I hope to make them recognize two things in addition. First, that Ruskin's aesthetic principles, which have often been connected to the style of his most familiar works, were developed partly in response to his earliest experiments in writing. And second, that the application of his principles to his prose contradicts his pronouncements as a man but not his achievements as a child.

. . .

Ruskin's intricate response to the child in himself is not typical of nineteenth-century writing about childhood. This is especially clear where he sounds most indebted to Wordsworth. When Ruskin undertakes to defend, against the authority of Sir Joshua Reynolds, the scrupulous rendering of specific detail in landscape painting, he declares that "There is a singular sense in which the child may peculiarly be said to be father of the man." In this 1844 adaptation, Wordsworth's language is a patrimony which allows Ruskin to grant the authority of patrilineal law to the artist's inheritance of his own past self. Ruskin's detailing of the singularity and peculiarity of this process opens up other differences from Wordsworth as well. First of all, Ruskin's child is not only the father of the artist but is already the artist: "the perfect child" is the beginning of art. He is simultaneously the "infancy" of criticism. Then the "absolute beginner in art" and the "Infants in judgment" of it yield to a "middle age" which loses hold of "a truth . . . which the grasp of manhood cannot retain." Only in "utmost age" will the man regain the "light and careless stroke, which in many points will far more resemble that of his childhood than of his middle age." For

the truth bears so much semblance of error, the last stage of the journey to the first, that every feeling which guides to it is checked in its origin. The rapid and powerful artist necessarily looks with such contempt on those who see minutiae of detail *rather* than grandeur of impression, that it is almost impossible for him to conceive of the great last step in art by which both become compatible.   (3.30–32)

Although writing anonymously, trying to sound older than he is, the twenty-four-year-old Ruskin could no more be mistaken for a man at the end of his career than for a precocious child. The middle years which he occupies are cut out from under him by his argument, whereas the thirty-two-year-old Wordsworth had affirmed his present (as well as his future) by connecting it to his past. The authority that

Ruskin borrows from "My Heart Leaps Up" is ultimately used to authorize the disowning of his art: writing with prodigious confidence in his mastery, Ruskin denies the master who has just emerged from youth.

Ruskin both exerts and survives this self-denial by redrawing chronological lines. There is a key to his new arrangement in an unpublished passage from the manuscript of *Praeterita*, in which he vilifies a middle period of his own history as a visual artist – and locates it between the ages of seventeen and twenty or twenty-one (35.621–27). When one turns from his scorn for his drawings of these years to the writings he completed during the same period of benighted "conventionalism," one finds an essay that is surely in his mind when he denigrates the young man of whom Wordsworth's child is the father. The context of both pieces is a celebration of the mature works of Turner. In "A Reply to 'Blackwood's' Criticism of Turner," written when he was seventeen, Ruskin has already fixed on the artist in whom "the means employed appear more astonishingly inadequate to the effect produced than in any other master" (3.637), and anticipated what the later passage will define as the single distinction between the work of childhood and utmost age: that "the consummate effect" is "wrought out by . . . apparently inadequate means" (3.31). But in the 1836 essay, Turner's consummate knowledge of landscape is put into parentheses, to leave more space for his painting "from nature, and pretty far from it, too": "he rushes through the aetherial dominions of the world of his own mind," and "changes and combines" what he finds there into images that are seen nowhere else (3.637–39). Ruskin does not quote himself seven years later, when such Shelleyan sentiments have already become alarming to him. But it is partly the memory of his earlier devotion to reflexivity and self-projection which moves him to ridicule those who believe that things are "'convertible by the mind into what they are *not*,'" and those who admire "combinations whose highest praise is that they are impossible" (3.52,25). What Ruskin is rejecting is his own young manhood.

As we will see in detail later on, this rejection includes not only his romantic reflexivity but also the sexual scenario that went along with it. In the earlier of the pieces I have been comparing, "Maga" (as *Blackwood's Magazine* was nicknamed) is figured as a female who has grievously surrendered "the magic ring of her authority" to a male reviewer who violates her "maiden[hood]" when he impugns the virgins of the painter Murillo (3.635–36). But Ruskin's beloved Turner is proof against the defiled and the defiler – in some moments eclipsing them with a self-generated light, in others shining like a moon which will never "bate of her brightness, or aberrate from the majesty of her path" (3.640). Of course Turner is still being figured as a beloved woman long after both this writing and *Modern Painters* I. In *Fors Clavigera*, for example, Ruskin says he relates to Turner as a child does to its "father or mother" (29.539). In 1852, trying to overcome his father's reluctance to spend very large sums of money, Ruskin sends him a letter whose language implies that his urgency to possess Turner's pictures is sexual, and that it competes with his feelings for his father.

But do you count for nothing the times out of time you see me looking at them morning and evening, and when I take them up to sleep with? I have fifty pounds' worth of pleasure out of every picture in my possession *every week* that I have it. . . . if I should outlive you, the pictures will be with me wherever I am.

(36.134)

As is suggested by these passages written before and after, the competitive and homoerotic dimension of Ruskin's relations to artistic fathering are more fully suppressed when he is

7

twenty-four, and bent on subordinating the "middle age" of artists to their "manly, broad" and pious achievements (3.32).

What is most remarkable about Ruskin's suppressions and evasions and denials is their preserving so much of his history intact: his very standoffishness from himself is the bearer of intimate communications. In fact nearly all of his expressions of self-alienation are eventually continuous with self-affirmation. The two come closest on those many occasions when he is introducing or annotating his earlier work. To take the nearest example to hand, his 1844 quotation of Wordsworth's line about father and child appears in writing that is literally a reassertion of himself, the preface to the second edition of *Modern Painters* I. He was particularly provoked to write this preface by an attack on the first edition of his book in *Blackwood's Magazine*. In private, his animus is suggestively competitive and phallic: "Put my rod nicely in pickle for *Blackwood*," Ruskin remarks in his diary while working up his rejoinder.[3] As he rightly guessed, his anonymous adversary was the very man whose previous attack on Turner had provoked his 1836 "Reply to 'Blackwood's' Criticism of Turner" – which was not only the beginning of *Modern Painters*, as his editors point out (3.xviii), but also a record of literary and sexual ambitions during the years that came before. So his 1844 preface is a reading not only of the source of *Modern Painters* but also of its fathering – and mothering. It is a reading that registers, even as it erases, the emotional and physical contests behind inherited images of parenting.

Nineteenth-century pieties about the ties between children and adults, or about their sad severance through time, are revised by the passage of experience from the past into Ruskin's present text. Not that he never makes use of clichés:

in fact he is so far from concealing the currency of his remarks that he repeatedly reminds his readers that the importance of childhood has been (to use a phrase I have already quoted) "universally acknowledged." Under cover of this acknowledgment, Ruskin is able to retain the currency while adjusting its value. So the veil of familiarity may purposively cling to his claims that "the whole difference between a man of genius and other men, it has been said a thousand times, and most truly, is that the first remains in great part a child" (11.66) – or that experience and education and industrialization and urbanity all make the survival of genius unlikely. But if we push past Ruskin's resistance and look closely at what lies behind the histories he has written of artists, including himself, we face an unfamiliarly sharp image of what it is in children's beginnings that makes for their ending as artists. Or not ending as artists. For Ruskin lays out the stages of an artist's development and of the progress of art, only to declare himself powerless before the unutterableness and unteachableness of what they have achieved: the glories and the dangers of artistic self-expression.

How are we to cross the breach between these assertions of inadequacy and his own prodigious past? What Ruskin says is that a man's earliest and latest opinions and works of art will "coincide, though on different grounds" (3.31). Coincidence comes only through difference. Here in the preface to the second edition of Modern Painters I, Ruskin makes his case by pointing to the different stages in the artist's representation of landscape. Forty-two years later, in Praeterita, it is discontinuities in the landscape itself that make visible the continuity between youth and age:

But so stubborn and chemically inalterable the laws of the prescription were, that now, looking back from 1886 to that brook shore of 1837, whence I could see the whole of my youth, I find myself in nothing whatsoever *changed*. Some of me is dead, more of me stronger. I have learned a few things, forgotten many; in the total of me, I am but the same youth, disappointed and rheumatic.

(35.220)

"Different grounds" become the grounds of his recognition of the future of his past. Things he has forgotten are subordinated by his syntax, but without having learned what to forget, he would not see that he is "in nothing whatsoever *changed*": the middle ground must drop out if extremities are to coincide.

Ruskin's certainty about what to subordinate lies behind his confidence in putting disparate materials together, whether in describing his own life or the history of art. Invention, he implies, has nothing to do with it. As he claims in the appendix to *Modern Painters* IV, a properly "Logical Education" would free *any* English youth from "the most pitiable and practically hurtful weakness[ ] of the modern English mind, its usual inability to grasp the connection between any two ideas which have elements of opposition in them, as well as of connection" (6.482). Yet to pursue the relationship among his ideas is to recover what he is silent about when he looks back on his own development: an art that makes connections on the site of opposition.

.   .   .

If the unevenness of Ruskin's "grounds" forces his reader across the lines that ordinarily delimit chronology and formal disciplines such as verse and prose, it also allows for a vista on the development of critical methodology itself. What becomes visible is that the very means of reading Ruskin as an artist lead into the argument about how he reads himself. The method partakes of and subsumes the material.

Consider, from this point of view, the method of reading back and forth between Ruskin's reminiscences and his juvenilia. The discriminations Ruskin provokes between actual beginnings and their retrospective construction by adults, including ourselves, are valuable in the study of many nineteenth-century writers, for their growing interest in early life begot multitudes of fictional children – in autobiographies as well as in poetry and novels – who were really adults in disguise.[4] Ruskin's work enormously complicates what we can see not only in contrasts between past and future but also in temporal leaps within childhood itself. As a seven-year-old, he was already representing time as a figure of speech which he could approach or back off from at will.[5] Ruskin's writing is evidence of just how early a child can realize that he is older than he was when he began a poem or a letter, and that he is younger than he sounds. He could readily evoke the future and the past in a single performance, like many another child, though he was quicker to realize that the younger he appeared to be, the more marvellous it would seem that he performed like an adult. His father's delight in his precocity spurred Ruskin to impersonate not only his elders but also boyhood itself – trumping it up and then peering at it sagely, as if from afar.[6] Once initiated in this way, the imbalance between his age and his verbal accomplishment never ceased to be an issue. When he was in his teens and eager to make his mark in print, he disguised his youth with a pseudonym. In his forties and fifties, he displayed a precocious old age. Later on, he gave readers cause to find him childish – or as childlike as the geniuses he celebrated in The Stones of Venice, who see "with the large eyes of children" (11.66).

Without a close look at the child who was already anticipatory and nostalgic, prospective and retrospective, it might seem easy to nestle the adult into place after Wordsworth and before Proust, who resemble him only from a distance. Although the three of them – and many others in between – made subjects of the reading that shaped their youth, no one drew as much attention as Ruskin to the rereading of his own writing, and to writing as a rereading of past writing. Among the precocious children who grew up to be famous as writers during the nineteenth century (including Tennyson, Mill, Elizabeth Barrett and Robert Browning), Ruskin stands out for the intensity and publicity of his rereading of himself. His reconsiderations are enacted in every genre and for every sort of audience – from the privacy of diary entries collating a given day with its anniversaries before and after, to publications in which he transcribes those entries for anyone who cares to read them. When, in *Modern Painters* III, he draws on the development of his own "landscape feeling" to define nineteenth-century attitudes towards nature, it is clear from his references to places that were subjects of his childhood poems that to describe the characteristic "movements of his own mind" is to recall a boy (quite unlike the one Wordsworth remembers in *The Prelude*) who was also self-consciously regarding those movements and representing them in language (5.365). That the language and movements were sometimes prompted by other peoples' (here, for example, Wordsworth's) only adds another layer to the history of his reading.

This interleaving is of course most apparent in Ruskin's book about his own genesis. A great deal has been made of Ruskin's deviations from the facts in *Praeterita*, and of his avoiding the family letters that he had in his possession; what must be more impressive to anyone who reads his childhood writing is how significantly the writing in *Praeterita* depends on his rereading of himself. Yet his method has implications which emerge when he is not an old and self-denying autobiographer, but the middle-aged biographer of other seers and artists, and of the physical world that they see and depict. There is a particularly telling passage in *Modern Painters* IV:

But, the longer I live, the more ground I see to hold in high honour
a certain sort of childishness or innocent susceptibility. Generally
speaking, I find that when we first look at a subject, we get a
glimpse of some of the greatest truths about it: as we look longer,
our vanity, and false reasoning, and half-knowledge, lead us into
various wrong opinions; but as we look longer still, we gradually
return to our first impressions, only with a full understanding of
their mystical and innermost reasons; and of much beyond and
beside them, not then known to us, now added (partly as a
foundation, partly as a corollary) to what at first we felt or saw.

(6.66)

To move back and forth among Ruskin's writings is to see
how a beginning can eventually lead not only to a corollary
but also to the discovery of its own foundation.

That a "foundation" may be "added" long after the
"beginning" it underlies is an idea which is further realized
in the process of following Ruskin back and forth across
generic lines. As with his chronological leaps, this process
expands our thinking about other writers too, for the
incorporation within single works, and within his oeuvre as a
whole, of aesthetic and scientific and political writing – of
poems, letters, diaries, and newspaper reports; of dreams and
recipes and descriptions of the weather – is (in part) an
expression of attitudes which rehearse and extend the
nineteenth-century debate about connections among different kinds of language. Given my own emphases, the most
important of these debates is the one which defines prose in
relation to poetry. The fact that he wrote a great deal of poetry
in his youth has mattered to readers (if at all) mainly as the
background to his giving it up, and putting what he had given
to and learned from it into the analysis of art created by
others. But the persistence of poetry in his prose might be
differently traced – not in one direction but in several.
Ruskin's 1836 "Essay on Literature" (written two months

after his "Reply to 'Blackwood's' Criticism of Turner") is conventionally romantic in its claims that poetry is the most inspiring verbal form, and that misery is the source of the greatest achievements within it. The "Essay" is also full of verbal gestures which imitate the writers on whom his views are based: hence his sniping at female (and unvirile male) readers as a shortcut to establishing his masculine authority; hence his enactments of reflexive ideology in figures of speech, and his association of writing with physical desire. His determinedly poetic language, with its inscription of his rivalry with other writers and of his love for Adèle Domecq, would certainly have been disqualified by Ruskin twenty years later, when, in Modern Painters III, he defined poetry as the employment of "expression" – whether in painting or writing – "for the noblest purposes" (5.31). Poetry, he concludes, is "the suggestion, by the imagination, of noble grounds for the noble emotions" (5.28).

Unlike Wordsworth, for whom the kind of emotion changes during the poetic process but not the grounds of it, Ruskin implies that the imagination may retrospectively supply an appropriately "noble" groundwork for emotions which came first. His formulation is revised and reinforced – "suggestion" becomes "arrangement," "grounds" become "motive" – in Ruskin's recollection of it in Praeterita, which may itself have been spurred by his recollection of visiting Vevay and Chillon, scenes permanently identified with the Byronic poetry he imitated in 1836 (35.483). The autobiography enlists his failure as a poet in its campaign to render him a failure in other things as well. But if we yield to his attacks and overlook his early poetry, we cannot see precisely what it was about his beginnings that he wanted to exclude, and – more importantly – we lose an opportunity to see him lay the ground for such exclusions in the argument that the past may be retrospectively rearranged. Reading across genres suggests that the differences of Ruskin with himself are obscured when poetry and prose are mistaken for the critically "different grounds" which separate his past from his future (3.31). Even in the 1836 "Essay," Ruskin was already celebrating "poetical prose," and quoting Bulwer in support of his own view that this hybrid is more capable than poetry of flowing beyond the "'hackneyed,'" "'common problems of human nature,'" and into the "'nice and philosophising corollaries which may be drawn from them'" (2.371–72). These "corollaries," as Ruskin would later say, might well be "added" later (6.66).

In order to follow Ruskin in his passages across time and genres, it is necessary to rely on a range of critical methods, as he did himself. My interest in his art has led me to begin with textual analysis, and to let that direct me (in the book's second part) towards biographical and social contexts whose effects are already perceptible in his language. At the same time, my findings are influenced by recent perspectives in linguistic and psychoanalytic and feminist criticism, as well as by paradigms derived from the new science of chaos. The bearing of these methodologies on the reading of Ruskin is not one-sided: his writing illuminates their development and implications, as well as the reverse. What it illuminates above all is how methods come together, and how much may be concealed as well as revealed in their interactions. In this context especially, it is worth recalling the analogy Ruskin makes between formal disciplines and the critical under-standing of them, as when he says, in *Modern Painters* III, that both verbal and visual art are "methods" of expression (5.31). The reader who admits of only one method, whether critical or creative, risks losing track of Ruskin's art – as does the reader who, in setting methods against each other, may become his co-conspirator in the concealment of invention.

There is no contest here between a single critical allegiance and an indecisive pluralism. I am seeking neither the dominion of one method over the others, nor the dominion of Ruskin as an artist over Ruskin in his other capacities, but a combination which will allow me to sustain a focus which Ruskin would rather break up. What I am trying to see is a writer who has the strongest motives to make art and to be identified as an artist, and the strongest motives not to be or to be identified as an artist; who produces some of the strongest, most extended accounts of making art and of being an artist, and some of the strongest, most extended accounts of the failure to be an artist or to comprehend the artistic process. How does such a person learn to write, and think about writing, and learn to think through the experience of writing? The methods necessary to answering this question can themselves advance the argument that the struggle to deny oneself in writing will start by shaping one's prose and one's theory of it, and end by constituting one's art and the bases on which one judges the art of everyone else.

PART ONE

LOOKING AHEAD

The way back to Ruskin's juvenilia almost always passes through the last book he wrote, because the revision of his youth in Praeterita has created much of the interest that is taken in his early writing, and because Ruskin's memories have the power to withstand the evidence (usually his own) that his past was not quite as he said it was. Yet Ruskin's relentless insistence in Praeterita that he was an entirely uninventive child – "I can no more write a story than compose a picture" (35.304), "I had not the slightest power of invention" (35.608) – has not encouraged his critics to hunt for signs of verbal originality in his first writings. Not many readers have in fact studied what Ruskin wrote before he retained "a certain sort of childishness" (6.66) and was instead a child himself.[1] The few, including Ruskin, who have read his juvenilia with care have often done so in terms of the reading to which he was "susceptible," and of which he claims (in Modern Painters III) that his responses were never "innocent" (5.365–67). But if the bible, Wordsworth, Scott, and Byron (to mention only some of what he studied) provide a necessary context within which to consider Ruskin's juvenilia, none of this reading can adequately account for that extraordinary "skill of language" (35.225) which was suspected before Ruskin could write and has never been denied since. His instinct to put into words what he thought

17

and saw was at least as remarkable as any he had, and was certainly the one among them that did most to bring him to terms with the sometimes enabling and sometimes maddening world that surrounded him, to bring into relationship what he thought he was, and what he thought there was to know. If there were an Edenic beginning, however eccentric, not only to the life he describes in Praeterita but also to the life of his writing – a beginning full of the press and bruise of constraining circumstance but full, too, of the sense of an infinitely inviting prospect and of the incipient power to meet it – then such beginnings must be apparent here, in Ruskin's earliest works. And Ruskin, who quoted and planned to reprint some of his first writings at the end of his working life, seems to have felt that to find such beginnings, and to find them telling, his readers have only to look (1.xxiii n.1).

INTERRELATIONS
(1823–29)

When we look at the first letter Ruskin composed, we may be disappointed to find that it is written in his mother's hand. And yet Margaret Ruskin's hand in the matter is not uninformative, and not merely because she explains to her husband, on the page below, that she has just transcribed "exactly word for word" what their son "pretended to read" from "scrawling" she thought too indecipherable to send as requested (RFL, 127–29). For the punctuation and paragraphing in her own letter are only slightly more orthodox than in her transcription, or in the letters he will soon be writing for himself. The point to be taken is not that Margaret Ruskin was inappropriately skeptical about her son's (or complacent about her own) editorial skills, but that she was rightly confident that her meanings – irregular punctuation notwithstanding – ought not to be in doubt. And this confidence bears a family resemblance to Ruskin's own. No one was clearer on this point than Ruskin, whose famous acknowledgment of his mother for "the one *essential* part of all my education" concerns her instruction of his ear rather than of his eye, her teaching him to sound the sense of a biblical chapter rather than to make visible his own meanings through a series of markings on his own paper (*Praeterita*, 35.40–43). In another of Margaret Ruskin's cover letters written six years after the first, her conviction that what is properly pronounced will eventually be properly attended to is implicitly part of the behavior of the son who, "you will be aware . . . does not know there is any difference in putting things on paper from saying them" (RFL, 172).

But for all its relationship to his mother, the letter Ruskin first dictated at the age of four is signally his own, and in no way more than in its extraordinarily precocious grasp of interrelationships. This grasp is so marked that the adult Ruskin might well have owned the letter with the same proprietary amusement that led him to annotate "My First tree! from nature, 1831 (J. R. 6th Jan. 1884)" [Illus. 3], or a letter and two poems written when he was eight "as evidently the first sketch of the Moral Theory of his work" (36.562). It may of course be fortuitous that the description of a child's model of Waterloo Bridge should open the first letter of the man who would celebrate the intellect involved in the building of a bridge (*The Stones of Venice* I, 9.66–67), and who would elaborate an argument "On Composition" whose third law, "The Law of Continuity," is illustrated with reference to bridge designs that not only relate the shores to the water and to each other, but also interrelate the varying constituents that make a bridge Ruskin's model of continuity in the first place (*The Elements of Drawing*, 15.170–76). But what is not fortuitous is the way that Ruskin assembles sentences that begin with the assembling of his toy bridge:

My Dear Papa
I love you – I have got new things   Waterloo Bridge – Aunt brought me it – John and Aunt helped to put it up but the pillars they did not put right[,] upside down   instead of a book bring me a whip coloured red and black which my fingers used to stick to and which I pulled off and pulled down – tomorrow is sabbath   tuesday I go to Croydon   on monday I go to Chelsea   papa loves me as well as Mamma does and Mamma loves me as well as papa does—
   I am going to take my boats and my Ship to Croydon   I'll sail them in the Pond near the Burn which the Bridge is over   I will be very glad to see my cousins   I was very happy when I saw Aunt come from Croydon – I love Mrs. Gray and I love Mr. Gray – I would like you to come home and my kiss & my love   JOHN RUSKIN
(RFL, 127–28, Burd's interpolation)

If Margaret Ruskin knew how easy it is to misassemble phrases one is only pretending to read, her son could make out that his elders had misassembled their parts too. His model bridge was so well made, and Ruskin had so thoroughly analyzed the structural principles that went into its making, that he remembered sixty-two years later that "I was never weary of building, unbuilding, – (it was too strong to be thrown down, but had always to be *taken* down) – and rebuilding it" (*Praeterita*, 35.58). At that time, Tuesday may have seemed too exciting to put in its proper place after Monday, and the colorful prospect of a new whip might have come between the memory of pillars and the fingers which could bring them down. Even so, the elements of his sometimes "upside down" letter are, like the bridge which it is about, basically sound enough to be reorganized into a more serviceable structure – especially by a boy who not only liked to match the days of the week with their appointed duties, but who showed such aptitude for rendering geometric ratios out of the experience of familial interrelationships. "[P]apa loves me as well as Mamma does and Mamma loves me as well as papa does": the sentence is balanced satisfyingly on the son in his parents' midst (a balance which remains untipped by Mamma's capitalization of herself). Yet the engineering of it is still less accomplished than in the sentence where the four-year-old imagines himself in Croydon. In this letter so full of feeling for connectives, a bridge once again makes an appearance near the end, buttressed this time by a relative pronoun and prepositions which deftly dispose the Pond and the Burn and the Bridge in syntax that repeats their remembered relationship in space. Far as his phrases have ranged geographically, they are shaped by a persistent impulse to mark or to make both physical and emotional interconnections. "[T]he signature," as Margaret Ruskin said, "you will see is his own."[1]

It is much the same signature as in works done three or four years later entirely in his own hand. Ruskin appears to have been helped by no one in producing his earliest surviving drawings, although he must have helped himself by examining what other people drew, much as he helped himself to write by using what he read and heard.[2] This quite ordinary instinct to learn from what has already been done was distinctively compounded in Ruskin's case by his having learned so many things, and by his having chosen to make drawings of what he wrote, and to describe in prose and poetry the subjects he had drawn. By the time he was twenty-one, he was fluent enough in translating from one medium to another to say, in recalling his own education, that "In Drawing only, I learned by *grammar* thoroughly" (36.21). The "grammar" of the untutored seven-year-old displays itself not only in the writing of his *Harry and Lucy, Concluded*, but also in the picture (of "harrys new road") which was designed to illustrate it and which Ruskin redisplays in *Praeterita* [Illus. 1], thinking it "my first effort at mountain drawing" (35.54–55). In it the arrangement of mass is coordinated not only with the small lines which give it texture and direction, but especially with the sinuous line of the road, which interweaves the sections it divides. It is the road which defines the contour and structure of the mountain, which suggests the continuity among discontinuous masses; and its winding, in *Praeterita*, across a page reprinted from *Harry and Lucy, Concluded* brings out its relationship to the writing from which the child had removed it in imitation of the look of separate "copper plates" (35.53).[3] For the progress of this road from one level to the next is a smoother realization of one of the impulses behind the rather jolting prose passage – "this piece of, too literally, composition" (55) – in which an "electrical apparatus," clouds, and dust give way to lightning and then to rain, a rainbow, and a mist which Harry's "fancy soon transformed into a female form." In calling his excerpt "an extremely perfect type of the interwoven temper of my mind" (35.56), Ruskin refers to the derivation of its subject from *Manfred* and Jeremiah Joyce's *Scientific Dialogues* (1809), and of its format from Maria Edgeworth's *Frank* and *Harry and Lucy Concluded*. But as the drawing suggests (and Harry had been drawing when Lucy pointed out the storm cloud), this interweaving is characteristic of the grammar as well as of the genesis of Ruskin's story. Comparison with the original paragraph in *Scientific Dialogues*, which Ruskin has taken care to quote in a footnote to *Praeterita*, shows how the child adapted the actions parcelled out into separate sentences by Joyce, and ran them together into a continuous sequence – except, significantly, when it came to one atypically complex and intervolved movement, which Ruskin found attractive enough to appropriate almost unaltered, only substituting "sky" for the final word: ". . . a flash of lightning was seen to dart through the cloud of dust, upon which the negative clouds spread very much, and dissolved in rain, which presently cleared the atmosphere." In dropping all the commas Ruskin brings Joyce's grammar into line with his own, and gives expression to his pleasure in the way things run together.

In another illustration made for the same volume, "harrys river" repeats, in the foreground, the double, progressively deepening bend that "harrys new road" makes around a mountain [Illus. 2]. The river cuts across the center rather than the edge of the terrain, again and again curving out of sight over the borders of the drawing as it sweeps from side to side down the page. As in "harrys new road," it is a circuitous line that defines both the declivity and the edges of the landscape whose elements it draws together. These elements most prominently include two peaks which appear to rise out of the land rather than being (as in many children's drawings) set down upon it – an effect which the artist enhances by wittily exposing a glimpse of the river behind at a height which shows that it did not, and could not, flow over the land that connects them. And this stretch of land in between is as carefully and continuously rounded as is the top of each peak, as is the river which sets them in relief. It is the curves which give to the still life of Harry's road and Harry's river an implication of progression, of movement. It is not surprising that when Ruskin drew his "First tree! from nature" he chose one whose bending trunk and relentlessly sinuous branches relate the parts to a unified, and animated, whole [Illus. 3].

An interest in animation is also obvious throughout the whole of what may be his first attempt at poetry. Ruskin's attention in this verse to subjects and modes that will engross him in the future is no more remarkable than the verbal energy, facility, and self-consciousness with which he explores them as a child. Neatly printed on the page facing the conclusion of Harry's adventure with lightning and electricity, "poem 1" shows off a readiness with complex interconnections that is astonishing in a seven-year-old:

> when furious up from mines the water pours
> and clears from rusty moisture all the ores
> then may clouds gather then may thunder roar
> then may the lightnings flash and rain sigh [sic?] may pour
> yet undisturbed the power alone will raise
> the water from the engine might be formed a phrase
> when as it drags the weight of fragment large
> it also drags the weight of smokey barge
> called by us a steam boat and a steam boat saves
> the beings scattered on the furious waves

by boilers bursting but a steamboat can
be the most useful engine brought to man
the grinding stones that by its force are whirled
and by their force the yellow grains are twirled
Bruised ground and thrown away in boxes small
While it doth thunder near the echoing wall
The whirring wheels arranged in whirling rows
And on the wheels the spinner cotton throws
Next moves the noisy beam the wheels do whirl
And next the wheels the cotton fibres twirl
The moving bellows that are made to roar
By its huge strength that melt the red hot ore
The copper mines that by it emptied are
And their blue metal now is brought from far
then it puts forth its power the rollers squeeze
the metal then another part doth seize
the flattened metal quick flies the circle round
And all is stamped at once Brittannia and the ground
then showers the water from the reservoir
and round the town it rushing now doth pour
then runs to cisterns large and fills them all
and turns back homeward in quantity but small
then forms the lengthening and putting link to link
makes a small chain and leaves of that flower the pink
    and so I end

                    [My interpolation][4]

The opening lines follow the "furious" upward flow of
waters mechanically raised (as opposed to the natural
downpour of a storm), and they come full circle when the
engine's "power alone will raise / the water" again at the
beginning of the sixth line. Much as the basic machine may
be compounded to perform various functions, the word for it
may also be combined with another and "from the engine
might be formed a phrase." Ruskin's double consciousness
of words and things (simple enough here but destined to

become deeply complicated, as we will see in the next part of
this book) now ramifies into an evocation of the compound
"steam boat" as both a destroyer and preserver, as a machine
which gathers those whom it has "scattered" on waters
which, like those at the outset, are said to be "furious." The
workings of the steam engine seem less dangerous but
remain reciprocal, cyclical, when harnessed on dry land; and
Ruskin's precision of diction and vigorous enjambment –
almost half of the rhyme words are verbs – work to create a
simulacrum in verse of the chain reaction in which "yellow
grains" are "twirled / Bruised ground and thrown" by
"grinding stones" that are themselves "whirled" by the
force of the engine. The vertiginous medley of responses
which the machine sets into play is matched by the virtuosity
of a child who can conduct alliteration so confidently that
sound is both related to and differentiated from the action
which produced it: it is easy to see why even Ruskin's
painstakingly accurate editors could have silenced his subtly
orchestrated "whirring wheels arranged in whirling rows"
when they transcribed them as "whirling wheels arranged in
whirling rows." The "roar" of bellows subsequently sounds
the recall of the "ore" that Ruskin has rhymed with it in the
second line. Only instead of being put through a purgative
rinse the metal is now subjected to that paradoxical operation
by which a rounded object renders another one otherwise –
an operation that caught Ruskin's interest earlier (when
rotary action wound up emboxing what it ground, and
wheels within wheels at length drew out what they had run
circles around), and will again later (when "the circle"
controls the stamping of a label flat on pieces of copper).
Everything turns on circuitous shapes – not only the engine
which drives the waters to circumnavigate the town but also
the poem, which turns "back homeward" with them, where
their "small" flow can still be adapted to the "small"

concerns of domestic gardening. And thus the verse which begins "when furious up from mines the water pours," and whose "lengthening" depends on the child's "putting link to link" in imitation of the sequences the engine sets in motion, at length comes to rest in the contemplation of a little flower. The pink might seem to displace all the sound and fury on which its life depends; but "having," as Ruskin would say forty-six years later, "their stems jointed like canes" (21.240), the very structure of the plant replicates that additive "chain" of events which the poem both refers to and repeats. "And so I end" with this final link between humanly controlled energy and the God-made nature it derives from and serves. It is what the adult Ruskin would often define as the end of progress.

The poem in itself partakes of the form of a riddle, as do several dialogues inset in the preceding volume of *Harry and Lucy, Concluded*. Thanks to circumlocution, the steam engine is never indicated by name; by its action, you will know it. The child makes no connection between the evaporation–condensation–evaporation cycle of a compounded steam engine, and the way that, in his poem, what waters a flower in the end flows back, in the memory, to the waters that pour through the beginning. But the syntax and versification attach themselves to and capture the transformations of matter wrought within the larger cycle. The punctuation superadded after Ruskin's death disguises his having bound his phrases each to each, and jams their movement back and forth in the mind. The poem is not, as his editors suggest, "as difficult to follow as most clever children's stories," but more so, for the problem is not that "the links in [the] train of thought are never supplied" but that they connect, as supplied, and as many organic links do, in two directions, on two sides, at once. What makes the poem on the steam engine so difficult, and so amazing, is that it aspires to the ambiguity of interaction in which connections are everywhere, and every ending is arbitrary.[5]

The second poem in the *Harry and Lucy* volume, "on scotland," is far less ambitious. Instead of the transforming animation of its subject (which is here subdued to a matter of dropping water and popping fish), the motion is supplied by the traveller who takes in the changes in terrain as he passes from one part of the country to another.[6] "Spring," copied out into a section labelled "poetry discriptive" (sic) in another notebook, elaborates a contrast between "waving" things that bloom in orchard and garden and those less fortunate "stiff" ones which are compensated with height or beautiful flowers. This poem is the second of two that Ruskin recopied in a letter to his father in May 1827 which he passed on to his friend Charles Eliot Norton with the comment, previously quoted, that it was "evidently the first sketch of the Moral Theory of his work by the great author of 'Modern Painters.'" But it was not only in the hindsight of 1869 that he saw something germinating there: during a trip to Scotland in 1853 Ruskin wrote to his father that the landscape was "putting me in mind of my baby verses" (12.xxi), and he quoted the last four lines of the other poem he had first sent to his father in 1827:

Wales

That rock with waving willows on its side
That hill with beauteous forests on its top
That stream that with its rippling waves doth glide
And oh what beauties has that mountain got
That rock stands high against the sky
Those trees stand firm upon the rock
and seem as if they all did lock
Into each other; tall they stand
Towering above the whitened land

(RFL, 158)

In 1853 Ruskin supposed that he had "meant the rocks looked whiter by contrast with the pines – a very artistical observation for a child" (12.xxii). But what is more artistical, and what probably locked the lines in his memory, is the way they interlock with each other just where their subjects do. When the great author of *Modern Painters* comes to lecture on the vital interrelationship among things, he will make it clear that their interrelationship is a sign of their vitality, and that they are vital in his sight partly because they are interrelated.[7] And it is his nascent sense of these truths that vitalizes the verse of the eight-year-old as he tries to represent their effects in words and rhyme and meter. The elements of the scene are so ordered that their individuality, and position in life, are at once precisely delineated and shown to depend, in their fulness of aspect, on what is nearby. After these elements are firmly characterized in the first four self-contained, alternately rhyming lines of iambic pentameter, the unrhymed (yet internally rhymed) fifth introduces both a change to more swiftly pronounced tetrameter and the sky against which everything stands that is locked into the subsequent pair of couplets. Even a detail like the small "a" which begins line 7 of the fair copy suggests Ruskin's eagerness to move the reader's eye continuously along the enjambment and the continuities which it represents without blurring, without confusion. And the distinction of such a detail is no more answered for by generalizations about the influence on the child of Wordsworthian intercommunion, than an awareness of Carlyle's Mechanical-Dynamical argument can answer for the fine points of a poem on the steam engine written three years before the "Signs of the Times" to which it can indubitably be related. For the question is not whether the spirit of the age made its way into the drawing-room niche where the child was "shut . . . well in" behind a "good writing-table'' (35.61), but what Ruskin made of it once it got there.

Appearing in the "poetry discriptive"collection just after "Wales," "The hill of kinnoul" also dwells on river, rock, mountain, and trees, but the grouping is complicated now by the phenomenon of reflection. The River Tay not only winds around the objects of Ruskin's attention (as in the drawings of Harry's road and Harry's river), but also mirrors what it flows beneath, so that the "high topped trees" are at once "above below."[8] By moving his body, or merely his eyes, the viewer can alter the appearance of what he sees, and set it into the motion of a narrative, creating that apparent animation taken on by a series of scenes when it passes rapidly before the eyes, or through the memory. No sooner does he sight "the glass tay" than he recalls seeing it when it was not "quite so smooth"; no sooner does he depict a rock rising from the river's surface than he gives the order to climb it and look down on the dizzying height from which the Tay "appears like a little rivulet . . . / dwindling into nothing mong / the distant mountains." That sound as well as sight can evoke and depend upon the position of those who respond to it is demonstrated in "Highland Music," which Ruskin presented to his father instead of "a small model of any easily done thing." With its awkward but deliberate preference for coordinating rather than the subordinating structures he has already mastered, this poem about a sequence of sounds and silence models Ruskin's awareness that poetry is itself a composition of sounds or writing that defines an experience as it occupies and develops in time. It is, not surprisingly, in her next letter that Margaret Ruskin is certain her husband "will be aware that John does not know there is any difference in putting things on paper from saying them" (RFL, 170–72).

Perspectival changes, and the ways that physical moves can

seem to activate a subject and render it audible, fascinate
Ruskin again in a poem in which the first pair of imperfectly
rhymed lines (9–10) end with the words "far" and "near."
Ruskin reprints it in *The Queen of the Air* (1869), commenting
that "It bears date 1st January, 1828. I was born on the 8th of
February, 1819; and all that I ever could be, and all that I
cannot be, the weak little rhyme already shows" (19.396).

Glenfarg

> Papa how pretty those icicles are
> That are seen so near that are seen so far
> Those dropping waters that come from the rocks
> And many a hole like the haunt of a fox
> That silvery stream that runs babbling along
> Making a murmuring dancing song
> Those trees that stand waving upon the rock's side
> And men that like spectres among them glide
> And waterfalls that are heard from far
> And come in sight when very near
> And the water-wheel that turns slowly round
> Grinding the corn that requires to be ground
> And mountains at a distance seen
> And rivers winding through the plain
> And quarries with their craggy stones
> And the wind among them moans[9]

Once again Ruskin's scene is variously yet interrelatedly
animated – waving, winding, turning round; even its sounds
are the sort – babbling, murmuring, moaning – that are
usually continuous. But Ruskin's being animated to write by
the animation he regards has a new dimension in "Glenfarg," a dimension opened up not only by his choosing to
keep his distance or to come in for a closer look, but
especially by his interweaving his own activity with the
activities that he notes. "And waterfalls that are heard from
far / And come in sight when very near": the approach seems

equidistant, mutual. The child drops himself out of the picture after pointing out its prettiness; but his movements in verse dramatize nature's own.

It is what Ruskin takes to be the anima in and behind "Glenfarg" that moves him to cite it in The Queen of the Air, just after insisting that his own "art-gift" derives "from the air of English country villages, and Scottish hills." The poem is unmarked by the kind of animus that actuates the earlier "Glen of Glenfarg" (1826), in which the inertia and activity of the landscape are a sermon to higher creatures to keep striving upwards in accordance with God's plan. His New Year's address to his father of 1 January 1827 develops this moral imperative to move on into a self-delightingly grotesque play on the quick and the dead. In "Papa whats time" it is not now a question of the interlocking elements of the landscape but of his own movements in relation to those of "the quick course of time," which relentlessly speeds minutes into hours, and hours into days, and days into years – and "past times gone for ever so he has a lock / of hair upon his forehead and the proverb is / take time by his forelock" (RFL, 150–51). This keen feeling for one thing's giving way to the next informs the composition of "On Skiddaw and Derwent Water," Ruskin's first piece of published writing. Appearing in 1830, and written in 1828 or early 1829 about scenes he saw on a tour to the Lakes in 1826, the printed text differs from both the 1829 fair copy and the original draft.[10] But all three versions share an opening in which the yielding of sunshine on the cliffs to a cloud, and of the cloud to the returning sun, is a prelude to "fancy's play" in which clouds resemble unmanned implements and architecture of war which appear to chase what precedes them and then to be chased off in their turn. Derwent Water's being "a looking-glass" is the occasion not only for a conventionally picturesque set piece in which nature has "painted" and "framed" a counterpart to the original,[11] but also for the implication that the image held by reflection can be released into action by it too. The mirroring surface is likened to a boy who builds a snowman, only to "play / At tearing it to pieces":

> Trees do first
> Tremble, as if a monstrous heart of oak
> Were but an aspen leaf; and then as if
> It were a cobweb in the tempest's blow.

Upon reflection, the aspect of nature takes on new activity, new life. Earlier poems like "The hill of kinnoul" and "Glenfarg" demonstrate how physical movement in the landscape is related to physical gestures of the viewer; "On Skiddaw and Derwent Water" suggests that it is not simply a change of position that can set things in motion, or seem to, but also a change of mind.

> Thus like Penelope thou weav'st a web
> And then thou dost undo it.
>
> (2.267)

By the time he was ten years old, this aspiring poet for whom writing was a favorite form of play had thoroughly understood how the "play" of a reflective surface could be like "play" in the snow of just such a boy as himself, and like "fancy's play" with the position, and disposition, of the objects of sight. To take things to pieces (whether in fact, as with a model of Waterloo Bridge, or in analysis, as with the operation of a steam engine, or a lake) is not just to see how they work but also to give oneself an opportunity to assemble them again, showing other people how they work. And every assembly is a sequence in time and in space of elements that may be as distractingly varied as they are satisfyingly related, and as diverse in their contours, and continuities, as they are coherent in one's own imagination.

In the "General Index" to *The Complete Works*, Ruskin's editors give forty-nine citations under the heading of "Invention" (39.280–81). The most compendious of them – "an arrangement, in which everything in the work is thus consistent with all things else, and helpful to all else" – describes his early writing at its best (*Modern Painters* V, 7.208–09).

CHAPTER 2

LAWS OF MOTION
(1829-33)

Neither Ruskin nor his editors convey an adequate sense of the interest he took as a boy in the relationship between his mind, his subjects, and the language with which he registered the animation of them both. This could be more than a relationship among entities separate in time, for to Ruskin a "subject" could simultaneously mean his own consciousness, his topic of the moment, and his writing's dependence on, its subjection to, the authority of his mind and his topic. Behind the adult who defensively parodied the "German" metaphysical preoccupation with the "Subjective" and "Objective" in his chapter on the pathetic fallacy (5.201–04), there was a youth with a remarkably full and subtle awareness of the power of an object to become a subject when it is subject to a subject. This awareness developed out of his first encounters with the issues involved in composition – issues raised for him by fundamental questions about what to write and how to write it; about how to start and continue, attaching part to part before he reaches a stop; about how to accommodate the range of his interests and to bring them into line with his strongest motives; about what to make of the relation between a topic and his responses to it, and between his thoughts (once he has them) and their almost instantaneous expression in language.

These questions begin to be considered in his earliest letters. From the time he was ten, Ruskin puzzled over and protested his needing a topic in order to be off and writing ("Well then to begin, but what shall I begin with, I dont know"); yet he was quick to recognize ("It really is singular how one makes substance out of nothing") that the want of a subject is itself a subject, or at least the beginning of one: "I think I have been writing about writing about nothing as I have been writing a poem upon the want of a subject."[1] He founded not one but several poems upon this subject, which preoccupies him in the beginning, and in the midst, of letter after letter.[2] Of course these writings might be considered in terms, or as proof, of Ruskin's claims in *Praeterita* that he entirely lacked invention. But there is often invention in the ways that he meets the sense of something missing in his equipment; and, more importantly, there is often something present that he prefers to working up a subject "'out of [his] head'" (*Praeterita*, 35.75).

Ruskin's experience with his drawing master, carefully detailed for his father, is a case in point. Although the adult Ruskin complained of Mr. Runciman that he "gave me nothing but his own mannered and inefficient drawings to copy, and greatly broke the force both of my mind and hand" (35.76), the boy of thirteen meant it (and possibly meant to double his words) when he said that in "drawing drawing [sic] there Im comfortable again" (RFL, 258, Burd's interpolation). At any rate, it was a new and significant departure when Ruskin was first directed by his teacher to invent his own subject:

I now proceed to communicate important information respecting my lessons . . . Well I took my paper & fixed my points, & I drew my perspective, & then as Mr Runciman bid me, I began to invent a scene; you remember the cottage that we saw, as we went to Rhaidyr Dhu, near Maentwrog where the old woman lived whose grandson went with us to the fall, so very silently. I thought my model resembled that so I drew a tree, such a tree, such an enormous fellow, & I sketched the waterfall, with its dark rocks, and its luxuriant wood, and its high mountains, & then I examined one of [his cousin] Mary's pictures, to see how the rocks were done, & then another to see how the woods were done, & another to see how the mountains were done, and another to see how the cottages were done, and I patched them all together, & I made such

a lovely scene. Oh I should get such a scold from Mr Runciman,
(that is if he ever scolded). (RFL, 262–63)

On the contrary, when Ruskin eventually showed him the
drawing and "told him how I had patched it up, . . . he said
that that was not copying" and decided his pupil was ready to
begin painting with color. What excited Ruskin about
painting as opposed to drawing was not that it would allow
him to be more inventive with distant or wild scenery, but
that it would allow him to be more veracious:

how much superior painting would be, if I wanted to carry off
Derwent Water, & Skiddaw in my pocket, or Ulles Water, &
Helvellyn, or Windermere, & Low-wood, Oh if I could paint well
before we went to Dover I should have such sea pieces, taken from
our windows, such castles & cliffs – hanging over the ocean, And
ships on those waters, in heaving commotion. There would be a
night scene, with the waters in all the richness, of Prussian blue &
bright green, having their nightly billows crested, with Reeves best
white, & the sky above, a very heaven of indigo, with the moon, &
attendant stars, pouring their bright rays upon the golden waters,
in all the glory of Gamboge . . . (RFL, 267–68)

As usual the prospect stimulates more than one of his favorite
activities, and he falls quite naturally into geography, rhyme,
and artistic techniques for producing effects from their
causes. In the meantime, the boy's sense of getting away with
something uninventive and naughty has yielded to his
finding himself in possession of a subject which will do his
talents justice, and to which he wants to do justice. The
command to compose a drawing, like the self-imposed
command to compose a letter, brings him self-consciously
face to face with the question of what there is to compose: in
discovering the connection between a subject and thinking
about a subject, Ruskin discovers that a composition may be
an arrangement of things that pre-exist their arranging.

This recognition, and his finding a vocation in *Modern*

Painters as a critic of the works of God and man, are separated by the experience of about ten years; but even in 1832 he is already his own critic, who knows that his lack of one kind of subject is his access to another which suits him better. The poem of 1831 which begins "I want a thing to write upon, / But I cannot find one," concludes, ten stanzas later, with a new insight into his uncooperative muse:

> And lest she urge her airy flight
> From my so drowsy brain,
> Upon no subject I will write,
> That so she may remain.
>
> (2.321)

The resolve is emancipating. As an Oxford undergraduate, full of his first major successes as a critic, Ruskin tells his father, "I dislike having things to tell – I would rather write about nothing, so I shall write again soon – less laconically" (RFL, 499).

Once begun, "Composing gets on too amazingly fast" (RFL, 227) – particularly in a letter written when he was ten in which he says he is bombarding his reader with the subjects which have fought with him and each other for his attention. The martial images he adopts in describing this competition are in fact less indicative of his response to it than are some lines from the poetry of Bishop Heber, who provides the main subject of his letter: "I suppose you know that when I repeat a line of poetry that I am much taken with I involuntarily keep repeating it the whole day my Rhyme today is [']I see them on their winding way, About their ranks the moonbeams play &c.['] . . . After all I shall not get what I have to say into this letter." Under the circumstances, the certainty of failure does not concern him very deeply:

by the by my discourse is not a regular one it is irregular . . . I believe my discourse has a conclusion, and a beginning too though that is not mentioned among the learned terms of Rhetoric . . . but to return to bishop Heber – The original port from which I set out and wandered over the world of Rhetoric. And yet I think that world is rather too large to let me wander over it in a few minutes though it may be something smaller than that province over which bishop Heber . . . of calcutta travelled. But pull up, pull up* observe this asterisk papa. What off at full gallop again, check, check, take care, pull him not in too suddenly. He's a capery fellow that, gently, let him have some of his own way, turn, thats it, thats it, now back, back, not too fast, not too fast, take care, Ay ay, thats it, come away gently, gently, Ay now . . .

[*] only a wee bit metaphor papa I found myself galloping off from the subject[.]   (RFL, 193)

He writes about writing here as if it were a mode or vehicle of progress which has a will of its own but is also controlled by Ruskin's will to have "some of his own way." Instead of resisting he authorizes his impulses to play themselves out, enacting movements of mind and subsequently of pen which seem to answer to the behavior of his subject, as if they rhymed in and of themselves, or corresponded to each other like two sides of "the quadrilateral plan" of his dominant interests (Praeterita, 35.120–21). And while his language is charged, and overcharged, with the implication of its being a direct translation from the terrain that he sights, Ruskin's writing is also its own terrain:

you would be overdone smothered under a mountain of words and of rhymes also if I wrote more. Oh you will groan under the weight of lines the sea of rhymes which I shall load you with on your return . . . But I shall not make you quite overburdened for as fast as I load you with mountain after mountain heaped gigantic I shall lighten you of your money Hurra Forty lines per day regularly as the sun goes down. We were very much delighted when we heard your intention of going to Dover . . . now we shall cut right up by Bath and Bristol and so into Wales Oh we shall have such fun such

39

delightful walks   It will be expensive   I shall be sure to make a
poem of it. Steamboats dashing, Paddles splashing, Coach a going,
Horn a blowing, Such a bustle, Crowd and tustle, Engines fizzing,
Steamboats whizzing, Oh gloriosities, Such curiosities, Hop sa sa
Fal lal la – Oh I shall make such a collection of shells Univalves
bivalves multivalves and sea urchins . . . O papa we are making you
out such a tour in Wales . . . We have dragged you over bridges . . .
over chasms some hundreds of feet deep with torrents roaring at
the bottom, over mountains which seem to have a mind to make
war with the stars   over over over   I am lost in the wilderness of
wonders in the ocean of overs   I write regularly a page of Clarke['s
Latin grammar] as you desired me   One thing puzzles me a little
When you say Anger will hurt me more than injury do you put the
Adjective or the Adverb More . . . if the Adjective what case do you
put it in.   (RFL, 220)[3]

He draws no more attention to the pace of his subject than to
his keeping pace with his thinking about it: once the impulse
is taken from his father's travelling, or from Bishop Heber's
mount, the Pegasus to whom Ruskin is fond of referring in
his letters breaks into some sequacious prose that not only
follows the sequence it regards but also regards itself in the
act of following.

It is the element of self-reference in this prose written in
propria persona which makes explicit a connection only
implicit in Ruskin's poems and stories between what he takes
to be the continuous movements of his own mind and those
of the world that is not himself. And as his verbalized
thoughts run on continuously, like their subject matter,
Ruskin begins to see that they are themselves internally
composed and interconnected in ways that can be transferred
intact onto paper, like the design of a road or river, or the
sequential operations of a steam engine. This is why Ruskin's
discourse is no sooner said to be irregular than it is affirmed
as an eventual course towards his desired destination, for the

wilfully "winding way" of his writing can provide Ruskin with a sense of expressive accomplishment even in passages where "I found myself galloping off from the subject." In the exuberant didacticism of these early letters – "think," as Ruskin pedagogically puts it, "(and in the thought find teaching good)" (RFL, 291) – the sense of an affinity between the behavior of his subjects and of his own responses to them develops into a principle of composition, a principle which links the composition of his prose to that of the spectacles it seeks to represent.

So that if "Composing gets on too amazingly fast," it is at least in part because being watchful of what comes to him, or of what he comes to next, does not simply deflect the pressure to invent his subjects but also suggests to him that they can be represented as, and as rapidly as, they have presented themselves to him. Not that he pretends his letters are unpremeditated, or unaltered once they are written.[4] Although he can draft a letter very fast – "as fast I think as I could speak it," says his mother (RFL, 270) – he is eager to show his father how much forethought goes into what he writes: "letters are of such importance that I always slate them first" (RFL, 235). Among the things he considers in advance, and records his consideration of, are the styles in which he might compose his subjects, having learned from looking, reading, and especially from his drawing masters that a given subject may be approached in various ways, and that it makes a difference in the results when he has found what he calls, in a verse letter, "a style and metre that looked knowing" (RFL, 294). And like the readiness of his rough-drafting, Ruskin's drawing attention to his preliminary choices sometimes makes him seem more expressive than he has thoughts to express.

Yet the distinction only serves to deepen the connection between the enumerated things that occur to him and the innumerable actions by which he modifies and makes use of them. As in the beginning of the section in *Modern Painters* III where he explores his childhood feeling for landscape, Ruskin's observation of his own mental moves discloses not only the elements they negotiate between but also a suggestion that the mind and its objects – the movement of the one and the fixity of the other, or the animation of them both – are somehow bound together:

> though there is much work to be done in the world, it is often the best thing a man can do, – to tell the exact truth about the movements of his own mind . . . The first thing which I remember, as an event in life, was being taken by my nurse to the brow of Friar's Crag on Derwent Water; the intense joy, mingled with awe, that I had in looking through the hollows in the mossy roots, over the crag, into the dark lake, has associated itself more or less with all twining roots of trees ever since. Two other things I remember as, in a sort, beginnings of life; – crossing Shapfells (being let out of the chaise to run up the hills), and going through Glenfarg, near Kinross, in a winter's morning, when the rocks were hung with icicles . . . Only thus much I can remember, respecting [this gift of taking intense pleasure in landscape], which is important to our present subject.
>
> First: it was never independent of associated thought. Almost as soon as I could see or hear, I had got reading enough to give me associations with all kinds of scenery . . . I also generally knew, or was told by my father and mother, such simple facts of history as were necessary to give more definite and justifiable association to other scenes which chiefly interested me . . .
>
> (5.365–66)

This prose of 1856 confidently entwines into a single passage the twining roots and the inalienable associations which clung to what he saw. The movement that was a cause of writing can also be discovered in its effect. Ruskin goes on just as confidently to insist that the "landscape-instinct" he felt as a boy was

entirely unaccompanied by powers of reflection or invention.
Every fancy that I had about nature was put into my head by some
book; and I never reflected about anything till I grew older; and
then, the more I reflected, the less nature was precious to me . . .

(5.367)

After the first semicolon, the longer sentence tends to
compensate Ruskin for what seemed like a deficiency at the
beginning, as it appears that there is something to be
preferred to "reflection." The denial of his originality
becomes a celebration of his ability "to tell the exact truth
about the movements of his own mind" over the world that
he sees. In the 1820s and 30s, Ruskin is more proprietary
about the ideas he expounds; but even so elementary an
exploit in language as the "wee bit metaphor" he produced
when he was ten gives evidence of some confidence that the
analogies which he makes can be treated as if they are not
merely private fancies, provided one goes deeply enough
into one's subject and one's own responses to it, or gives
them room enough to grow in.

But if it requires a free rein to follow the mind's pursuit of
its interests, Ruskin has also discovered that the burden of
having too much space and too much time when he was at a
loss for a subject has now been replaced by the frustration of
having too little of either. "I believe you will find that in most
of my former letters, the great subject is want of time" (RFL,
263). And since "time is, in fact, just as we feel it" (RFL,
279), Ruskin continually experiences time as space that is too
small ("a little spare scrap of time" [RFL, 353]), as well as
finding space insufficient in itself: "I have had more to do
than I could do without all possible cramming and ramming
and wishing days were longer and sheets of paper broader,
though that is a wish which has nothing to do with time."
The constraint does have its incentives and compensations. In
addition to his certainty that "in common things it is having

too much to do which constitutes happiness and too little unhappiness" (RFL, 200), Ruskin's feeling "forced to write . . . as it were by inches" (RFL, 325) contributes to the pleasing conclusion that his meandering lines of prose may be counted as a composition, a work which occupies space and time like the lines of verse which he carefully numbers and amasses, or the drawings which he executes inside boundaries that define or contain them.

It is in those letters which he regards as compositions that Ruskin most clearly affirms his attachment to the manner of writing which not only cleaves most closely to the movements of his mind, but is also the mind's best solution to the problem of how to make his surface hold all he has to say. For Ruskin's insistence on drawing out his lines of thought is precisely what makes a habit out of his attraction to the "winding way" – admittedly attractive in itself, like the serpentine or undulating double curve which Hogarth, and Ruskin's drawing master J. D. Harding, celebrated as "the line of beauty"; and arguably appropriate to retracing many favorite courses of study; but most welcome for its expanding the amount of ground he has to cover within the perimeters of any given subject.[5] It is as he observed of his route in Iteriad:

> One thing in the prospect alone us did bore, –
> A tedious hill lay our noses before, –
> Up-turning, long, tedious, and toilsome, but yet
> We surveyed it, half joying and not with regret –
> For our slowly ascending its windings, we knew,
> Must give us more time for beholding the view.
>
> (38)

"[E]very curve divides itself infinitely by its changes of direction"; like the gradations of shades and colors, the curvature of lines "is their infinity, and divides them into an infinite number of degrees." These axioms do not appear until *Modern Painters*, where Ruskin's assertion that the visual and the verbal arts are governed by the same laws suggests a relevance to his own prose of his claims that curves are always more beautiful than straight lines, and that almost all natural forms are composed entirely of curves (4.87–89).[6] But some of the experience from which he derives these arguments and their adversarial fervor is already evident in his boyhood remarks, and in the figures cut by his circuitous letters as they proceed amidst his cousin's and especially his mother's complaints that he is going on too aimlessly in his writing, and too long.

Ruskin records these complaints not only because he is a dutiful son who knows that the first reader of his letters to his father is his mother, and because he knows that his father will indulge what she calls self-indulgence, but also because he thinks that his writing can stand up to the protest.[7] Far from concealing the structure of his letters, Ruskin repeatedly points it out, making so much of the multiplication of his turns that at times he seems to be deliberately attenuating his thought in order to demonstrate (while risking) its remaining continuous. That adversarial fervor just mentioned sometimes makes itself felt in recurrent adversative conjunctions like "but," "yet," and "though" which signal changes in direction which give their pattern to his prose. The silently curving passages of his drawings and the often mute juxtapositions of his poems become, in his letters, undauntably loquacious transitions – "By the bye (how often Ive said < that > you must be quite tired)" (RFL, 259) – that enhance the impression of a mind on the move which draws the distance it covers along in its train.

But Ruskin's transitions do not simply link his thoughts

end to end. They display what to him is the extremely
amusing fact that one remark can be drawn out of another,
and nestled back in, as relentlessly as a curve can be
subdivided into an infinite number of degrees:

(. . . this whole page and a half through which I have dragged you
by the nose, has been a parenthesis, though perhaps you do not
know it, you will find the first hook of it about in the middle of the
first page (I have made it black, that it may catch your eye and be of
importances proportionable to the length of the parenthesis) and
am just going to put the other, only I judge it expedient first to give
you fair warning that I am going to resume the thread of my
lucubrations, because I am often much puzzled by Thucydides,
who interrupting himself in the middle of a sentence, and perhaps
giving the whole history of a nation, in a parenthesis, recommences
or rather continues his original sentence, taking it up where he left
it off, without warning you.) There.   (RFL, 342–43)

As writing travels through a medium that is at once writing,
the topic of writing, and Ruskin's consciousness of them
both, the compositional difficulty of how, technically, to
relate part to part in his letters seems to go the way of his
search for the subjects he found he had already got. This is
true not only of their overall design – of the sections or
digressions, whether parenthetical or not, which declare
their attachment to a pre-existing "hook" – but also of the
patterns of his individual sentences, whose syntactical
involutions and shifting verb forms are made to take in the
turns within the grander sweep of an imagined scene, and
within the sweeping movements of his eyes and thoughts:
"the mountain ridges would be peaked & crested with snow,
throwing their summits against the clear blue sky, and the
torrents whose force the frost is totally unable to bind,
fringing their banks with icicles" (RFL, 269). Ruskin was
barely thirteen when he wrote the relative clause in this

sentence; unsustained as it is compared to the syntax of inter-relationships that he mastered three years later in his geological diary, it has the advantage of self-consciously appearing in a letter written expressly to show off what he is learning about art.

This letter, previously quoted, in which he describes his first lesson in water colors, and then his having been thrown off his high-flying poetical course by his now "reinless Pegasus" (RFL, 268), begins and ends with attempts "to picture" his father who is travelling on business. Once the father's movements have moved the son to write, the separation and its anxieties are relieved by the image of a reunion: "Oh I do like to picture all this!" But not completely relieved, for his imagery – drawn from Gray's "Elegy" and *Hamlet* – draws attention back to the way that Ruskin plays with verbal connections in contemplating a physical and emotional separation. The first sentence of his letter refers to his father's "last paper conversation, or communication, or in common language, letter"; and his continuing to assemble and reuse words emphatically related to each other in sound and in meaning makes a special occasion of the likelihood that any sentence will relate to something that precedes it. While it is in part Ruskin's management of repetition, synonyms, assonance, alliteration, and other visual and aural patterns that leads his reader to what is nearby, Ruskin himself seems to be led by the inherent properties of words – by a "reinless Pegasus" which flies on without him:

all those letters, that have come before have only been accounts of anxiety, of terrible anxiety, of sleepless anxiety, caused by the cholera, & your love for us, but the last told us that, that same anxiety was abating, was decreasing, was retreating, retiring, departing, and running away. Great was the joy occasioned by the abridgment of your journey. I believe we may thank anxiety for that. I like when I am snug in bed, & the candle retiring, "which leaves the "room" to darkness, & to me" to picture our meeting "in my mind's eye Horatio" . . .   (RFL, 266–67)

Verbal play like this can seem aimless; or it can seem overdetermined by the aim to give to language the responsibility for his own need to make connection with his reader, and to find connections among the elements of the world. It is a responsibility that the boy seems to think language can easily bear. For he treats verbal association as if it were not just a matter of his relating words to each other by their look or sound or definition, but of their already being so complexly interrelated and so deeply attached to the thoughts they evoke that a word can bring a word in its train – a word a thought or a thought a word. As he had with the separate parts of his letters, Ruskin finds evidence inside of his words that their continuity with each other corresponds to his own mental figures and figurings. So that his best sequences tumble forth as if he need not add his words one by one because the connections between them are built into the language of his thought: they are part of his inheritance as a speaker of English. "Mamma says you are spoiling me," Ruskin tells his father about his birthday gift of books; "I say I am spoiling, despoiling, and taking the spoil of your pocket" (RFL, 278). He seizes what he considers to be there for the taking – whether worn-out homonyms like the one about the "tail" of his letter of which "unluckily one cannot say . . . that thereby hangs a tale" (RFL, 271) or the rewarding knowledge of those familiar words whose etymological careers can take him around as many bends as his own careering Pegasus.

It is for some of the same reasons that puns roll on and on in his boyhood writing, like ball bearings that smooth the friction between separate surfaces, or like the relentless rolling of his own prose over the things that he regards. This process and Ruskin's consciousness of it are worked together over the long stretch of a remarkable letter which, more than any other, sums up the compositional theory and practice of them all:

Tuesday, 15 Jany 1833

My dear Papa

I would write a short, pithy, laconic, sensible, concentrated, and serious letter, if I could for I have scarcely time to write a long one. Observe I only say to write, for as to the composition 'tis nothing, positively nothing. I roll on like a ball, with this exception that contrary to the usual laws of motion I have no friction to contend with in my mind and of course have some difficulty in stopping myself when there is nothing else to stop me. Mary declined writing to you for a reason which gave me peculiar and particular offense, namely, that I wrote nonsense enough, and she had nothing else to offer, as if my discreet communications, merited the cognomen of nonsense: However I did not quarrel with her as she surrendered her half sheet to me which space I was very glad to fill up with my nonsense as this additional space gave me much greater freedom & play of cogitation, as I had then not to compress my ideas, like the steam of a high pressure engine but was enabled to allow them to flow forth in all their native beauty & elegance, without cramping, by compressing, or confusing by curtailing   I like elbow room in everything. In a letter it is essential and in a stage coach I should opine, that before these sheets can have reached you, you will have found the want of it, as Dogberry says "very tolerable and not to be endured." In time I know the trouble occasioned by the want of it. If the maxim which mamma is always inculcating upon me, that nothing is well done in a hurry, is without exceptions, this letter is fated for I seldom have been more pressed. Yet letters never thrive on mature consideration. The same impulse continued or ought to continue from the "my dear" at the top to the "your affectionate" at the bottom. The momentum once given and the impetus obtained, the word is forward, and it is enough to guide, without restraining the Pegasus of thought.

49

I can sympathise with you in your present situation as mine is similar in a great degree. You are bogged amongst the marshes (horrid things those bogs in this season, horrid sir horrid), and I am sadly bogged in my algebra. I cant get over division, it appears to me very long-division. It is positively not to be understood and I dont like to be made a fixture of, not by no means, and I have come to a very unhandsome fix. Mr Rowbotham will pronounce my head to be − understanding, and I pronounce his lessons to be + difficulty and yet with all my algebra This minus & plus will not add & make nothing. If they would I should be on my four wheels again progressing onward to fractions which look as if they would as the Doctor says crack anybodys skull and reduce it to fractions. But I will not anticipate difficulty.

Really Sir I think the drawing room, withdrawing room or room into which I withdraw to draw, owes all its beauty to your presence. We have sat in it two nights and the vacancy of the throne which you are wont to fill and from which thou are wont to impart the learning contained in the volumes of literature enlivening it by your conversation and facilitating its comprehension by your remarks, the vacancy of that chair I say made the room appear vacant and the absence of that conversation made conversation flag. Return, oh return from thy peregrination, fly from the bosom of the bogs to the bosom of those who wait thee in anxious expectation. As the eagle returns to its eyrie, as the bird that wanders over distant climes returns to its place of rest so < do > thou return to us who are sorrowing for thy presence. < . . .> winder up!!!! Factas meas admire   And now $X\alpha\hat{\iota}\rho o\tau\epsilon$, as Anacreon says pour la présente pro non quantum sufficit temporis ut literam longam scriberem I remain

Your most mightily affectionate son

John Ruskin
(RFL, 274−75)

He finds his first subject in reflecting on his composition − in reflecting, that is, on the "positively nothing" with which he is so fully compatible that he can describe it as himself: "I roll on like a ball." The only counterforce comes from without −

not from his mind's interaction with his subject, which seems to involve as little "friction" as its articulation in prose, but from resistant phenomena like time and space and his cousin Mary. Unlike the latter, time and space will not move in on him but they are more stubborn in holding their ground when he starts to get expansive. And one of them can stand in for the other, so that his experience of a tight fit remains after Mary vacates the premises because the continuing lack of time reminds him of what it is like to lack space ("In time I know the trouble occasioned by the want of it"). Even his quickness to embrace time and space as subjects leaves them still unabsorbably around him, constricting the "flow" which is necessary to demonstrate that his prose is the very "play of cogitation." It is not because "greater freedom" improves his thought but because it does not impinge on virtues that are "native" to it that Ruskin's partiality to this condition displaces his conditional desire to write a "short," "pithy," "laconic," "concentrated" letter. Displaces not replaces: a reminder of the advantages of concentration persists in the simile likening the compression of his ideas to "the steam of a high pressure engine" which, in his first memorable poem, was seen to generate numerous fruitful activities, including his own writing. And that expansive and vigorously enjambed verse seems all the more energetic for its being held within his chosen couplet form. Like the steam engine, the constraint which he writes under is a preserver as well as a destroyer, making it likely that if his "impulse" survives at all it will continue as it "ought to continue" from the top to the bottom of his letter. This is why his mother's stricture against hurry, instead of being suppressed, becomes the setting for his own maxim that "letters never thrive on mature consideration." The pressure he complains of has "pressed" him into writing the kind of letter with which he has reason to be pleased. The lack of "elbow room in everything" protects and enhances the "momentum" which is a sign that he is writing on, as well as about, Pegasean wing.

But if "the word is forward," there is still the question of exactly how to accommodate unrestrained movement within the fixed bounds which he has come to consider advantageous as well as ineluctable, "'very tolerable and not to be endured.'" This is where what Mary calls his "nonsense" comes in – and he plays on it as ironically as he does on the variants of "pressure," first disowning "the cognomen of nonsense" and then taking it up as a cover under which to bring in what is actually "sensible" and "serious." His "nonsense" comprises not just jokes and puns but also mental turns which they express or facilitate, and which make them continuous with each other. Whether the turns in this letter are disconcertingly short and sharp, as on a word, or open out over a longer stretch as he revolves an idea in his mind, they participate in a single extended meditation on the "laws of motion." The obstacles presented to his own rolling on like a ball bring to mind his father's rolling on in a stage coach, which brings on a second paragraph in which he associates his father's being "bogged among the marshes" with his own "bogged" progress through the fields of mathematics. The matter of algebra is assimilated to his previous discourse on how one makes one's way through a letter as "the Pegasus of thought" carries him "over" one algebraic difficulty only to deposit him "on my four wheels again progressing onward" towards another. His refusal to dwell on this destination prompts him to recur to his present situation without his father, whose movements back home he imagines in a final paragraph which returns Ruskin to his opening complaint that he has "scarcely time" to write a long letter. In the meantime he has managed to produce a letter which is not "short" yet is "concentrated." He has made something substantial enough to occupy space and time out of the "nothing" he calls the process of composition, substantiating his paradoxical claim that it is "positively" nothing. In fact he thinks pervasively in terms of this kind of paradox, in which the absence of one thing (a subject, for instance) is experienced as the presence of something else that suggests it. From the first the "I" which identifies itself with an act which is "nothing" nonetheless demands, and fills, all the "elbow room" it can muster – the absence of which makes its presence felt as the incentive to get it, or as duress. The "no means" by which Ruskin finds himself able to "make nothing" by way of progress is a mathematical operation which constitutes so palpable an obstruction that Ruskin finds it not merely hard to understand but "positively not" comprehensible.

As they draw in the various and obviously related images of moving through time and space, these paradoxes eventually give to them a wider reference, a subtler coherence. This becomes clearer when the letter writer who relentlessly multiplies his words and his turns declares that what he cannot "get over" is "division." The believer in the continuity of a single impulse is alarmed enough by the prospect of "fractions" to decline to "anticipate difficulty." But the difficulty already tells in the next paragraph, where his father's being withdrawn from the "withdrawing room" leaves the family a fraction of itself – and introduces another instance of the way that being "minus" something can paradoxically amount to being " + difficulty." Once again "This minus & plus will not add & make nothing," and the nothing that they make is the composition of his paragraph. For in the absence of a Papa who can fill with meaning those "volumes" of literature and of space that he has vacated, his son must – and can – fill them up himself. Like the pressure created by the lack of ample time and space, absence (whether of a subject or of his father) has a double valence, conducing not just to an uncomfortably positive presence that is a sign of what is missing ("the absence of that conversation made conversation flag"), but contributing also to the presence of a compelling opportunity. In both cases the sense of what he lacks helps to "guide, without restraining the Pegasus of thought." The shortness of time and space works to maintain the coherence of the expansively winding way of writing which they tend to induce; the experience, or even the anticipation, of division or fragmentation, of a separation between his thoughts or a "vacancy" in the wholeness of his world of Herne Hill – all of these are controlled by writing that makes and emphasizes connections, that sustains the one impulse that "ought to continue from the 'my dear' . . . to the 'your affectionate.'" Out of the negative experience, something positive is generated, something that reticulates and extends itself far beyond the initial connection made by a letter to an errant father. It is partly under the pressure of division and separation that the fragments of his composition coalesce.

As do his ideas about composition. To write about writing, as well as to write, is to move through time and space, contending with the pressures they create and with those that set one in motion in the first place. Ruskin naturally imitated what he heard and read about how a writer "ought" to compose, but his early letters are distinguished by the great ingenuity with which he also learns, and teaches, from his own processes of composition. It is partly on the basis of his own writing that he theorizes about writing itself and about the writing of others – a method that will come to fruition when he undertakes to draw Turner's subjects as an approach to understanding what Turner aimed at and achieved. Those were working studies, and this prose is merely "play"; but when he lays down his pen in allusion to Anacreon's taking his leave, it is because Ruskin believes that he has not only played for the amusement of his audience, but has also produced a kind of composition. At the end of his letter he translates its beginning into an array of languages, the real point of which is no longer that he lacks the time to write a long letter but that he has mastered several means of having his say.[8] But what is most impressive about his letters is not the profusion of words which he finds to express a given idea, or to express the givens he takes on when he writes. The achievement of his best letters is their demonstration that any composition worthy of the name is put together according to "laws of motion" that are discernible in it ever after. The laws are built into it along with the words.

.   .   .

"Factas meas admire": and his father did admire his achievements in the long letter quoted above, choosing it to forward to friends as the one "by which you will best see how John goes on" (RFL, 276). But none of his readers saw better than Ruskin that it is the way he goes on which "of course" produces his "difficulty in stopping myself when there is nothing else to stop me." These difficulties are acknowledged as often as are his problems in starting, and with a similar implication that to represent the problem may be to find its solution. He takes leave of his subjects by saying, in the last words of two of his poems, "I must take leave of you" (2.256 n. and 259). In his earliest verses he expects the last word to be taken for the deed: "And so I end" (2.255), "I quickly end" (2.256). His later methods of stopping and starting are so closely related to each other that he can even provide himself with a beginning he seeks by making use of his characteristic self-reference in ending. "Rhyme is a

difficult thing to conclude in, so I fall into plain prose,'' says
Ruskin at the end of eleven irregular stanzas whose first
concludes

> – A thing that's begun
> People say – is half done,
> That is only a mental illusion
> Most proverbs are false, & you'll find this is one
> If you look for my letter's conclusion.
>
> (RFL, 321–24)

The announcement that he intends to be done often comes as
a new departure, as in the penultimate stanza of another long
rhyming letter which previously had a different end in view:

> Twas in this stanza that I did intend
> To terminate my letter, if I could.
> How very difficult tis to conclude,
> From the high flights of rhyming to descend.
> Either my endings are abrupt and rude,
> Or else my poems never have an end.
> I seldom find a stanza a real poser
> Save that one which I wish to make the close, sir.

As if this requires a demonstration, Ruskin allots himself
another stanza:

> Then this will be a puzzling one, I know.
> I want a rhyme: the first that comes I pop
> Down, and my Muse's soaring wings I lop.
> I wind my watch up when it will not go,
> And wind my verse up when it will not stop!
> I've three lines only to conclude in, so
> You see that this, the next approaching line, is –
> This very verse is positively
>
> FINIS   (RFL, 362–63)

The central metaphor is predictive: having been wound up so
tightly, his writing ticks on for another paragraph after the
"FINIS," in prose.

Ruskin's references to the difficulty of concluding obviously answer to his mother's requests that he write shorter letters, and to his own relentless sense of the shortness of time and of pieces of paper. But his answer's being so ostentatiously long and good-humored reminds the reader that still more is in question – even where the matter is apparently as trivial as his display of vexation that an address usurps space in a letter:

And then how provoking when you come to the end   How one hates the direction for taking up such a quantity of room as if it thought itself of such mighty consequence as to turn out all the thoughts which might have blackly rested on the snowy couch of paper   Oh one could kick it downstairs.   (RFL, 227)

With every afterthought his space shrinks, and his pleasure grows. When, for example, his "mamma says its wasting my time" to write a verse travelogue, Ruskin counters with a poem in which his admission of "wasting and beguiling time / And spinning out line after line" is linked to the closing assumption that his father "must excuse / The capricolings of the muse" about which he goes on for another four lines (RFL, 233–34). The poem displays the speed and ingenuity with which Ruskin has always been able to make of frustration and self-deprecation a drama of achievement and self-assertion. What this poem more distinctively demonstrates is how he ties his confidence in self-justification to the movements of forces at once inside and outside of himself – here, a muse whose "unbounded wing / . . . never never will remain / Bound to earth by any chain." His feeling attached to something "unbounded" suggests why, when time, space, and his mother do not close in on him, Ruskin writes with a will to close in on them. Going on about the opposition brings him closer to those boundaries he can sooner find than he can find it in himself to make.

In Ruskin's writing of the early and middle 1830s, the centrality of self – whether as culpably deficient of ideas, or as being the inventive subject of them – is posited at the outset and used in order to get going, but is then identified with, submerged into, the process of composition ("I roll on like a ball"). So that the compositional will can no longer stop itself because it can no longer command itself, and writing purports to be in its own control, or at the mercy of animated and animating subject matter over which it rolls or with which it is fused in the act and fact of composition. Coming to the end of its subject will not necessarily mean that a composition is over. Even as a fourteen-year-old decreeing that "The same impulse . . . ought to continue from the . . . top to the . . . bottom" of a letter (RFL, 275), Ruskin already knows that what makes it so difficult to find the bottom is that the "impulse" can migrate between the subject, the writing, and the self. The very definition of a "top" and a "bottom" depends upon where the impulse is said to be at work, or in play. The poem he attributes to his "unbounded" muse is set in the midst of a letter that begins with his declaring "I really do think I shall soon be quite exhausted run out of subjects" – which exhaustion is understood to have no bearing on his "cantering away" in the meantime with the subject of his four-hundred-line travelogue (RFL, 233). His language implies that it is not the letter writer but the writing which puffs up a "direction" into something substantial enough to be kicked downstairs. His ornamented salutations make him wonder whether he will have space for what he has to say, yet his regret that he must confine himself to "paper talk" gets lost in the delight of describing the travels of the mail and of his pen: "I think my pen must be out of breath," he says, fully in possession of his own; "It has run such a wild goose chase over the snow white sheet of paper" (RFL, 256–57).

This migration of the "impulse" can prompt the design of

an entire literary project, as it does in a composite of pictures and writing he produced between the ages of nine and ten. Part of the drama of "The Puppet Show, or Amusing Characters for Children" comes of Ruskin's reliance on his characters for the stops and starts of his writing (they are "puppets" in this sense too, obedient to his compositional will).[9] In his ten-line verse "Introduction," self-reference gets him going: "Once by a little boy a puppet show was made." But Ruskin quickly identifies himself with the characters who are his subject, as he had in *Harry and Lucy, Concluded*, where Harry spoke for him in alluding to creating "a Punch's Show or Pantomine [sic] to please his father" (2. xxxiii). Then the characters take over, making a departure which puts Ruskin in possession of an ending:

> Such were the figures acted in this pretty
>   little show
> And as the figures went away so from it
>   I do go   (1)

The subject ends itself, and the authorial presence along with it. This precisely predicts what happens in the subsequent series of verses. In the midst of them, he is carried by Cruikshank's illustration and the movements of a fox − "GETTING OVER THE GROUND" of the book as well as of the page [Illus. 4]; and by the last verse, the "I" of John Ruskin is entirely lost in the movements of a character named "Curdken" who has lost his hat in the wind:

> And while high the breezes blow
> After it I swiftly go   (31)

The utterance of the poem has been assumed by the utterance of its subject.

The complexity of what he is doing here is compounded in a poem written two years later whose subject is poetry. The five stanzas of "To Poesie" suggest why the young Ruskin was attracted to personification as a means of fusing an idea or an object with human verbal expressiveness.[10] He envisions poetry only to call it – as he has so often called composition – "nothingness," precisely because it is so fully the expression of the writing self which has no presence here:

> Thou art a thing of nothingness,
> Thou art fancy's wayward child;

At the same time that poetry is the expression of the self, it is also identified with its subject and with the expression of its own impulse in language:

> Thou art the bursting of the heart,
> The language of the fiery soul;
> Thou art nature's voice and tone:
> While as thy numbers higher roll,
> In mystic harmony,
> With soundings all thine own. (2.318)

Having absorbed both the poet's self and his subject, in the last stanza the notes of poetry can be said to sing themselves:

> Mingle thy voice with the thunders,
> And notes of woe, and notes of dread,
> In various lyrics sing.   (2.319)

As these and other instances suggest, even more than their openings, the closings of Ruskin's poems bring into focus what he considers to be the relationship between the composition of one's subjects and one's writing, and the composition of one's identity. Although in his prose Ruskin does not cling to the simile of rolling on like a ball, his idea persists that one's own volition can appear to disappear in one's writing, becoming the "nothing" which is composition. In a letter written when he was barely thirteen, an allusion to Pope's *An Essay on Criticism* enhances with animal life the graphically "winding way" of his writing. His comparison between the form of a snake and that of his serpentine prose will be sharply vexatious in his work as a man, but it strikes the boy as a promising means of prolonging his "fun."

> ... I was beginning to think, that my store of conversation and fun, was run out, & exhausted, & that another letter if I attempted one, would be a thing with a beginning & an end, but no middle, a head & a tail but no body, and besides unluckily one cannot say of that tail, that thereby hangs a tale, nor that it like a wounded snake drags its slow length along, for although I always understood that the possession of a tail indicated the possession of a body, yet this tail not only wants a body, but it is a tail that is taleless; which although it appears a contradiction in theory, is nevertheless very true in practice, as you may see from this example, as I dare say you are now thinking, that this tale about a tail, has neither head nor tale, but only too much body,   ergo it is a tale without a tail, which proves it to have an existing nonexistence (perhaps it would be the better for nonexistence) like the famous letter, which is always invisible, yet never out of sight ...   (RFL, 271)

Ruskin makes a subject of the ending of a letter which begins by seeming bodiless, but he can change that subject with the mere substitution of a letter in one word, so that the "tail" or ending can be seen not only as the beginning of his letter but also as its middle ("tale"). Yet whether he sees it as a beginning or a middle, Ruskin's ending seems without end – like the endings of other letters which he cannot quite attain yet always keeps in sight, "an existing nonexistence." The reference to Pope brings with it a suggestion that some endings may be as superfluous as "A needless Alexandrine ... / That, like a wounded snake, drags its slow length along" (Book II, lines 356–57). It also brings with it reminders that writing can resemble, as well as discuss, its chosen subject, and that writers have good precedents for thinking that "The sound must seem an Echo to the sense" (Book II, line 365).[11] So it follows that later in the letter Ruskin's "treatise" on his "thundering knocks" at the door claims that "they distinguish my arrival from that of any other person" – as they did in those letters he wrote as a ten-year-old which begin "Ha ha ha, he he he, ho ho ho" (RFL, 177) or "Hollo hollo papa . . . no boy except myself would have dared address his papa with . . . hollo . . ." (RFL, 174–75).

The physical resemblances between his language and its subject are more palpable, the echoes between them are more audible, because Ruskin's experiences as a child involved remarkably little alienation of his writing from his speaking, and remarkably strong connections between his own marks put on paper and what he could see elsewhere. To begin with the relationship between writing and speaking, Margaret Ruskin has already been quoted as observing, of her nine-year-old son, that he "does not know there is any difference in putting things on paper from saying them" (RFL, 172). As we have also heard, Ruskin felt so little difference, or "friction," between the modes of speaking and writing that he continually describes his poems and letters as "talking," or "talking on paper" (RFL, 256, 313, 324, 357).[12] It remains to be said that this was possible for him partly because of his mother's clearly articulated principle of not criticizing or altering his writing (RFL, 176, 185, 409). For all his references to her requests that he end his long letters, there is no suggestion in them or in hers that she ever touched anything he wrote; and there is a great deal of evidence that she was right to assume that "to check or point out faults . . . might make that a labour which is at present done with perfect ease & delight" (RFL, 176). She assumed that her son inherited this fluency from his father (RFL, 171, 176); yet her own transcript of his first letter is a reminder that it was she who gave him his confidence in the inalienable meaning of

words and the Word, she who taught him to sound the sense
of a biblical chapter, and to feel certain that what is rightly
pronounced will be rightly understood. It is also important to
remember that the bible was not the only book she read.
When Ruskin was ten she was enjoying John Horne Tooke's
The Diversions of Purley (RFL, 208), a speculative dialogue which
moves from the Lockean view that language enables thought
to a specific consideration of how it is that "winged words"
enable the *speed* of thought. During the same year she was
reading to Ruskin and his cousin from Adam Smith's *Theory of
Moral Sentiments*: "it may be the means of making them even
now observe something of the working of their own minds
and this may lead in time to more & more knowledge [of]
themselves   at present they appear both to understand and to
like it . . ." (RFL, 186).[13] As is clear from the opening of this
paragraph, her readings were intended to enhance her
husband's: "I let Johns letters come just as he writes them
that you may not be misled in your judgment as to his hopes
and feelings" (RFL, 185). It was in part because his verbal
facility reminded her of the husband she adored that she
could give to the very young Ruskin what she could not allow
in herself, a prodigious confidence in the workings of one's
own mind.

His mother's witness is also significant when it comes to
the physical aspects of Ruskin's writing. When he has just
turned four and dictates the first letter which "he pretended
to read from his paper," Margaret Ruskin notes that "he is
beginning to copy from his books and will soon learn himself
to write I think – " (RFL, 128). It is difficult to tell from her
account of "our reading" when he is not quite three – he has
"perfectly" memorized all of the Lord's prayer and nine of
the Ten Commandments – whether Ruskin's writing therefore comes after he can read by himself or whether he is still
remembering the words she so carefully reads aloud (RFL,

109). What is clear is that Ruskin's learning to read is based in some important ways on what he has learned from his experiences of learning to write.[14] This is because his visual apprehension is at least the equal of his aural apprehension, and because the two are inseparably bound together in his response to graphic marks which he regards as things in themselves, as well as means of signification. Margaret Ruskin's comment on the first letter written in his own hand, and on several thereafter, that he may be even more concerned with the way his writing looks than with what it says, does not just reflect his assumption of her own concern with the correct appearance of a letter. She no doubt has some share in his apologies when his writing is untidy. But it is his own idea to think of his pen as a "tool" and himself as a "workman" (RFL, 173); to labor over minute replications of printed copperplate hand (2.529) [Illus. 5, 6]; to design so elaborate a "finis" for a poem that its flourishes make it seem that there is no "beginning of that end" (RFL, 259) [Illus. 7], and to draw out salutations until it seems there is no end to his beginnings.

John James Ruskin takes up the emphasis placed by his son on writing as a physical act and object when he praises the "beautiful flourish . . . you commence your Epistle with":

You have put your Papa in a frame of filagree work or of the age of Louis 14th as they say at Mr. Snells [the upholsterer] of all those fine carved Works exhibited to our admiring Eyes Your Letter is expression of high Spirits & is witty in its turns – extremely well written as to legibleness or legibility or readableness & I think your capitals improve. They are numerous & to me as expressive as poetry for I see they are each followed by some Town that I am to drag your Honour through before Summer be come & gone. You may Sing Fal lal la. You are to dance away over Hill & Dale & I am to pay the Piper. (RFL, 221. Part of the letter to which this one refers is quoted above, pp. 39–40)

For all the father's responsiveness to the look of language – for all his punning on capital letters and cities, or his having previously heaped them both into the shape of a "Pyramid" (RFL, 210) – he is right to regard his son as "the Piper" in this matter. Behind Ruskin's jokes about kicking writing downstairs, or tracing it like a goose's tracks in the snow, is an exceptionally powerful sense of the materiality of language and its movements, and an exceptionally powerful sense of how the physical world and its movements might likewise be seen as a language. Writing literally taught him about the world about which he would write. Maybe not while he was making the flourishes in his early poems and letters for his father, but surely on the basis of them, Ruskin was later helped "to understand that the word 'flourish' itself, as applied to writing, means the springing of its lines into floral exuberance, – therefore, strong procession and growth, which must be in a spiral line, for the stems of plants are always spirals" (28.525).

Not that words are the things which they signify: as Ruskin says in a verse set into the letter whose tail, or tale, has "an existing nonexistence," "'twould be a great deal better, / If you were yourself the letter" (RFL, 272). But his letters and the words of which they are composed are nonetheless things in themselves, not mere compensations for the presences he misses. So Ruskin can do more than point to the volumes that his Papa leaves empty: he can make them companionable – so companionable that there is little space left for anybody else, including the person to whom he addresses himself (RFL, 275). The irony of this situation is literalized when Ruskin complains that an address seems to think "itself of such mighty consequence as to turn out all the thoughts which might have blackly rested on the snowy couch of paper" (RFL, 227). Although the provoking words were not inscribed by the son to the father but by the father to the son,

Ruskin's witticism registers his realization that the actual whereabouts of an addressee might be as inimical to the comfortable couching of one's own thoughts as an unwelcome guest.

I will return to this realization when I consider how Ruskin's language marked his separate ways of contending with his father and his mother, not only during their lifetimes but also when he was living with their deaths, and with the death of his earlier confidence in language. The reminiscences about his past in which Ruskin revises these losses will add tremendous practical and theoretical complexity to what we have seen thus far about how children learn to write. But his early work has important implications of its own for readers who would set individual practice against twentieth-century theories of language and language acquisition. For it strongly suggests the destructiveness of segregating a child's experience of visual and verbal signification, or of pictorial and scriptorial signs – and it strongly suggests the arbitrariness of locking them into an inevitable chronological sequence.[15]

To Ruskin as a boy, the audible echo and graphic isomorphism between writing and its subject are less frequently, and less meaningfully, results of the writer's attempts at imitation than they are results of the properties of language itself. Many years before Modern Painters laid out his objections to mimesis and advanced instead an expressive theory of art,[16] Ruskin was finding that language is always inherently expressive – about its own nature, about its topics, and about the writer who attends to them both. Rather than being a mere manipulable object, language seems to be a subject which is itself subject to a subject matter and to a writer (to adapt the terms I used at the outset of this chapter). The consequence of these interrelations is the opposite of that swallowing up of everything into one subjectivity which

Ruskin parodied in his analysis of the pathetic fallacy. For if Ruskin's boyhood writing was deeply self-expressive, it was also expressive of an obedience to other things. This is the message of the nameless child in "The Lamp of Obedience," who preserves the freshness of what Ruskin first felt when he thought he was moving freely within the laws of the language.

It is almost impossible for us to conceive, in our present state of doubt and ignorance, the sudden dawn of intelligence and fancy, the rapidly increasing sense of power and facility, and, in its *proper sense*, of Freedom, which such wholesome restraint would instantly cause throughout the whole circle of the arts. Freed from the agitation and embarrassment of that liberty of choice which is the cause of half the discomforts of the world; freed from the accompanying necessity of studying all past, present, or even possible styles; and enabled, by concentration of individual, and co-operation of multitudinous energy, to penetrate into the uttermost secrets of the adopted style, the architect would find his whole understanding enlarged, his practical knowledge certain and ready to hand, and his imagination playful and vigorous, as a child's would be within a walled garden, who would sit down and shudder if he were left free in a fenceless plain.

(*The Seven Lamps of Architecture*, 8.259)

When Ruskin wants to convince his readers of the advantages of their settling on a single architectural language or "style," he adduces – in the paragraph just before this one – the example of a child who is learning to write. Obey the language that already exists, Ruskin says. Originality depends on it.

CHAPTER 3

DISCIPLINES
(1833–35)

"The effort to express sentiment in rhyme; the sentiment being really genuine"; "the real love of engraving, and of such characters of surface and shade as it could give"; "the violent instinct for architecture"; "the unabated, never to be abated, geological instinct": these together made up, to the autobiographer considering his boyhood, "the quadrilateral plan of my fortifiable dispositions" (*Praeterita*, 35.120–21). It looked different to the one who appointed himself to man the fort – more polygonal, less infiltrated with longing to concentrate power on just one side. When, for example, the sixteen-year-old set himself up to produce "The Ascent of the St. Bernard, A Dramatic Sketch" (1835), he at once called into play these four instincts and more – in planning the action, in designing the roles, in characterizing young Master R, who sketches, geologizes, writes poetry, speaks poetically, and is in other respects very like the author of the verse account in which he appears. The playwright caricatures, more or less genially, each undisguised member of his own family and of the entourage with which they had actually travelled through the same Alpine scenes a few months before. Then he goes out of his way to regard the caravan from the point of view of a soliloquizing Mountaineer, who breaks free of the alternately rhyming lines of their conversation to wish "the hills had souls, / That they might crush these emmets, who pass by / Tracing these most ignoble portraitures / Of our free Icebergs!" While the speeches of an Augustinian Monk set the Ruskins' travels into a more broad-minded evocation of time and eternity, the most enlarging perspective is the one provided by the elaborate stage directions in prose, prose which expresses

Master R's designs upon a setting which Mr. R said his son "could not / Express" as an artist and misrepresents as a naturalist ("Why, the snow's a little dirty, / And he calls it pink") (1.513,519). This arrangement allows the author of the "Sketch" to seem good-naturedly ironic about his abilities while setting his family down in a place so stupendous that it makes them look small.

The manuscript breaks off after six scenes, but Ruskin began again, in the same vicinity, with Chronicles of St. Bernard (1835-36), now entirely in prose and equipped with an "I" who directly describes what he sees. In the meantime Ruskin's impulses to geologize and to draw are personified and parodied in an English geologist insensitive to effects ("the man of stone" [1.525]) and an English artist uninterested in causes ("and falling on hands and knees on a smooth, wet, round block of this foreground, as he called it" [1.533]), while his impulse to venerate is embodied in a monk, and his impulse to socialize, in a young Oxonian. What the speaker is left with is an inclination to observe the others, and to respond to their setting in prose whose intermittent excesses might be measured against the monk's efficiently energetic discourse on the same subject. What is still more interesting than Ruskin's irony about aptitudes like his own is his recognition that each of them may involve a different style of self-expression, even while engaged with aspects of the same thing. And Ruskin's projection of several of his own abilities onto separate characters makes one think about how and how long they coexist in a composition in which they each go their separate ways. Yet the characters disperse only to reconvene in the shape of subject matter elsewhere. The failure of their conversation is worth the success of Ruskin's translations from mode to mode, or so he seems to think. For his self-irony coexists with confidence that excerpts from his 1833 travelogue may enhance an 1834 number of the *Magazine of Natural History*, and that its editor may profitably cull the diary of his continental tour of 1835 for passages to publish in 1836.

As was the case with many others in the nineteenth century, Ruskin's confidence in crossing boundaries between disciplines was enabled by inherited convictions that the physical creation and human artifacts are both inherently languages, the one of God and the others of men.[1] Corollaries of the linguistic metaphor that connected them could be discovered within individual disciplines themselves. Far from concealing his assumption of assumptions he found elsewhere, Ruskin enjoys giving evidence that what he has taken in is then laid out according to its own designs, not his. This ingestion and display are reflexively dramatized in *Chronicles of St. Bernard*, when the Oxonian (and Ruskin is soon to go up to Oxford himself) rhapsodizes on "the good deal of imagination" discernible in the stomach of a corpulent English gentleman.

"I can read at this moment the thoughts of his inside: there is a light of other days illuminating his interior; and beautiful dreams, yet not all dreams, are passing over the mirror of his – mind – I was going to say, – stomach, I mean, and it's a large one. First comes a vision of a plateful of the turtle – the fair fat, transparent as a chrysophrase, beautifully green, lustrous as an opal, floating swanlike on the richness of the exquisite brown ... Now the vision is changed: in imagination he is about to cut into the sirloin of beef. All over the beautiful brown, with soft and gentle distillation flowing like spontaneous pourings forth of the spirit of poetry from some mighty mind, descend the streams of crystal gravy, melted ruby, in soft, soft silence descending, the voiceless flow of meadow waters by night not more soothingly sublime. In goes the imaginary knife with a sweet, rich sound, as it buries itself in the pure marrow ... and lo! the exquisite shading from the outward brown to the interior rose, that rises over the white bone like the blush of the dawn of the morning upon some snowy Alp."

(1.528)

In a single caricature, Ruskin incorporates conventions drawn from natural history, visual art, and literature – especially the writing in which Percy Shelley uses mental operations as figures for physical phenomena. For all its farcical carnality, the boy's burlesque deserves to be read in relation to the seriousness with which, sixteen years later in Venice, Ruskin describes his own insatiable desire:

[T]here is the strong instinct in me which I cannot analyse – to draw and describe the things I love – . . . a sort of instinct like that for eating or drinking. I should like to draw all St. Mark's . . . stone by stone – to eat it all up into my mind – touch by touch.[2]

Like St. Mark's in *The Stones of Venice*, each of the disciplines with which Ruskin works not only has but is a language – a language which can be taken in by the mouth while remaining outside the body, a language which is materially present as well as signifying what is not, a language which functions according to laws that are already built into it and that demand obedience from anyone who would regard it with imagination.

So that when, at the end of his letter naming the "laws of motion," Ruskin expresses himself by deploying a number of national languages, he does not imply that their differences from English are swallowed up in the process (RFL, 274–75). On the contrary, it is their differences which make it possible for the English speaker to say what he wants to say. This is also what happens when Ruskin sets himself to master the three dominant disciplines – of science, visual art, and literature – in terms of which he wrote as a boy, and to each of which I will now turn in sequence.

.   .   .

Ruskin's study of science, like the religious training with which it was compatible, defended him against a suspicion of solipsism even as he took in the world beyond himself.[3] The more fully he puts the natural world into his own language, the more certain he seems that he is not its artificer. So that his verbal self-consciousness can buttress, rather than undermine, his sense of his own objectivity.

I have thought sometimes that though there always *appears* a richness, a melancholy, a fatigue if I may so say, in the light of the afternoon, and a freshness, coldness, cheerfulness, and vigour in that of the morning, yet that these changes were more in our feelings than in the light itself, and that a person waking from sleep in the evening would not be able to distinguish it from the morning, and this is true to a certain extent, but these changes of light [I have just described on] the Alps show that it is not altogether so.

Here a truism about the power of the mind over what appears to the eye is actually corrected, not confirmed, by his having set the daily passage of Alpine color into the pattern of his prose (*Diaries*, 58–59). Language again becomes a mode of evidence when Latin, which "beautifully distinguished" degrees of sentience in creation, structures Ruskin's opinion – fortified by "Some philosopher or other," by "many an observer of nature," by the behavior of three kinds of plants – that "anima" as well as "vita" exists in vegetation (RFL, 354). The finding that plants experience pleasure and pain supports his tentacular analogy, reaching through two letters about his translations of the classics, between students' feeling nourished or emboxed by instruction, and the "vegetable life" of plants that burgeon while he works at home or are stunted outside the window at school (RFL, 350–57). His study of languages and of botany together authorize his verbal display of "the living banks of leaves . . . all quiver, quiver, quivering," and of laurels standing moribund in his teacher's courtyard, like "Antigone, immured in a rocky cave" (RFL, 355–56).

In the second of these letters, the one celebrating his

retention of "that sine qua non of translation, presence of mind" (RFL, 357), Ruskin also parades his mastery of the language in which a mineralogist might describe the panes of glass that face the "dead brick walls" of the courtyard. He isolates the technical idioms – one color "passing" or "running" into the next, a medium that transmits light more or less "feebly" – which suggest activity in what is apparently inert; so that what began as mockery of a classmate for staring through such a window ends in the possibility that he might find "epigrams in bricks, sermons in stones" (RFL, 356). His translation from minerals to syntactical meaning is not eccentric: Robert Jameson's three-volume *System of Mineralogy*, which Ruskin studied as a boy and honored as a man, is a book whose very format enforces the idea that minerals may be arranged like a linguistic system. Studying Jameson and the minerals in the British Museum led Ruskin to begin his own "Mineralogical Dictionary" when he was twelve, organizing it alphabetically like Jameson's but, as he puts it in *Praeterita*, "writing my own more eloquent and exhaustive accounts in a shorthand of many ingeniously symbolic characters, which it took me much longer to write my descriptions in, than in common text" (35.121).[4] On two other occasions Ruskin draws attention to the writing in his dictionary: in 1864 he recalls that he "invented" for it a "shorthand symbolism for crystalline forms" (26.553), and in 1875 he notes his "shorthand composed of crystallo-graphic signs." The variation in these accounts between forms and signs depends upon the compound meaning of "crystallography" itself, which refers to both the forms under study and the written systems in which men have classified them.[5] His "Mineralogical Dictionary" draws on, and substantiates, his impulse to make analogies between his subject matter and his language, and to find a natural bond – whether in a snail's shell or in a stone – between a figure and a letter that may be seen and sounded. The combination of "crystal" and "graphy" (or of "geo" and "graphy") came to Ruskin with its meaning intact and vivid – as did those terms like "geology" whose suffixes refer not to the written but the spoken word.[6] The bible says that creation is inherently written and spoken. It is the fault of his translation if Ruskin's boyhood characters are "now entirely unintelligible to him" (26.97).

Following Jameson, Ruskin focussed on the "External Character" of minerals rather than on what chemistry might disclose about them.[7] But his concentration on the visible in minerals led to an explanation of what might otherwise be invisible in the scenes of which they were a part, and led to refinements in his grasp of interrelationship that were derived from the conventions of scientific writing. "Enquiries on the Causes of the Colour of the Water of the Rhine" (1834), Ruskin's first published piece of prose, shows what the lucidity and course of his characteristic syntax (beginning with the four-year-old's memory of "the Pond near the Burn which the Bridge is over") owe to his tracing the effects of a scene back to causes associated with a mineral: "There is a lake in a defile on the northwest flank of Snowdon, which is supplied by a stream which previously passes over several veins of copper" (1.191). Mineralogy led Ruskin to see exactly how stones compose, in space and through time, the larger composition in which they appear, for minerals are no more inert than the words in a sentence, and their position and juxtaposition are no less consequential. So he can dramatize the paradoxical durability of medieval ornaments and tracery as a mystery whose solution is the behavior of sandstone: a casual observation in his diary about Basle Cathedral is worked up into a publication portentously titled, "TO WHAT PROPERTIES IN NATURE IS IT OWING THAT THE STONES IN BUILDINGS, FORMED ORIGINALLY OF THE FRAILEST MATERIALS,

GRADUALLY BECOME INDURATED BY EXPOSURE TO THE ATMOS-
PHERE AND BY AGE, AND STAND THE WEAR AND TEAR OF TIME AND
WEATHER EVERY BIT AS WELL, IN SOME INSTANCES MUCH BETTER,
THAN THE HARDEST AND MOST COMPACT LIMESTONES AND
GRANITE?'' Once he discovers the inherent logic of a
composition, Ruskin can readily reverse the order of his own.
A mountain may be verbally decomposed into granite,
quartz, and mica, as in "FACTS AND CONSIDERATIONS ON THE
STRATA OF MONT BLANC . . ." (1.194–96); or deduced from
them, as in his 1835 verse "Journal of a Tour through France
to Chamouni" (2.411–12).

In the prose diary he kept of the same trip Ruskin
approaches the valley of Goldau through an analysis of the
materials which constitute it (Diaries, 36–37). All of the
elements are here of the chapter in Modern Painters IV called
"Stones," which declares that a stone is "a mountain in
miniature" (6.368), and dwells on "the straight and even
slope of bank" where the experienced eye detects a danger
greater than in the wilder, more curvilinear scenery to which
Ruskin is so deeply attracted (6.378). Ruskin facsimiles and
describes Turner's 1843 drawing of the valley of Goldau in
order to define both these ominous "lines of rest" and
Turner's genius in exaggerating them into "a form explanatory
of" the catastrophic rock fall of 1805:

even the slopes of the Rigi on the left are not, in reality, as
uninterrupted in their slope as he has drawn them; but he felt the
connection of this structure with the ruin amidst which he stood,
and brought the long lines of danger clear against the sunset, and as
straight as its own retiring rays.

(6.380)

This passage is evidence not only of the "Turnerian
topography" that gives prominence to truths that "lie
deepest in a scene and are most essentially linked together"

(6.380), but also of Ruskin's anticipation of it seven years before Turner's "Goldau." Within the space of twenty lines in his diary, Ruskin describes "a considerable slope," "the steep precipices which descend from Rigi Kulm," the "escarpments . . . which descend steeply into the lake of Zug," "the strata . . . (as I before remarked) very steeply inclined and . . . sloped down towards the village of Goldau." To anyone who knows stones, disaster is imminent – which is how Ruskin wants it. For the narrative in Ruskin's diary makes the Rossberg Fall into the sequel, not the preface, to his findings in the rubble.

"The interest of that pass to me / Lay in its mineralogy," he jauntily declares about St. Gothard in a verse letter to a friend (2.435 and n.3). In the combination, here as in his diary, of mineralogy with geology Ruskin was profoundly influenced by his study of Horace Bénedict de Saussure, whose four-volume *Voyages dans les Alpes* gave him a map, in dramatic illustrations and prose, of his favorite landscapes in the world.[8] Having requested and received these books for his fifteenth birthday, Ruskin thanks his father in a letter which moves from Saussure as subject, with his capacity "for carrying me again over the summits of the higher Alps," to his own descriptions and analyses of mountain scenery, to the explicit idea that writing is itself topographical: he concludes with a lament that his "geological poem [is] knocked up on the humps and bumps of the road, and brought to a standstill, else should be sent" (RFL, 278–80). In an obvious way, the progress of this letter literalizes and rehearses the habitual continuum between Ruskin's subject, his own occupations, and his writing. But Ruskin's sense of interrelation was affected in much less literal, more pervasive ways by the argument that Saussure advances in his "Discours Preliminaire":

Les hautes montagnes au contraire, infinement variées dans leur matiere & dans leur forme, présentent au grand jour des coupes naturelles, d'une très-grande étendue, où l'on observe avec la plus grande clarté, & où l'on embrasse d'un coup-d'oeil, d'ordre, la situation, la direction, l'epaisseur & même la nature des assises dont elles sont composées, & des fissures qui le traversent.

En vain pourtant les Montagnes donnent elles la facilité de faire de telles observations, si ceux qui les étudient ne savent pas envisager ces grands objets dans leur ensemble, & sous leur relations les plus étendues.

[The high mountains on the contrary, infinitely varied in their material and in their form, present in broad daylight natural declivities of very great extension, where one observes them with the greatest clarity, and where one encompasses in a look the order, situation, direction, density, and even the nature of the layers of which they are composed and of the fissures which cross them.

In vain however do mountains offer the opportunity of making such observations, if those who study them do not know how to consider these great objects in their overall effect, and in terms of their most extended relations.]   (I.ii–iii; my translation)

The coup d'oeil is intensive, as in mineralogy, but also takes in the extensive spaces of geology.[9]

> City, and hill, and waving wood,
> Blue glaciers cold, and sparkling flood –
> All that was marvellous or fair
> Seen at a single glance was there.
>
> (2.437)

Ruskin's response to the continuity between detail and panorama was enabled no less by Saussure's own syntax than by his organizing *Voyages dans les Alpes* as a series of tours which connect site to site. Ruskin chooses for translation in *Praeterita* a passage of "my Papa Saussure's description" of a vista taken in by a coup d'oeil and laid out in a series of interdependent clauses:

"A semicircular rock at least two hundred feet high, composed of great horizontal rocks hewn vertical, and divided by ranks of pine which grow on their projecting ledges, closes to the west the valley of Valorbe. Mountains yet more elevated and covered with forests, form a circuit round this rock which opens only to give passage to the Orbe, whose source is at its foot. Its waters, of a perfect limpidity, flow at first with a majestic tranquillity upon a bed tapestried with beautiful green moss, Fontinalis antipyretica; but soon, drawn into a steep slope, the thread of the current breaks itself in foam against the rocks which occupy the middle of its bed, while the borders, less agitated, flowing always on their green ground, set off the whiteness of the midst of the river; and thus it withdraws itself from sight in following the course of a deep valley covered with pines, whose blackness is rendered more striking by the vivid green of the beeches scattered among them . . .

"Ah, if Petrarch had seen this spring and had found there his Laura, how much would not he have preferred it to that of Vaucluse . . ."   (35.162)

The scene Saussure describes could have been no more hospitable to Petrarch than its interdependent syntax was to Ruskin. As when he drew and colored his own set of geological maps for his coming tour, or translated the bulk of Jameson into a "Dictionary" he could carry on the road, Ruskin drew on Saussure to create his own Alpine tour (35.lxxx–lxxxi, 152 and n.6).

Having learned from Saussure that what you see depends upon where you are, and that this arrangement can be charted in prose, Ruskin considered himself to be in position to see and write still more than his "Papa." Among the many perspectival studies in his 1835 diary, the one begun at the base of the Jura best shows Ruskin using *Voyages dans les Alpes* to gain perspective on Saussure (*Diaries*, 6–9).[10] Ruskin first presents the conformation of the mountain chain, then the views from its first slopes, and from the high pass through which his family continued to Geneva. It is while going back over this ground, and that covered in his verse "Journal of a Tour through France to Chamouni" (1835), that Ruskin creates one of the passages of greatest visual and verbal intensity in *Praeterita*. In the chapter called, like the pass, "The Col de la Faucille," the achievement of perfection comes – as it does so often in *Modern Painters*, *The Seven Lamps of Architecture*, *The Stones of Venice* – at an apex on either side of which are development and descent. What makes possible the ecstatic vision which closes the chapter is his sense that geological composition supports his own compositional instincts:

It is worth notice, Saussure himself not having noticed it, that this main pass of Jura, unlike the great passes of the Alps, reaches its traverse-point very nearly under the highest summit of that part of the chain. The col . . . is a spur of the Dôle itself, under whose prolonged masses the road is then carried six miles farther, ascending very slightly to the Col de la Faucille, where the chain opens suddenly, and a sweep of the road, traversed in five minutes at a trot, opens the whole Lake of Geneva, and the chain of the Alps along a hundred miles of horizon.

I have never seen that view perfectly but once – in this year 1835; when I drew it carefully in my then fashion, and have been content to look back to it as the confirming sequel of the first view of the Alps from Schaffhausen. (35.167)

Not only his drawing but especially his writing "in my then fashion" preserves the finding that shapes the revision of the view in *Praeterita*. For in the 1835 diary his bird's-eye view discovers the highest summits of the Jura at its southern border, "which a transverse section of the range of the Jura might present" (*Diaries*, 7). And his subsequent verbal account of his actual progress on the road brings him to "that illustrious corner, that looks across the broad and beautiful valley of Geneva, to the eternal ramparts of Italy" – and to the certainty that "this [is the] highest part of the pass." "Nothing" – not even Saussure – "could better illustrate the

79

form of these minor ranges of mountains" (Diaries, 8–9).

In the view of Charles Lyell, Saussure contributed valuably to what was known of the structure of the Alps and Jura, but "The few theoretical observations which escaped from him are . . . mere modifications of the old cosmological doctrines."[11] The influence of Lyellian geology on Ruskin's writing is usually postponed by his critics until it becomes obvious in Modern Painters IV.[12] Ruskin's boyhood works tell a different story. This story is graphically laid out in the pages of his geological manuscript dated 1831 by a cataloguer and still so striking that they have been reproduced in a recent biography of Ruskin and also as the endpapers for a collection of critical essays about him. But these pages are in fact his meticulously miniaturized rearrangements of text and illustrations from the third volume of Principles of Geology (1833) [see Illus. 8–12].[13] Ruskin's appropriation suggests not simply that consequences of his study of Lyell came earlier than many have noticed, but that from the first that study was of an interrelationship between visual and verbal representation.

The implication is that one person can import another person's accounts of geology into his writing much as he can use his own prose and drawing to import geology itself. Like his other movements back and forth between disciplines, Ruskin's apprehension of Lyell was enabled by their shared inheritance of the conviction that the physical world is itself a language. One language renders another, both of them visible – a project made manifest in the very title of Lyell's work: Principles of Geology, Being an Attempt to Explain the Former Changes of the Earth's Surface, by Reference to Causes Now in Operation. And the title also suggests the compatibility of Lyell's documentation with Jameson's insistence that conclusions be based on the visible, not invisible, character of things, and with Ruskin's belief that his eyes, and the texts and tools of his own making, are all he needs to comprehend what is before him. Lyell too relies on metaphors of decipherment, reading the "living language" whose "characters" are rocks, vegetation, animals.[14] Without reading the earth in the same way as Lyell, without supposing that Lyell was the only one who could read it, Ruskin was spurred by Lyell's language to make his syntax of interrelationship knowingly temporal as well as spatial. To the example Saussure gave him of the workings of physical perspective, Lyell would have added the perspective of history.[15] The present is the clue to the past, and the past is the explanation of the present aspect of things. Ruskin's religious training would have made him all the apter in mastering this mode of thinking, for biblical exegesis taught him to move back and forth with great speed between a present reality and its type in ancient story. There is, of course, an obvious alliance between historicism and nine-teenth-century geology, or between religious orthodoxy and the tendency of eighteenth-century science to focus on order and structure in nature rather than development. But Ruskin crosses those lines, as Lyell had before him.[16]

A cataclysmic theory of creation, consistent with the biblical time-scale, does remain in evidence in Ruskin's diary: he is caught by the spectacle of "veteran crags . . . telling to every traveller a wonderful tale of ancient convulsions" (22), rock deposits that stand as a "memorial of a series of successive and powerful deluges" (36). It is not until 1856 that his theories accord with Lyell's view that the earth's surface is constantly being elevated and eroded,[17] or that he announces he will "adopt the order, in description, which Nature seems to have adopted in formation" of mountains (6.214). But his language has enacted parts of Lyell's drama for years, arranging objects in space in terms of sequences in time. His first descriptions of the sights from Abbeville to Rouen and, a week later, from Paris to Soissons, are determined by the course of their formation as well as by the order of his perception:

The road from Abbeville to Rouen passes over a series of elevated plains, intersected by considerable vallies; these high, but level chalk downs, on the approach to Rouen sink suddenly down into a wide and richly cultivated plain which they surround on three sides, but which spreads away towards the south in uninterrupted distance. Round this champaign flows the Seine, skirting closely bases of the hills, which it has washed away in many parts into lofty chalk cliffs, and in the centre of the horse shoe thus formed, at the bases of the hills, and between them and the river, lies the town of Rouen . . .

Some distance from Paris the road passes over an immense sandstone tract, which extends to a great distance in the direction of Fontainbleau. It consists of low rounded hills covered in most parts with forests, but here and there heaving up naked summits of grey rock, partially covered with turf, from among the trunks of the tall trees by which they are surrounded. The whole of this district, from here to Fontainbleau, is covered with huge rounded blocks, apparently waterworn, of the sandstone by which the hills themselves are composed. These masses lie tossed among the trunks of the ancient trees, half buried in the turf, covered with moss, or tinted with various lichens. (Diaries, 4−5)

Language covers the ground between the spectacle and its catastrophic origins. While differing with Lyell's view that the pace of geological change is usually steady and gradual, and that the continuous changefulness of the earth is in the long run nonprogressive and nondirectional, the artist in Ruskin would still have been responsive to Lyell's implication that it is by gradation that continuity is achieved between things spatially or temporally disjunct.[18] When he takes up his diary to make sketches of ''three dispositions'' of ''veteran crags,'' Ruskin is finding in their own composition the links between ''ancient convulsions'' and what he sees now, in 1835 (Diaries, 22). Is the lake of Lucerne simply the water-filled breach between cliffs catastrophically severed, or the result of ongoing subsidence (Diaries, 38–39)? Either way, Ruskin can trace the lines that matter. They are all laid out before him, and he knows as well as Lyell how to make them extend into the past and future as far as his eye can reach.

Ruskin's knowingness involves theory as well as practice, and especially the interaction between them. From very early on he saw that gradations mediate not only between physical phenomena in the natural world but also between empirical observation and the theory that is allegedly based upon it – between, that is, two decidedly different things whose chronological relation is subject to change. He thought that Lyell had exploited this situation, to his discredit. Hence Ruskin's 1836 aside: "(I assert this as Lyell asserts his *well grounded* geological facts, upon very vague conjecture)" (RFL, 336). But Ruskin's "assertion" was presented as a joke, a pseudo-Lyellian observation that the rusty gown worn by one of his teachers had long ago been black. Elsewhere he regards his own rhetorical ordering of "conjecture" and "facts" as the expression of a justly deliberated "principle." Thus he writes to his editor at the *Architectural Magazine*, in 1838:

My tour in Scotland has, I hope, afforded me too much information to be kept in a detached heap. I have already referred it all to its regular heads, and I hope it will add interest to my future papers. I think if I were to put it in the form of a journal, it would lose much of its interest for want of arrangement. A fact always tells better when it is brought forward as proving a principle, than when it is casually stumbled upon by the traveller.   (36.15–16)

For Ruskin, the expressiveness of the conjecturing observer is all in the arranging of the "facts." He so reads the laws of the physical world and of English that a "fact" can follow the very "principle" to which it supposedly led.

. . .

If, as he puts it in one of his first scientific publications, "The granite ranges of Mont Blanc are as interesting to the geologist as they are to the painter" (1.194), the reverse is also true. The "composition" of and within stones, the "disposition" of cliffs, the "coup d'oeil" of an observer who makes out "gradations" between masses – all of these words point to issues no less relevant to art than to geology. And that drawing, like natural history, was associated in Ruskin's mind with the mechanics of writing is suggested by the lessons he gave to his college friend Henry Acland on the principles of composition: "In Drawing only, I learned by *grammar* thoroughly – and it is only as a grammarian that I speak to you" (36.21).[19] Ruskin plays as well as works with these connections, as in a letter in which news about his literature examination, his sketch-book, and his reading of Saussure is prefaced by jokes about the startling "coup d'oeil" of his "very longitudinal essay" (RFL, 386–87). And in general his sense of drawing and of writing do tend to be linear. His gift for line drawing (35.120), combined with his keen experience of the physicality and expansiveness of writing, help explain the remarkable individuality with which he seizes on the traditional notion that art is "nothing but a noble and expressive language" (*Modern Painters* I, 3.87).[20] For Ruskin, both visual and verbal "languages" are material; both interconnect their objects in space; and both involve a placing, a fixing of what is transitory.

He demonstrates as much in a piece of writing about a painting composed while he was under the instruction of the president of the Water-Colour Society, Copley Fielding:

Terror and peace, and calm and storm
Yet all before the tempest flee
From morn to eve, from eve to morn,
Changing their vain and fickle form.

Indeed; I've thought of taking down
In Copley Fieldings style, you know,
The blue and black, the smile & frown
Tornado, tempest, summer glow . . .

(RFL, 311)

Writing and painting are just as intimately linked in those moments when he creates, with great delight, a sense of animation or activity in what seems fixed by and within the form of composition. This link structures the previously quoted verse letter in which he justifies the "capricolings" of his muse in "line after line" of writing:

May I not employ my brain
In calling past delights again
Remembering thoughts recalling sayings
In fancy's never wearied playings
Joys succeeding pleasures flown
Till the last ray of light was gone
To image scenes left far behind
On the frail canvass of the mind
And raise in colours rich and bright
That mountain scen'ry to the sight
And make the placid waters flow
In seeming majesty below

(RFL, 234; italics mine)

It was in the spring of 1831, when he was twelve, that Ruskin began his lessons from Charles Runciman in the techniques for accomplishing in drawing the kinds of fixing, and animating, he writes of here. Ruskin parodies his own bustle in preparing to "invent a scene," and laughs at himself

85

for looking at his cousin's pictures to see how to draw rocks, woods, mountains, and cottages; but he is significantly silent about how he managed the waterfall, which is the central attraction of the scene (RFL, 262–63). Ruskin's talent for drawing falling water – a quintessential composition of motion which he implies he has performed here from memory – may well have been what Runciman had in mind when he said of Ruskin's drawing "that there was something in it, that would make him totally change the method he had hitherto pursued with me." For Runciman's next step was to paint a sea scene for his pupil to copy, and Ruskin's next step was to produce a long paragraph verbalizing the ways in which he might "carry off" the moving waters of England on paper (RFL, 267–68).

In *Praeterita* Runciman is credited with having taught Ruskin perspective – so impressively that he "drew [his] perspective" even before he "began to invent" the scene of the waterfall (RFL, 262). Since the late 1820s, when he was making perspectival studies in poems like "on scotland" and "The hill of kinnoul," there had been a steady growth in his sense of how one's physical position determines both the scene to be composed and the composition one makes of it. By the time he writes *Iteriad* (1830–32), the verse travelogue of his family's 1830 tour of the Lake District, he shows a self-conscious mastery in posing his subjects and in using their movements to activate his scenes.[21] Writings like these bring to mind the claim he makes about his drawings of the mid and later 1830s: "I was now . . . entirely master of perspective, and had great sense of position, and composition, in a subject" (35.623). This comment from the manuscript does not appear in the published version of *Praeterita*, where his acquiring a true *sense* of composition is put off until 1842 and he himself never learns to compose. *Praeterita* instead commemorates Runciman's failure to cultivate "the strong accuracy of my line." But in learning perspective from him, and "the habit of looking for the essential points in the things drawn," Ruskin has, as his writings of the 1830s clearly show, learned some of the elements of composition (35.76–77).

At least a year before he began lessons with Runciman, Ruskin's sense of position and composition were affected – to a degree unregistered in *Praeterita* – by the visits he made with his father to exhibitions of the Society of Painters in Water-Colours. The Society (whose members included Samuel Prout, David Roberts, and J. D. Harding, with whom Ruskin studied between 1841 and 1843) placed an emphasis on scrupulously accurate observation and imitation of nature, usually aided by a scientific study of light, color, and vision: doctrines and practices which bear fruit in Ruskin's later teachings in *Modern Painters* and *The Elements of Drawing*.[22] In the meantime, the dynamic perspectives of Turner, which Ruskin first studied in 1832, and, to a lesser extent, the deep spatial recession of Copley Fielding, both leave their mark on drawings Ruskin made during the continental tour of 1835.[23] The effect of his teachers is still more striking on the writings that came out of the tour. The greatest drama of "The Ascent of the St. Bernard, a Dramatic Sketch" is in the spatial and temporal perspective of its stage directions:

A wide, stony, and desolate plain among the mountains, sur-rounded by dark and bare peaks, half-covered with cloud. The Drance, now diminished to a mere torrent, foams among the rocks which lie scattered in the foreground. A slight vestige of a path among the stones and turf, which zigzags to the summit of a huge rock on the left, turns sharply round its overhanging top, and disappears. Immense sweeps of snow on the flanks of the mountains, which descend into the plain, crossing the mule-path in some places; in others forming precarious bridges over the torrent of the Drance, whose dark waters have worn a way beneath them. In front, the plain is compressed into a dark and silent gorge, running up among the mountains, and hidden in mist and cloud.

(1.518)

In the diary he kept of this trip Ruskin's geological knowledge leads him to perspectives which disclose external and internal composition at once:

The Jungfrau rises whitely and beautifully, marked calcareous by its wavy domelike outline, although such an outline is not always a certain criterion of the composing rock . . . But among the Bernese Alps the form of the Jungfrau is peculiar, for they are mountains of straight lines, and sharp angles, and inaccessible peaks; the highest is a regular, but craggy and inaccessible cone; the Wetterhorn is a pyramid, pointed, and surrounded by aiguilles; the Shreckhorn a bare and perpendicular rock; the Eigers are sharp ridges formed by precipices almost vertical; but the Jungfrau is all curves and lines of beauty, presenting in the ranges of the Silberhorn that figure assumed by the waves of a rippling sea under the influence of opposite currents, that of ridges with regular concave sides, which quite prevents any of that lumpishness which spoils the Chamouni view of Mont Blanc.   (Diaries, 57–58)

What Ruskin is doing in his diary is clarified by a treatise On the Theory of Painting, the second, enlarged edition of which was published in 1835 by T. H. Fielding, a member of the Society and brother of Ruskin's drawing master. There are points in the treatise with which Ruskin would have disagreed, and there is in any case no proof that he ever read it, although it is very likely that he was familiar both with the ideas it espouses and with their sources in other writers. What Fielding argues is that a viewer's initially "unconscious" apprehension of external and internal properties eventually becomes both conscious and accurate through the process of learning to represent a given form; and he quotes an 1829 speech reprinted in The Edinburgh Review in support of his view that the very process of drawing promotes the knowledge on which it most importantly depends.[24] As the means of art is a "language" which the artist learns to use "as persons learn to write" (19), the "coup d'oeil" in which the artist encompasses everything needed may be likened to the "one short monosyllable" of a naval officer in an urgent moment of command (33). Fielding subordinates the strictly manual techniques of art to the "effort of mind" and "those principles in all things that have any similarity in their uses" (19). Influenced by Coleridge's idea that mind and nature function according to interactive and congruent principles, Fielding's exegesis strongly suggests an analogy between the matter which is the subject of art and the manner in which the artist composes it. He finds further support for this analogy in Quintilian's phrase about "true manner," which he takes to refer both to the manner of art and to all manner of *things* in nature which it represents:

Now this "true manner" is of infinite importance: nor can it be obtained by any labour of the hand, being dependant [sic] alone on judgment, or a right mode of seeing and thinking; and when we are so fortunate as to hit this happy method, we discover that Nature's principles of working are based upon the most perfect and solid reason. Such is the yielding resistance offered to the elements by every plant, with a sufficient and appropriate adjustment, as the plant increases; giving a similarity and beautiful fitness of construction to all vegetable matter. We find this in every thing that Nature does, from her chemical operations on what is considered inert matter, to the construction of the most intelligent beings; and it is the discovery of this reasoning power in the formation of things at which we must aim . . .

(19–20)

Some of the resources for such a discovery are no farther away than the artist's own body, for knowledge of the "true manner" in which his eyes are constructed and function is crucial to knowledge of the matter which is seen: the

89

unconscious but perfectible "reasoning power of the eye" is built into it (53).

The implications here about learning from the operations of one's own mind and body recall Ruskin's early education, and behind that the ideas of George Berkeley and Adam Smith.[25] Because it is at once derivative and contemporary, Fielding's treatise suggests why, under the combined influence of his study of art and science, Ruskin would see that "the reasoning power in the formation of things" is the key to representing those things, and that the representation of them would allow the viewer to reason on them too. Hence his advice to Henry Acland in the 1840 letter quoted above, in which Ruskin insists that he speaks as a "grammarian" of drawing. Acland should make his art "more of a science," Ruskin urges:

And your success in this study will depend far more on yourself, and on the education you give your own mind, than on any instruction from men or books, if you accustom yourself, with every shadow and colour you notice, to inquire – Why is this shadow of such a form, and such a depth? . . . Most artists learn their rules mechanically, and never trouble themselves about the reason of them. You had much better arrive at the rules by a process of reasoning – you will then feel as well as know them. (36.19–21)

Three years later, this is precisely what Ruskin is claiming that Turner has done:

In fact, the great quality about Turner's drawings which more especially proves their transcendent truth is, the capability they afford us of reasoning on past and future phenomena, just as if we had the actual rocks before us; for this indicates not that one truth is given, or another, not that a pretty or interesting morsel has been selected here and there, but that the whole truth has been given, with all the relations of its parts; so that we can pick and choose our points of pleasure or of thought for ourselves, and reason upon the whole with the same certainty which we should after having climbed and hammered over the rocks bit by bit. With this drawing before him, a geologist could give a lecture upon the whole system of aqueous erosion, and speculate as safely upon the past and future states of this very spot, as if he were standing and getting wet with the spray. (3.487–88)

The process is reversible, Ruskin discovered as a boy. He would not have been the least bit surprised to learn that in 1984 one of the world's leading physicists, who studies turbulence in air, waves, and waterfalls, would be reported to

have begun going to museums, to look at how artists handle complicated subjects, especially subjects with interesting texture, like Turner's water, painted with small swirls atop large swirls, and then even smaller swirls atop those. "It's abundantly obvious that one doesn't know the world around us in detail," he says. "What artists have accomplished is realizing that there's only a small amount of stuff that's important, and then seeing what it was. So they can do some of my research for me."[26]

In his 1835 diary Ruskin does both kinds of research for himself, using the one to spur the other. "The opening to Airolo is beautiful," he begins, facing the prospect of describing the descent on the Italian side of the Col St. Gothard; "but what is the use of describing it" (Diaries, 41). In the perspective of his own Alpine travels, and of numberless descriptions by artists and tourists, it seems "we have had all that before. Objects on paper are always the same, it is by the disposition of them that nature gives variety, and therefore you can say no more than that – the opening to Airolo is beautiful." With his closer approach, picturesque conventions fall away and the "peculiar character" of the view emerges, along with an inviting difficulty in saying "exactly in what it consists." He catalogues contrasts with the Swiss side: less snow, richer color, more villages, more zigzags in the route. As Ruskin takes in "the essential points in the things drawn" (35.77), the panorama, with its "low line of rocks of picturesque and beautiful forms," gives way to an analysis of the minerals it contains. Half way down to Airolo, where "The rocks look most tempting," they have accumulated into the scene it seemed useless to describe. The "disposition" of the rocks guides the disposition of his prose; their "decomposition" gives its color and structure to his composition of "the middle of the descent."

> . . . the slates are exceedingly soft and in a state of half decomposition and the road which was based on them has been a good deal washed away by the torrent, and the quartz veins stand out white and beautiful mixed with green chlorite and running into imperfect crystallization. (*Diaries*, 42)

The order of his perceptions is conditioned by what science has taught him – whether at home or on tour – about how things come to look the way they do. In the space of an entry or even a sentence, Ruskin can move from a general vista, to those external and internal facts which disclose its formation, and back to the newly comprehended aspect of the scene. In the end, an aspect comprehends its own past: the reasoning power is in the formation of things.

Near the close of his diary, when he descends at last into Italy, the drama of the scene is history's:

> Far down this enormous chasm the promontories of perpendicular rock jut out from behind one another, like the side scenes of a theatre, their bases lost in an abyss in whose depth the river is not seen, their summits rising so high above you, and so steeply, that you feel as if the convulsed earth had yawned and let you down into a chasm from which there was no egress, and the road is carried along their sides in a fearful terrace, passing through the rocks, which are cut out into long caverns, or under vaults built to bear the burst of the bounding avalanche. (*Diaries*, 70)

But is this the drama of nature's architecture or the architecture of human drama? In his autobiography Ruskin says that the act of drawing a tree in 1842 led him to a revelation of "the bond between the human mind and all visible things" (35.315). The famous and intensely dramatic passage in which this happens is designed to protect what are allegedly facts from what are allegedly prejudicial theories of composition, and to separate his own belated discoveries from the conventionalism that he deplores in his masters.[27] "With wonder increasing every instant," he sees that the branches "'composed' themselves, by finer laws than any known of men. At last the tree was there, and everything that I had thought before about trees, nowhere" (35.314). Yet it is the early drawing lessons he disowns which suggest how deeply Ruskin's writing was enhanced by a discipline which linked the composition of the natural world to the grammatical "laws and rules" (36.20) which govern the hand and mind of the artist.

.   .   .

When, in Modern Painters III, Ruskin speaks of his lacking "powers of reflection or invention" as a boy (5.367), it is in the context of his experience of "the pure landscape-instinct" which he says he lost after he was about twenty (5.365). There are several things which are indefinite about this instinct: "there was no definite religious feeling mingled with it," God was in heaven, not immanent in the landscape (5.366); and there was an indefinite, "continual perception of Sanctity in the whole of nature," like a "disembodied spirit" which often made him "shiver from head to foot" (5.367). What is entirely definite about this instinct is its association with knowledge of the past – whether via hearsay, as in "the charm of romantic association" that comes with history lessons (5.369) or, most especially, through his reading of writers like Scott and Wordsworth. "Every fancy that I had about nature was put into my head by some book" (5.367).

The act of thinking of a present place in terms of reading or a memory is thus firmly associated with what he later calls "the instinct which leads us thus to attribute life to the lowest forms of organic nature" (5.385). Genuine though the feeling was, nothing in Ruskin's early writing can seem more like posturing – like a haunted but unhaunting impersonation of other writers (or of his own past self) – than some of his expressions of belief that a spirit is in nature. This is particularly evident where the chain of Ruskin's readings involves phenomena of which he has little or no sensory experience of his own.

There is a voice in all nature. List to the rave of the mad sea; speaks it not eloquently; does it not tell of its green weedy caverns and its coral towers, and the high hills and shelly vallies far, far beneath its cold blue? List to the song of the summer breeze; does it not tell of the blue heavens, and the white clouds and other climes, and other seasons, and spicy gales, and myrtle bowers, and sweet things far away? (2.360–61)

> And if thou ne'er hast felt as if
> The ocean had a mind,
> Nor held communion with the deep,
> And converse with the wind,
> When broad, black waves before it roll,–
> I would not think thou had'st a soul.
>
> (2.379)

But he is convinced and convincing (as in the letter discussing plant behavior quoted near the beginning of this chapter) about the animation that he can see stirring in what is apparently inanimate (RFL, 354–56). At its best this writing suggests a reconciliation between his mother's "unquestioning evangelical faith . . . [which] placed me, as soon as I could conceive or think, in the presence of an unseen world" (35.128) and his insistence that he was not "vitally and evangelically religious" as a boy (35.42 n, 45). It is in his prose about the things he has seen that the unseen world is most vitally present. And what this prose most strikingly brings into view is not Ruskin's sense of God but of a strong structural affinity between the methodologies of science, of art, and of literature that expresses the "landscape-instinct."

Ruskin was not unique in recognizing these affinities, nor did he wish to seem so – especially given the importance he attached to their existing outside of himself. But he did develop unique and influential ways of expressing them. Two of Ruskin's most ambitious undertakings will illustrate this development, the more effectively as they were written about two years apart, in consciously different styles. Produced when he was between fourteen and fifteen, "Account of a Tour on the Continent" is composed of passages of verse set between prose description, fair-copied and illustrated with vignettes drawn in imitation of those by Turner in Rogers's *Italy*. Although Ruskin's editors have had to piece it together out of manuscripts apparently written at different times, it is evident that the section on Chamouni is the climax of the "Account," as it was of the tour. His knowledge of scientific method, of art, of other literature touching the subject all shape not only what he sees in the Alps but also the syntax in which he envisions it, the interrelation of one thing to another in space and time. This is particularly clear in two splendid passages to which the next chapter of this study will return, one in prose on Mont Blanc itself, and the other in verse, on the source of the Arveron. In the two prose passages that precede them, Ruskin's approach is to meditate on his approach. In both of them, verbal and syntactical repetitions which may seem like filler, or meandering, are purposive attempts to hold himself up so that he can reflect on his reflections.

95

And this is our last excursion on Swiss ground, thought I . . . I have always a sort of kindred feeling for these beautiful blue hills; they ever look half English, and I love them for it. They may not be so wonderful, so majestic, so mighty, or so beautiful, but they are more like home, sweet home, and it is pleasant, very pleasant, to meet a friend in a foreign land. We are going to Chamouni, *c'est vrai*, but it seems exceeding strange. Before we left home, I had read of Chamouni, heard of Chamouni, and seen some few drawings of Chamouni, but never so much as dreamed of going to Chamouni, it seemed so un-come-at-able; and for the Mont Blanc, it seemed in another world, in fairyland, and of course had a magic halo thrown round it, and aetherialness that can never be joined with reality. That halo comes again on looking back. And this is our last excursion on Swiss ground, thought I, the last, and the wildest, and the sweetest, because – because, perhaps it is the last . . .

"Voilà les aiguilles," quoth our char-à-banc driver. How I started, I believe I was dreaming of home at the time; it is odd you always think it would be very pleasant to be where you are not; it can't be helped, but it is very provoking, the charms of a place always increase in geometrical ratio as you get farther from it, and therefore 'tis a rich pleasure to look back on anything, though it has a dash of regret. It is singular that almost all pleasure is past, or coming. Well, I looked up, and lo! seven thousand feet above me soared the needles of Mont Blanc . . .   (2.380–82)

What a delicious thing is a reverie, that total abstraction from all things present – that stilly, dreamy, waking vision that places you where you are not, that carries you where you wish to be, that presents the past to your recollection, and the future to your fancy, so forcibly, so impressively, so lovelily, throwing a glow on every circumstance, and a halo on every feature, giving the vivid, the magic colouring of the dream to the defined and distinct recollection of the reality. It is thus that I look back upon our first walk at Chamouni, to the Source of the Arveron.   (2.386)

Two years later Ruskin parodies, preserves, and illuminates the mode of these passages in the "Journal of a Tour through France to Chamouni" (1835), the two completed cantos of which are written in wittily extended Byronic *ottava rima* stanzas.[28] What he has previously read about the site – in Byron and other poets but especially in Saussure – makes him strain to see Jura:

> Long had I looked, and long I looked in vain
>> For the pale mountains in the distance showing . . .
> Is it a cloud, that yon pale, azure chain
>> The whole, wide, low horizon round is throwing?
>>> (2.404)

Reading – the anticipation created by reading – produces the mental movement which tends to animate the scene. What turns out to be Jura looks to be "throwing" the horizon around itself – much as, some twenty stanzas later, it is his dreaming over the daylit foreground (st. 40), and then his nocturnal dreaming of Mont Blanc when he is elsewhere (st. 42), which make it seem to "rise" of its own volition when it actually does appear. The imagination of it preexists the reality but also, later, coexists with it. The mental movement between the two – so deeply a part of the landscape feeling he describes in *Modern Painters* III – makes Mont Blanc seem to "call" to him, makes it seem to "rise" before him. The expression of verbal inadequacy which is conventional in encounters between romantic poets and the sublime is brilliantly replaced by Ruskin's expression of delight that the mountain provides its own figurative response to itself:

> for thou hast stood
> Unrivalled still, thine own similitude!
>> (2.412)

The imaginative movement, the "reverie" behind the landscape's movement, is not opposed to science or the techniques of art, but allied to them. Science is precisely what accommodates imagination in the face of the present reality to be compassed; it is itself "the defined and distinct recollection of the reality'' (2.386). Imaginative reverie does not shut its eyes but, in an intricate rethinking of "Tintern Abbey" (11.45–49), becomes – as it must for an artist – all eyes: facing the "magic" of a prospect at the end of "A Tour,"

> Sometimes, when such a glory you espy,
> The body seems to sleep, – the soul goes to the eye.
> (2.428)

Ruskin does not blanch – as he says his reader will, or as Wordsworth does in Book VI of The Prelude – in the face of Mont Blanc because his approach to it, unlike Shelley's, involves a reverie which replaces the stupendous whole with a humble foreground which allows him to "dream / Of greater things associated with these" (2.411–12), and because his scientific and artistic skills have helped him build a "similitude" in his mind of which he can more readily take the measure (2.412).[29] In Ruskin's uses of literature, of science, and of art there is an analogous and homologous movement of mind, spatially and temporally, between two different aspects or modes of the same thing.[30] Religion first and then science more complexly taught him to see the past in the present, to look back and forth between them. Art taught him the fixing of what is animated and the animation of what is fixed, and taught him to envision the two states at once. It is the contrast between them that is at the heart of the landscape feeling – whether reverie and nostalgia develop a distance between past and present or, as in Modern Painters III, between the country and the city (5.369).

These elaborate analogies and homologies contribute not only to Ruskin's sense of animation in nature but also to his sense of how to represent it in writing which repeats the designs of his favorite scientists, painters, and poets. Ruskin's travelogues are just such composites. But in making his sources his own he implies that they are not wholly his property. His translations are valuable, he thinks, because they bring him back to "the original": "I have not looked at my Pope's Homer, since I began translating, the original is so much superior" (RFL, 263). In 1855 he said that poetry cannot be translated in rhyme, since that would rearrange the thoughts.[31] In the 1830s, arrangement is what the boy's translations are especially keen to preserve. This is true whether he is translating from one verbal language to another or from one discipline to another. Again, Ruskin did not claim to have discovered the principle that there are affinities between the arrangements of different things. Behind him were generations of clichés about the sister arts, as well as Coleridge's more recent speculations about the "harmony" between words and things, and between the composition of language and that of the natural world.[32] It was not until *Modern Painters* that Ruskin produced his profoundly innovative substantiation of the view that art is a language, a substantiation which makes a definitive link in his work between the order of nature and the order of visual or verbal designs.[33] Yet Ruskin was already working towards this achievement in those boyhood writings in which he discovers rather than disguises the affinities between his own readings and those of other people.

This is why his writing is most fully, idiosyncratically his own when his appropriations are least covert. In an article on water temperature published in the *Magazine of Natural History*, Ruskin breaks, mid-sentence, into Byron's *Manfred*, which he follows with citations of Saussure (1.202–03). His "Journal of a Tour" would be impossible without Lyell as well as Byron and Saussure, but none of them could have anticipated the way they would work together:

So, on the heights of Jura, as I said,
    I stood, admiring much the setting sun
Taking a bath before he went to bed
    Out of the mists, that, indistinct and dun,
And dark, and grey, and colourless as lead
    Along the horizon's farthest outline run
Like velvet cushions for his weary head;
    Or like a sort of scene, for him to slip off
Behind: And a long line of ruby red
    Zigzag'd along their summits, like a strip of
Dutch gold upon a piece of gingerbread
    After the happy urchin's gnawed the tip off
The finger, after long deliberation
Between his appetite and admiration.
    . . .
Such are the dreams of the geologist!
    He sees past ages of the world arise;
Strange sounds salute his ears, prepared to list,
    And wondrous sights, his rock inspired eyes.
Before him solid mountains wave and twist,
    And forms of life within them fossilize;
The flint invades each member as it dies,
    And through the quivering corse on creeps the stone,
Till in the mountain's hardened heart it lies,
    In nature, rock, – in form, a skeleton . . .
Thus on the Jura dreamed I, with nice touch
    Discriminating stones . . .

                    (2.406–08)

What finally matters most in Ruskin's development as a writer is neither his sources nor his use of them, but rather his reflections on the mental and physical process of his combinings and recombinings. While mediating between the present aspect of his subject (whether nature or a text) and some other version of it, Ruskin makes a study of the relationship between "the original" and his imaginative recomposition. Both the mediation and his study of it are compacted in Ruskin's best compositions.

When, as in the scientific article just mentioned, Ruskin wants to suggest "the perpetual downward movement of glaciers," it is Byron that he cites; and when, in *Praeterita*, he rereads his works of the mid-1830s he again quotes this passage from *Manfred* (35.149). What Ruskin returns to in his autobiography is not simply Byron's scientific accuracy – which he verifies against the findings of James Forbes – but its being "measured and living truth" (35.148). The "measure" is partly the "natural flow" of Byron's language, which "interested me extremely," and which "I followed . . . instantly in what verses I wrote for my own amusement" – reserving the "structural, as opposed to fluent, force" of Pope and Johnson "for all serious statement" (35.151). And the "life," Ruskin says, is there in the way Byron "animated" mountains and sea "with the sense of real human nobleness and grief," and then "reanimated for me, the real people," long dead, who had looked on those scenes before him (35.150–51). Ruskin's quotation and requotation of Byron point to his view that a composition has life when nature is animated within it. That is why, in the first of the pair of letters on translation cited early in this chapter, Ruskin's description of entering a library is like his descriptions of entering scenes where he experiences the landscape feeling in *Modern Painters* III, as well as being like his descriptions of meeting writers inside their books in "Of Kings' Treasuries" (18.58–59). For language can incorporate not only the practitioners of science, painting, and literature but also the phenomena they observe.

Books are the souls of the dead in Calf Skin. when I enter a library I always feel as if I were in the presence of departed spirits, silent indeed, but only waiting my command to pour forth the experience of their lives; the thoughts and imaginations, the feelings and the passions; which have long since ceased in reality, but they continue to think & feel to me. Even as I look up to the rows of volumes in my little library, they seem turning into living beings and the ancients and the moderns seem rekindled into contemporary life.   (RFL, 350–51)

The opening of this letter likens sentience in nature to sentience in books. "Look[ing] up to the rows of volumes" seems to animate them, as "Lifting my eyes off the paper" leads him to sight the animation in nature. In the sequence of vignettes that follow, works by classics and moderns become the visible, historical self of each writer. The first to appear is an old man, "but there are no wrinkles on his brow, for there is no care there." He is "conversing in his mind," Ruskin imagines, with the movements and "singing" of the stream, the breeze, and the insect "intoxicated with day dew" on the bough – as the students, in the paragraph before, are "full of the rich dews of instruction," as the trees are "all full of that delicate day dew, glittering and glancing and shaking off showers of jewels onto the moistened ground: and their vegetable life seems strong in them; I could fancy I saw them growing." Ruskin describes and achieves an interanimation no less complex in his own writings about nature. It seems entirely right that, in the last sentence of the vignette, the old man should turn out to be Anacreon – the very writer whose "singing" Ruskin had incorporated into his own three years before, at the end of his great letter inscribing the "laws of motion" (RFL, 275).

CHAPTER 4

LEADING LINES
(1830–36)

In the process of following connections between disciplines
and their chosen subjects, and among disciplines themselves,
Ruskin's writing answers simultaneously to aspects of the
physical world and to the languages of natural history,
painting and literature which represented that world in the
early nineteenth century. Predilections of style become
epitomes of his grasp not only of the available means of
representation but also of what they were designed to
represent. In order to make this point more clearly, I return to
the non-fiction, verse travelogues, diaries, and poems Ruskin
wrote between 1830 and 1836, focussing first on images of
mental and physical movement, then on images that
structure contrasts between movement and fixity, finally on
images that suggest his discernment of natural and literary
form in the flux of its own creation.

. . .

The first of these stylistic predilections may seem to be little
more than a mark of his early infatuation with lines of
expression in British romantic poetry. Especially for readers
who come to his juvenilia through his dismissals of it in
Praeterita, it is no surprise that in his works of the early and mid
1830s Ruskin is conspicuously fond of figures which liken
aspects of nature to people and their artifacts, and vice versa –
sometimes with self-serious literariness (as where the
"portal" of the Arveron "Seems . . . an ancient forteresse, /
All shattered in its mightiness" [2.387]), sometimes with
self-delighting comicality: although "quite refractory" on
learning that one of the Alps is shaped "exactly like the
ridge / Of some spare, lean old gentleman's olfactory"

(2.417), Ruskin is nothing loath to measure the "comprehension" of Saddleback while winding around "his forehead" (*Iteriad*, 95) or to liken his own sneeze to a clap of
thunder in the midst of the "deep, still silence" of his
thought (2.408). Ruskin's anthropomorphizing does of
course suggest the influence of picturesque conventions as
well as of the self-projective locutions of Wordsworth,
Byron, and Percy Shelley.[1] But it is also the result of his own
zany, quasi-scientific sense of the intertextuality of people,
things, and language. At a meeting of the members of the
Geological Society, Ruskin "phrenologize[d] upon the
bumps of the observers of the bumps of the earth" – making a
mental journey over the physical manifestations of "the
eminences of mind which calculate the eminences of earth"
(RFL, 414).

We have already seen that Ruskin's written travels are
provoked by, and provoke, movements of the body as well as
of the mind. As early as 1831 his writing declares itself its
own terrain (RFL, 220), and further down the road it has
sufficient vitality to take itself on tour (RFL, 280). Ruskin's
fusion of poem and journey, of a place in writing with the
place that is written about, owes much – as he said his
"Journal of a Tour" did – to "the style of *Don Juan*, artfully
combined with that of *Childe Harold*" (35.152). At the end of
the long first canto, Ruskin arrives at Geneva,

> a pleasant place
> Whereat to make a week's or fortnight's stay,
> To rest and to enjoy yourself at; and to
> End a long journey, and a tiresome canto.
>
> (2.416)

When things are not restful *enough*, Ruskin resorts to
Byronism to banish Byronic rapture. Byron does this too, of
course, but always to initiate what will be his next move. On

the contrary, when Ruskin makes a show of stilling himself
and other poets, he leaves the reader with the impression that
it is because the scene (rather than the poet) will not stand
still. Thus it is that Mont Blanc can so "floor"

> Your very feelings, that you will not move
>   A muscle of your body, nor will dare
> To breathe the breezes that about you rove.
>   You could chastise the movement of the air
> While drinking in the beauty that you love!
>   Some cannot that delicious rapture share;
> Those who feel little, talk, and rant, and vapour,
> Kick up their heels, prance, frisk, curvet, and caper.

At the beginning of this stanza, Ruskin turns from his
satisfaction with a humble scene of rock, stream and tree, and
the imagination they can evoke of a mountain, to look up and
see Mont Blanc:

> I'm going to turn a corner, – which I've done
>   A hundred or a thousand times before!
> But this is really a distinguished one,
>   And needs a little preparation, for
> The shock of it is quite enough to stun
>   You, like a box upon the ear . . .   (2.412)

Romantic poetry, as well as Mont Blanc, administered that
"box upon the ear" which helps Ruskin look to what he has
seen, not just to what he has heard. And it is where he has
seen that a landscape has artistic and geological as well as
literary dimensions – as when he analyzed the aspect and
measurements of "that illustrious corner" where the gallery
of the Dôle looks across the valley of Geneva to Italy (*Diaries*,
8) – that Ruskin's view of the relationship between what is
topical, topographical, and typographical turns Byronism to
his own best advantage.

Ruskin's mental and physical movements are not only

followed in the sequence and design of his travelogues as a whole. They are also, with marked deliberateness, repeated in the very figures of his writing:

> And all along that hill's steep breast
> With snake-like coilings, wound our way
> On narrow shelves of rock, that lay
> Almost o'erhanging, and so sheer,
> 'Twas terror to look down, so near
> To such a precipice of fear.　　(2.372)

> And there, having passed by a bridge o'er the stream
> Whose fierce tumbling tide at the fall we had seen
> There still we continued our mind-charming route,
> Still winding and turning and twisting about . . .
> But, in order that we to the inn might attain,
> We were forced to turn down by a long, narrow lane.
> But it twisted and turned so, to left and to right,
> With its hedges obscuring the inn from our sight,
> That we, all its troublesome windings not knowing,
> Were all the time wondering where we were going!
> 　　　　　　　　　　　　　　　(Iteriad, 35–36)

The "winding way" of his own early prose is here mapped onto his route. Or is it that his serpentine figures of writing inhere in the figures his writing describes? In either case, both his matter and his manner go on cutting the same figure that Ruskin sees himself cutting as poet. For emotions – especially emotions about his own literary performance – are among the physical and mental movements retraced as his writing advances.

> Let every pert miss interrupt me in middle,
> With a proper, school-bred, and genteel kind of giggle –
> "I, I," – oh, dear me! – But I'll make a confession
> I'm digressive when I do but talk of digression.
> 　　　　　　　　　　　　　　　(Iteriad, 99)

Thirty-six, and again twenty-eight, lines earlier, Ruskin had
jokingly acknowledged that "I am not a lake-poet" (98). The
reader of the willfully Byronic – and "Hudibrastical" (99) –
Iteriad will have no doubt of that. But we should not let
Ruskin's jocularity pass by too quickly, for it makes a
meaningful connection even as it makes a meaningful
distinction. Nowhere in the work of those who really are
Lake Poets, or of Byron either, is the writer's construction of
the natural scene so little subordinated to his mental
constructs as is the case with Ruskin. And nowhere in their
work is there so much detail about natural structures
themselves, or about the mental process of pursuing them.[2]
Yet for all of these writers, the route of digressive mental
movement coincides with the mind's passage over the shape
of the route. Consider, for example, the lines that precede and
prepare both for Ruskin's denials that he is a Lake Poet and for
his acknowledgments that he is digressive. Poetry, he says, is
constituted by "Good rhymes," "good measure," and
"sense":

> But never allowed, I am sure, is digression,
> So of my great sins I will make a confession
> And hope that for them I may swiftly atone
> To the reader impatient by now going on.
> 'Mongst those beautiful woods now was winding the way,
> For here they held almost tyrannical sway.
> Near Gowbarrow Park, on the steep, rising heights,
> Forest on forest, the vision delights;
> Half nature, half art, had those forests upreared
> Till richly, they now on the mountains appeared,
> And crested the crags, as the plumes of red
> Wave o'er some warrior's helmeted-head.
>
> (Iteriad, 97)

Unlike Byron or the Lake Poets, Ruskin moves past verbal
digressiveness only to find outside of himself an instance of

his own "winding" "way." The route is determined,
"almost tyranical[ly]," not by the writer but by the forests
through which he makes his way. Yet the forests are
themselves "Half nature, half art" – like some of Wordsworth's scenes, and like those "plumes" which, once a part
of the natural world, are now human artifacts and symbols.

The coincidence Ruskin seeks between mental and physical structures is also approached in the long sequence of *Iteriad*
that surrounds his visit to the place called Friar's Crag, which
he lovingly remembers in *Praeterita*. This visit, and possibly the
verses, were previously remembered in "The Moral of
Landscape" (*Modern Painters* III), where they are introduced by
the passage (some of which was quoted above) in which
Ruskin echoes his childhood lessons in reflecting on the
associative processes of his own mind.

I cannot, from observation, form any decided opinion as to the
extent in which this strange delight in nature influences the hearts
of young persons in general; and, in stating what has passed in my
own mind, I do not mean to draw any positive conclusion as to the
nature of the feeling in other children; but the inquiry is clearly one
in which personal experience is the only safe ground to go upon,
though a narrow one; and I will make no excuse for talking about
myself with reference to this subject, because, though there is
much egotism in the world, it is often the last thing a man thinks of
doing, – and, though there is much work to be done in the world, it
is often the best thing a man can do, – to tell the exact truth about
the movements of his own mind; and there is this farther reason,
that whatever other faculties I may or may not possess, this gift of
taking pleasure in landscape I assuredly possess in a greater degree
than most men; it having been the ruling passion of my life, and the
reason for the choice of its field of labour.

The first thing which I remember, as an event in life, was being
taken by my nurse to the brow of Friar's Crag on Derwent Water;
the intense joy, mingled with awe, that I had in looking through the

hollows in the mossy roots, over the crag, into the dark lake, has associated itself more or less with all twining roots of trees ever since . . .   (5.364-65)

The "movements of his own mind" in this chapter are such that the "twining roots of trees" also take in his preceding image of a natural object surrounded by "fancies" about it which are vitally intertwined in "a garland of thoughts." Wordsworth's figure of "Yew Trees" – "Of intertwisted fibres serpentine / Up-coiling, and inveterately convolved" – becomes Ruskin's figure for the way a powerful mind, encountering a group of trees, will subdue, balance, and interweave the typical responses to it of the artist, the engineer, the sentimentalist, and the idealist (5.358-59). Ruskin is incipiently all four by the time he writes *Iteriad* (1830-31/2), in which Friar's Crag is literally and meta-phorically involved in a "net"-work of roots. In the hope of gaining an overview of the scene, the verse in fact replicates – doubles and doubles back on – the traveller's experience of intervolvement:

> No part of the scene the confusèd eye sees,
> Save copses on copses, and trees upon trees:
> Till, the path in the forest bewild'ringly tost,
> All points of the compass completely were lost
> . . .
> Thus wond'ring, we, serpent-like, twisted about,
> Till just where we got in, 'twas just there we got out.
> And we this occurrence determined quite by
> Not any more by-paths uncertain to try.
> We left the fair lake where, so azure, it flowed,
> And hotly set off by the Borrowdale road . . .
> The track it was steep, thorny, rugged, and rocky,
> As it angled and turned round the oak trees so knotty.
> Some, decaying, were but a vast, gray, hollow shell;
> Of former young grandeur and might they did tell:

And the soil which hung thick round their huge roots
  far-spreading
Formed steps, trunk-supported, where'er we were treading.
We pulled up the hill, and we turned round about,
And we crossed and we recrossed within and without . . .

(53–54)

It is Ruskin's repeated figures of repetition that force comparisons to precedents "within" this poem and to lines by others "without" it. His feelings about his own performance in *Iteriad; Or, Three Weeks Among the Lakes* are finally inseparable from his self-consciousness about writers who took the same steps before him.

As in the case of his responses to scientists and artists, it is particularly in his acts of appropriation that we can see what is new, and will be lasting, in Ruskin's literary beginnings. Or cannot see, for their being so ostentatiously derivative is one reason why Ruskin's early writings are rarely taken seriously. What might look like another reason – his self-proclaimed unseriousness, his expansive jocularity – is actually part of the first, for Ruskin does his best to associate his playfulness with the work of other writers. "But though you may think me prodigiously assical, / I do like some fun – something that's Hudibrastical" (*Iteriad*, 99). None of the romantics wrote landscape poetry in the rollicking triple rhythms of *Iteriad*,[3] but the example of Byron is nonetheless crucial to Ruskin's sense, here and elsewhere, of the possibilities for "fun." Ruskin followed Byron beyond individual turns of phrase and direction to a sense of how spur-of-the-moment play, and self-reflexive replay, could lead – for those tenacious of their own mental movements – to the expression of things that will permanently matter. Given Ruskin's upbringing, self-conscious playfulness was vital to his success – not because his mother was especially grim (her letters show that she was not) but because his father praised him for being "effervescent" (RFL, 265); not because he was ordered to to be original (there was sometimes a protective pretense that he was not) but because his father rewarded him for being prolific (1.xxvii–xxviii). Literary comicality and writing-to-the-moment helped Ruskin solve compositional and emotional problems that were neither comical nor momentary, including the problem of how to hold his reader long and close. Whatever it accomplished in his life, the sense of "fun" led him to important discoveries about what could be accomplished in language. As we shall later see, the "fun" he had as a boy is one of the things behind his discovery that the "bitter play" of Fors Clavigera (29.197) and the tragi-comedy of Praeterita (35.179) will allow him to express what is otherwise inexpressible. At least as much as its seriousness of focus on the world that is not itself, the self-reflexive fun of Ruskin's early writing leads to patterns that will last when he is no longer young and no longer willing to admit the scope of his own power or of his literary inheritance.

For Ruskin, it has often been remarked, was the author of one of the most powerful critiques ever made of romanticism.[4] His early admiration of Wordsworth passed through a series of revisions which mark the stages of his own advance as a critic.[5] The same can be said about his enthusiasm for Percy Shelley, which belongs to the slightly later period to which I will turn in the next part of this book. But the reflexivity of Byron (who influenced him more deeply than either Wordsworth or Shelley during the period I am now considering) is not discussed by the older Ruskin at all. In none of the passages celebrating him in Praeterita does Ruskin acknowledge Byron's mastery of reflexive figures for physical, mental, and emotional movement, much less the strength of his own boyhood grasp of them.[6] Nor – more telling still – is his genius for comedy among the "essential qualities" (35.145) in Byron that Ruskin names as influences on his youth.[7] Although he certainly approves of Byron's "sarcasm," his "bitterness or irony in a jest . . . if it were just" (35.144), he is much more insistent that Byron's "melancholy is without any relief whatsoever; his jest sadder than his earnest" (34.341). He is the great animator of the landscape "with the sense of real human nobleness and grief" (35.150); he is "the truest, the sternest, Seer of the Nineteenth Century" (34.397). The terms in which he praises Byron tend to reflect Ruskin's own self-image at this time, especially his image of himself as a teller of the truth; but they also obscure certain truths about the art that he made as a child. What is more, the brilliantly witty effects of his writing in Praeterita are often achieved at the expense of a child who is comical only unwittingly – who is never the self-regardingly funny and high-spirited author of the poems and letters I have quoted. While Ruskin's changing attitudes towards romantic self-regard have been effectively assessed in terms of his development as a critic, his connections with Byron suggest what still needs to be said about the significance of those attitudes for his development as an artist.

· · ·

The stops and starts of Ruskin's early routes go on bearing some of the weight of his reflections on how to begin and end a composition and keep it going in the meantime. But his most profound representations of the composition of both subjects and writing about them emerge in his evocations of the relationship between movement and fixity within a given scene, and within the individual elements that compose it.

The progess of Iteriad is arrested when "now in our front our low road seemed to check / In a chaos of hills, a dark mountainous wreck": the vigorous, portentous animation of the cliffs and rocks is contrasted with the level calm of the water — "Hanging o'er the dread dell their huge summits they hurled, / At whose foot the fair Derwent so crystalline purled" (62). This approach prepares for the confrontation to come with the Bowder Stone. What also prepares for this spectacle are the similes commonly applied to it – in Clarke's *Survey of the Lakes* (1789); in Father West's *Guide to the Lakes* (1812), where the "loose stone . . . of prodigious bulk . . . lies like a ship on its keel";[8] or, more compellingly for the young Ruskin, in Wordsworth. In an appendix to *A Guide through the District of the Lakes*, Wordsworth refers to "the huge mass of Bowder Stone, lying like a stranded Vessel whose hour of danger is no more";[9] and, in *The Excursion*,

> Upon a semicirque of turf-clad ground,
> The hidden nook discovered to our view
> A mass of rock, resembling, as it lay
> Right at the foot of that moist precipice,
> A stranded ship, with keel upturned, that rests
> Fearless of winds and waves.
>
> (Book III, lines 50–55)[10]

But for Ruskin, "Astonished, we passed through that wilderness lone, / Till burst on our eyesight dark Bowder's huge stone." The rock is first seen as "bursting" with energy, pushing back not only the astonished Ruskins but also the momentum of a torrent that is "fierce" in its own right: "A dark rock its high summit right forward did force, / And altered the fierce torrent's rock-beating course." Unlike Wordsworth's image of a stranded vessel, keel upturned in an image of pathos, past water and past danger, Ruskin's stone is breasting the flood, creating danger as it powers itself. When he backs off and fully takes in the way the stone composes the scene, what Ruskin fixes on is its poise: he balances into a single sentence the experience of a motionlessness and stability that are themselves in sustained balance with the ceaseless animation they create, as a fast-moving boat makes a pattern that persists in the water. Ruskin's composition is designed to bring out and show off the paradoxical creation of movement by fixedness.

> High raised on its brink, frowning down on the flood,
> A vast mass of mossy rock dreadfully stood:
> It seemed from the heights high above as if torn,
> And down to its wonderful resting-place borne.
> But nature most queerly contrived has to hitch it,
> And, poised on a narrow edge, managed to pitch it;
> And yet though so balanced, so firm is the rock,
> You may mount by a ladder quite up to the top,
> As when some vast ship the blue ocean divides,
> Her keen arching bow stems the breast of the tides;
> The wondering waves 'gainst her stern dash their spray;
> The waters enraged yet are forced to obey;
> And back from her sides the huge billows are thrown –
> So sternly triumphing appeared Bowder Stone.
>
> (Iteriad, 62–63)

Ruskin wrote this just around the time that Runciman "cultivated in me, – indeed founded, – the habit of looking for the essential points in the things drawn, so as to abstract them decisively" (35.77). Some of the same points again strike Ruskin as essential when it comes to representing a geological structure that is far more overpowering than the Bowder Stone. The approach to the description of Mont Blanc, referred to near the end of the last chapter, involves Ruskin in the backward movement of reverie about home, and of mental images – composed elsewhere – of what he is about to see; so that when it comes, the shock of disorientation creates that highly contrasted double vision which aptly introduces what he is about to represent. In his sight, the stationary needles receive the blows of six thousand years; the "flanks" of the everlasting mountains plunge and rise before his eyes; the sea of snow is set into a motion that unrolls its own history, accounts for its own astonishing appearance before him now. The "essential points" of the composition are not simply powerful movements and strong contrasts, but rather the temporal and spatial relationship between action and the steadfast scene.

Well, I looked up, and lo! seven thousand feet above me soared the needles of Mont Blanc, splintered and crashed and shivered, the marks of the tempest for three score centuries, yet they are here, shooting up red, bare, scarcely even lichened, entirely inaccessible, snowless, the very snow cannot cling to the down-plunging sheerness of these terrific flanks that rise pre-eminently dizzying and beetling above the sea of wreathed snow that rolled its long surging waves over the summits of the lower and less precipitous mountains. Then came the stretching gloominess of the pine forests, jagging darkly upon the ridge of every crag, strangely contrasted with the cold blueness of the peaky glaciers that filled the huge ravines between the hills, descending like the bursting billows of a chafed ocean tide from the desolate dominion of the snow, and curling forward till they lay on the green fields of Chamouni, which stretched away, one unbroken line of luxuriance, till bounded by the lonely desertness of the Col de Balme. There is not another scene like Chamouni throughout all Switzerland. In no other spot that I have seen is the rich luxuriance of the cultivated valley, the flashing splendour of the eternal snow, the impending magnificence of the bare, spiry crag, and the strange, cold rigidity of the surgy glaciers so dreadfully and beautifully combined. There is silence unbroken, no thunder of the avalanche comes crashing from the recesses of the hills, there is no voice from the chasmy glacier, no murmur from the thousand mountain streams, you are in solitude, a strange unearthly solitude, but you feel as if the air were full of spirits.   (2.382)

Already Ruskin is powerfully attracted to what he will most famously celebrate as the fifth element of Gothic – "not merely stable, but *active* rigidity; the peculiar energy which gives tension to movement, and stiffness to resistance, which makes the fiercest lightning forked rather than curved, and the stoutest oak-branch angular rather than bending, and is as much seen in the quivering of the lance as in the glittering of the icicle" (10.239). And already he has comprehended this aspect in terms of the energy that produces form, grows into and is preserved in it, intact, alive. When, shortly after the passage on Mont Blanc, his "Account of a Tour" arrives at the source of the Arveron – also introduced and made more striking by the backward movement of his imagination – Ruskin composes what he will describe as "the glittering of the icicle" in *The Stones of Venice*.

> And now his chafèd surges see
> Bound high in laughing liberty! . . .
> And, that its form thou now couldst trace,
> Froze to an icy wilderness:
> And that, its portal vast and old,
> All archèd by the crisp ice cold,
> And through whose chasms of paly green
> The shivery sunshine shot between,
> Or trembling with a meteor light,
> Or dancing in the billows bright,
> Smiling aetherially through
> The ghost lights of the crystal blue.
>
> (2.387)

Again in the Alps in 1835, Ruskin's eye follows as red walls of rock rise above him towards a vision in which centuries of action are fixed in the precipitous poise of the scene right now.

[A]bove our heads rose walls of perpendicular rock, red and bare . . . immeasurably high . . . – and over them, as the foam of a breaking wave hangs over its smooth and polished side, impends an

enormous precipice of ice . . . that seems to rest on it like the dome
of a mighty temple on a Corinthian column of Marble.

(Diaries, 53)

Animation seen *as* architecture is only a movement of
mind, or location, away from animation seen *in* architecture.
Near the beginning of his "Journal of a Tour through France
to Chamouni," on terra firma in Rouen, Ruskin writes a
serio-comic complaint about mounting a clock on the facade
of a "Gothic work," and then watches as time – the time it
takes a flower to blow, the time it takes a hand to carve
garlands – is stopped in stone.

> So, as the Rouen architects thought fit
>   To go upon a plan entirely new,
> They built an arch on purpose every bit;
>   Chiselled it over, till gay garlands grew
> Beneath their hands, where'er their mallets hit,
>   And open flowers along the granite blew
> Unwitheringly.   (2.400)

The finesse of the handwork is caught by Ruskin's own: his
rhymes and enjambment sustain the flow and overflow as
garlands "grew / Beneath their hands" and flowers "blew /
Unwitheringly." The very polysyllables of that last word
unfurl with the delicate, exact sequentiality of a flower's
petals, while "bit" and "hit" interlock as sharply as granite
rings under the chisel. By the time he sees "Gothic ornament
. . . germinating into a blossom" in *The Stones of Venice*
(10.240), Ruskin's knowledge will have grown, his opinions
will have changed; but "the essential points" remain. It is as
he said in his diary of 1849, while he tried without success to
draw the animation he perceived in the aiguilles of
Chamouni: "I can't do it yet, but I have the imagination of it
in me, and will do it, some day" (*Diaries*, 404). He is, of

course, already doing it in his writing, aided by the feeling –
which *Praeterita* says he first had in 1842, about Turner – that
"Nature herself was composing with him" (35.310).[11] In the
Alps, in 1835, the fields of snow are "tossed into rounded
and wreathed masses like the foam of a rock-beating sea,"
"dashed . . . against the mighty pyramids which rise beetling
over its billows, until they drip with its whiteness." Amidst
the tumult, Ruskin again comes to focus on the paradoxical
stillness of the glaciers that hang above him; and here, in a
grotesque and deeply characteristic compound image, the
"rooted" icicles – like the rigid ones that glitter in *The Stones of
Venice* – suggest not only the vitality and corruptibility of
nature, but also the definitively vital and corruptible artifice
of man, the painter's tool, and the writer's:

Down came two glaciers hanging from the snow above in such
vertical ravines, that they look like two ultra-gigantic icicles,
radiant at their roots with blue chasms and glancing pinnacles,
sapphire and silver, but black as ink at their extremities . . .

(*Diaries*, 67)

"Nature herself was composing with him," Ruskin seems to
imply in some of these brilliant early compositions in which
movement and fixity, flux and form, make each other
perceptible, visible, intelligible: describable, drawable,
legible.

.   .   .

Ruskin's contrasts between movement and fixity structure
some of the most sensational and idiosyncratic passages in his
prose; yet they provoke recognitions that seem analytically
exact and impersonal – much as the self-regarding winding
way of writing is an access to things that exist outside of the
self. The recognition, the access, is at its most elementary and
discernible in passages where the means (and at least part of

the end) present themselves as scientific observation or techniques of the visual arts. But it is in the same passages that Ruskin's distinctively verbal designs culminate in the pattern that characterizes them all.

At the fall of the Aar – "the very finest fall in Switzerland" – Ruskin's eye is again caught by dramatic contrasts, anomalous shapes. But here his imagination is not setting a fixed thing into motion – imagining the movement in fixity – but seeing the movement that makes for stability in form. Within a single sentence he accounts for – by giving an account of – the congruity between lines of water and their incongruously circular impression in rock:

> The rocks around the fall are remarkably chiselled by its spray, not only worn into a sort of tunnel by the wash of the water itself, but polished and full of circular cavities, apparently formed by the beating back of the spray only – water against granite, water and time against very obstinate solidity, very particularly unaccommodating durability. (*Diaries*, 48)

At Grindelwald, the form that catches his eye is also in bold contrast to the dominant action: "The ice of the glaciers has been often described and still it remains very incomprehensible ice." The "essential" action is swiftly found where Ruskin had not at first looked, and the prose that made motion visible in solid ice the day before now discovers in ice the motions of the invisible air:

> The arches in the glaciers whence run the streams formed by their melting are remarkable, because they do not resemble passages torn by the violence of the waters, but beautiful and regular arches melted away around them and high over them, as if by a warm air rising from the water itself, which indeed may be the case, for the glacier streams are not what you would call bitterly cold ... and in winter, when the water is colder, the arch is not only smaller in proportion to the diminished quantity of water, but barely enough to let the stream out ... (*Diaries*, 56)

The explanation must have struck the editor J. C. Loudon too, when he perused this diary for sections worth working up for publication in his *Magazine of Natural History*. For about a year later, in one of Ruskin's first pieces of published prose, his "Observations on the Causes which Occasion the Variation of Temperature between Spring and River Water" were substantiated by reference to forty- or fifty-foot high "vaults" under the ice –

formed, as a glance will show, not by the force of the stream, which would only tear itself a broken cave sufficient for its passage, but by the heat which radiates from it, and gives the arch its immense height, and beautifully regular form.   (1.202)

The form is wrought by what appears formless. The leading line Ruskin sights is an intimation of form in the flux of its own creation.

Like a shell which retains the same shape as it grows, the "beautifully regular form" of the vaults is sustained by the air and the water that move. What Ruskin sees in ice in 1835 will be theorized in his diary thirteen years later. "I was struck in looking over the Shells at [the] Brit[ish] Mus[eum] yesterday," he begins.

Now I think that Form, properly so called, may be considered as a function or exponent either of Growth or of Force, inherent or impressed; and that one of the steps to admiring it or understanding it must be a comprehension of the laws of formation and of the forces to be resisted; that all forms are thus either indicative of lines of energy, or pressure, or motion, variously impressed or resisted, and are therefore exquisitely abstract and precise. Variegation, on the contrary, is the arbitrary presence or absence of colouring matter and the beauty is more in the colour than the outline . . . so that we shall have three kinds of Form: that of mere stains on a surface, shells and skins; that of organic structure on a surface, serpent scales up to most beautiful plumage; and real form, the most precise of all in muscular or other separate developments . . .

all final forms, as of animal bodies, or of shells, are absolutely
perfect.   (Diaries, 370–71)

The lesson of the shell shapes what he sees when he is back
among the Alpine peaks in Modern Painters IV:

The hollow in the heart of the aiguille is as smooth and sweeping in
curve as the cavity of a vast bivalve shell.

   I call these the governing or leading lines, not because they are
the first which strike the eye, but because, like those of the grain of
the wood in a tree-trunk, they rule the swell and fall and change of
all the mass. In Nature, or in a photograph, a careless observer will
by no means be struck by them, any more than he would by the
curves of the tree; and an ordinary artist would draw rather the
cragginess and granulation of the surfaces, just as he would rather
draw the bark and moss of the trunk. Nor can any one be more
steadfastly averse than I to every substitution of anatomical
knowledge for outward and apparent fact; but so it is, that, as an
artist increases in acuteness of perception, the facts which become
outward and apparent to him are those which bear upon the
growth or make of the thing.   (6.231–32)

These passages may linger in the mind when he recollects his
learning to read and write in Fors Clavigera, and teaches his own
readers to write by having them trace the form of a shell (see
below, p. 216). But what I want to stress here is that, for
Ruskin in 1835, the connection between the visibly fixed
forms and movements of nature does not exist merely as a
paradox or image in the mind. It exists as a fact in nature. He
has access to this fact through his deepening conviction that a
subject's genesis through time expresses, and is expressed by,
the truth of its present aspect. His substantiating this
conviction through his study of nature and the visual arts –
"leading lines" is also a key phrase in the instructions Ruskin
gives for drawing landscapes in The Elements of Drawing[12] – does
not, of course, mean that it is a conviction drawn from only
those studies, or pertinent only to them.[13] No matter what he

considers, understanding what he sees in terms of how it came to look the way it does eventually leads him to seize on those aspects or moments in the history of his subject most abstractable from and expressive of that history as a whole. Ruskin's fixing on "essential points" – so often involving contrasting shapes or conditions of aspect – just as often resolves itself into a will to interrelate two apparently disparate things (or modes of regarding them) in a narrative which imagines the one term as gradually generating the other. Whether he is showing how the manipulations of "Turnerian topography" tell the truth (*Modern Painters* IV), or disclosing mythology's gradual embodiment of fact (*The Queen of the Air*), or teaching that handwriting should take shape as does the form of a shell (*Fors Clavigera*), these resolutions naturally take a long time to achieve; but by the mid 1830s he is already taking the time to search for them, and referring to time as the medium through which such resolutions, such evolutions, are achieved.

Ruskin's writing both explains these evolutions and is the most compelling evidence of how they work. In embodying what is behind it, in enacting what it advances, in representing the syntax of interrelations among and within its every subject, Ruskin's writing creates curves within straight lines, ripples within stone walls, movements of all kinds, within all kinds of fixed bounds, that he delights to see. And all the while he is satisfying his acutely self-conscious need for a subject of his own, and for a sign of his own inventiveness. His movements are freed by the confidence that he is writing within the defining forms of the subject and of the language as he finds them. It is because he thinks the language as he finds it is served by his analogous and expressive rearrangements of his subjects (rather than being traduced by attempts at mimesis) that Ruskin's security is enhanced, not undermined, by the recognition that writing represents not only its subjects but also the "position, and composition" (35.623) of the movements of his own mind and hand. As when it is retraced to its root in another of the languages that he studied, Ruskin's "invention" inheres in his "finding" the genesis of things – whether of his subjects, his self, or his language. "For you cannot find a lie; you must make it for yourself. False things may be imagined, and false things composed; but only truth can be invented" (7.250). The form of writing that discovers the history in the aspect, the "winding way" in the pattern to which it tends – this form of writing, whatever its plot or theme might be, was for Ruskin an access to the only story there was to tell. And if it did not always retain for him the authority of Genesis, still to him it was not fiction.

This is already clear by the time he has reached the end of the "Introductory" section of his semi-autobiographical *Chronicles of St. Bernard* (1835–36). Having returned to the Hospice after a day spent climbing to a view of Mont Blanc, the speaker is entrusted with a chronicle set in Venice which he proceeds to title *Velasquez, The Novice*, and to re-narrate in what has been called Ruskin's only attempt to write a novel (1.lv). This attempt lasts for just fifteen pages, in spite of its being elaborately framed to avoid the implication that it is what it is. Not only is it denied (by the truthful monk) that the story is fictional, but it is conveniently said, by the one who speaks for the diversely talented author of the *Chronicles*, to be written by diverse hands. After exploiting the Byronic pretense that the manuscript of an excruciated soul actually looks the part, the burden of proof is certainly eased by the announcement that this "broken, scratched, ... blotted" and intriguing document has been rewritten in prose that corrects its "want of connexion and ... [its] disjointed style" (1.536).

In fact the most interesting thing in *Velasquez* is precisely the role of "connexion." At the center of the fragment is a very long paragraph describing "the general features of the scene" which abstracts and formalizes the "essential points" previously presented; it even includes a tableau of three anonymous Venetians whose aspects stylize the three major characters – two English, and one "a stranger" – through whose eyes the reader allegedly sees (1.538, 544–45). What the reader is shown is a "scene . . . of such rapid change and singular beauty, as to compel the eye to keep in an almost disagreeable state of activity." Yet what makes this perception of change and activity possible is itself almost imperceptible. The "black crowd" of gondolas spreads so thickly over the water "as almost to conceal it"; the rise and fall of water over flights of marble steps is "almost invisible."

Farther on might be seen a narrow opening between the fronts of the palaces, where the deep water lay black and motionless, and some narrow and silent canal retired from the brightness of the daylight into a dim and twilight shadow, where the occasional gleam of some bewildered sunbeam was seen far through the distant darkness like a star; and the deep cry of the gondolier, as he turned the prow of his shadowy vessel into some yet more sunless chasm, came wandering along the damp, still air of the obscurity like a lamenting spirit.

What is "disjointed" by the rapid gliding from site to site – the silence and the sounds, the brightness and the dark – is connected by it too: Ruskin's imagery gives to water the imperceptible circumambience of air.

. . . above, in the shade of the Moorish windows, was seen, here and there, the flash of bright eyes, or a white arm resting on the marble balcony; and in the quiet of the air there was something like the sound of sweet, low voices, which made itself sensible, without being heard, as the eye perceives a glimmering in the twilight sky of a summer evening, though it cannot distinguish a single star.

(1.545)

124

Water is always the medium in descriptions of Venice, of course. At about the same date when *Velasquez* is set, Venice is "Rising" "fresh from ocean" and sinking back into it in *Childe Harold* IV, repeating Byron's vision of the rise and fall of empire which involves (like his vision of the same thing in himself) little gradation in between.[14] In Rogers's *Italy* – Ruskin's momentous birthday gift when he was thirteen – Venice is "in the Sea" and the sea is in it, dividing and connecting the land in "the broad, the narrow streets."[15] In Ruskin's first prose description of Venice, the objects of his sight seem not merely interconnected but interanimated by water. It is the course of waters which materializes the continuity between the dazzlingly bright scenes in *Velasquez* and the ominous undertow of the narrative, between the characters who are quick with life and those preoccupied with the dead. The language associates water with life – as does the heroine Ada when she imagines herself as a "wave of Venetian water" – and also with what Velasquez, who is thinking of desolated buildings, calls "a life in death": the same phrase that Ruskin uses in the "Introductory" narrative to describe "The rocks on the shore of the small lake" in the Alps (1.523). In the central passage in *Velasquez*, "the crowds of travellers of different nations" have, like water, "lately inundated Italy" – and though Venice retains "much of its original character,"

> its change of government and withering state of prosperity had brought the shade of melancholy upon its beauty, which is rapidly increasing, and will increase, until the waves which have been the ministers of her majesty become her sepulchre.   (1.554)

"The links between dead matter and animation drift everywhere unseen" (19.362),[16] like the waters through Venice.

Later I will come back to what is left marooned by the circumambience of *Velasquez* – the disembodied "white arm resting on the marble balcony," the "disjointed" and fragmentary manuscript itself, the deliberately distanced emotions of the writer who put these parts asunder. But it is clear in the meantime that the power of the contrasts in Ruskin's early writing depends on the power of his imagination of what interconnects the elements being opposed, what holds them in opposition. As in his sustained contrasts between the English cathedral close and St. Mark's in The Stones of Venice, or between the Venetian boyhood of Giorgione and Turner's London youth in Modern Painters V, the middle ground in some of his spectacular comparisons seems to drop out; and it is sometimes the spectacle of what is missing that takes the breath away. But Ruskin's will to know the gradations in between – whether between moving and fixed things, or between two fixed things, or between past and present – his will to invent a narrative in which the terms can be said, or imagined, to have developed: this is what gives the drama to his prose of high contrasts, as it is what gives the "strange, cold rigidity" to the "surgy glaciers" he beholds in the Alps (2.382). At their best, Ruskin's abstractions have a vibrancy and authority that come of his conviction that they have been generated and exist within a pattern as meaningful as the history of the earth, or the system of the English language – a pattern which is exposed by the very process of their abstraction from it. In the early writings where composition is "positively nothing," and the intense presence of self coexists with the ability to drop oneself out of sight, narrative continuity can also drop out from between the subjects it connects. It is important to see that this is true not only of his most fragmentary, unsuccessful pieces, but also of those that are most whole. It is Ruskin's early writings which most clearly display the evolution of his evolutionary narratives – in which those eclipsingly brilliant studies which stand out in the memory so demonstrably depend upon Ruskin's having gone over the ground in between – as the boldly framed views which burst upon his sight depend upon his passage through the rocks on the route at the end of the 1835 diary:

the road is carried through them in ranges of long and magnificent galleries lighted by openings blasted through their sides, which startle you with a sudden burst of light and beauty of landscape as you pass them. (*Diaries,* 72)

The leading lines of Ruskin's early writing are the ones that relate the forms he describes to the movements that gradate towards them.[17] What matters most are not finally his contrasts of form with form, nor of form with flux, nor even his displaying the continuities among them. His most powerful invention is his grasp of the pattern in flux itself – including the patterns described by, and in, the winding way of his own writing: his seeing its tendency to gradate towards form. The child who was fascinated by the relationship between fixity and movement and the "winding way" of his own language, and the man who enunciates the laws of composition in *The Elements of Drawing* and *Modern Painters* V, are both visible in the youth who makes out that his theories of composition may be abstractions from the growth of his writing through time.

But the youth who makes all of this out for himself may or may not be visible. For if the principle is already in the practice, if the design is already in the data – if geological theory is fossilized in the facts to be examined, if reasoning power is perpetuated in the formation of things to be drawn – then subjectivity may disappear in the depiction of the subject. The drama that seems to be produced by the disappearance of the self may actually be a consequence of its reappearance in the subject matter. The inventive young writer both is and is not to be caught in the act, for it is in the act of his invention that he is hidden best.

This is why, for all its self-expressiveness, Ruskin's juvenilia can underwrite his later self-denials. Out of the unconstrained and unconstraining practices of his earliest work come some of the more constrained and constraining principles according to which truth is related to invention in *Modern Painters*, or truthfulness is separated from invention in *Praeterita*. Ruskin would seem to be acknowledging this genealogy when he looks to his past for the justification of his present views. Though the past, once he turns back to it, is no longer as it was, what he has learned from his writing in childhood is forever immured in his prose:

Where [the slaty crystallines] are, they seem to form the world; no mere bank of a river here, or of a lane there, peeping out among the hedges or forests: but from the lowest valley to the highest clouds, all is theirs – one adamantine dominion and rigid authority of rock. We yield ourselves to the impression of their eternal, unconquerable stubbornness of strength; their mass seems the least yielding, least to be softened, or in anywise dealt with by external force, of all earthly substance. And, behold, as we look farther into it, it is all touched and troubled, like waves by a summer breeze; rippled, far more delicately than seas or lakes are rippled: *they* only undulate along their surfaces – this rock trembles through its every fibre, like the chords of an Eolian harp – like the stillest air of spring with the echoes of a child's voice. (6.150–52)

ILLUSTRATIONS

Lucy soon called him away and bid him observe a great black cloud from the north which seemed rather electrical. Harry ran

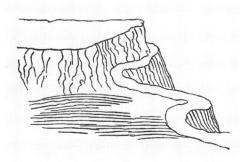

for an electrical apparatus which his father had given him and the cloud electrified his apparatus positively after that another cloud came which electrified his apparatus negatively and then a long train of smaller ones but before this cloud came a great cloud of dust rose from the ground and followed the positive cloud and at length seemed to come in contact with it and when the other cloud came a flash of lightning was seen to dart through the cloud of dust upon which the negative

2 JOHN RUSKIN, *harrys river*, 1826–27

My First tree! from nature, 1831

(J. R. 5th Jan. 1834)

3 JOHN RUSKIN, *My First tree! from nature*, 1831

GETTING OVER THE GROUND

I am a man sitting on a foxes tail

And away I go over hill and over dale

Go quicker my fox bear me swiftly along

And gallop away while I sing out my song

BARON MUNCHAUSEN

4 JOHN RUSKIN, page of ''The Puppet Show,'' 1828–29

My dear papa

A good Newyear to you. I at first intended to make for your Newyears present a small model of any easily done thing and I thought I would try to make an orrery but at length I gave it up on considering how many different things were wanted and composed the inclosed poem with another short address to you but Mamma disliking my address and telling me to write a small letter to you I attempted though I will not say I have succeeded to do it which thing I hope you will accept however unworthy it be of your notice

dear papa
your affectionate son
John Ruskin

Herinhill
December thirty first 1828

5 JOHN RUSKIN, letter to his father, 31 December 1828

ITERIAD

or

AMONG

the

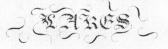

6 JOHN RUSKIN, title page of *Iteriad*, 1831

As departing we rode from the islanded wave
We looked towards Coniston looked to Scawfell
And bade to those lakes and those mountains farewell
15 Then swiftly away from the waters we flew
Till the towers of old Kendal appeared on the view
We past by those hills we had mounted before
When our path lay direct for old Windermeres shore
But with different feelings we now them beheld
20 As following ridges successively swelled
And the sounds of farewell floated wild on the wind
Returning to scenes we were leaving behind
Farewell to the lake and farewell to the mountain
The tarn and the torrent the fall and the fountain
To the deeps of the dell and the wood shaded shore
Thou land of the mountains I see thee no more

Finis

7 JOHN RUSKIN, finis page of Iteriad, 1832

can be observed in the entire thickness of subjacent beds of sand and clay.

The dip of the marine strata, at the base of Etna, is by no means uniform ; on the eastern side, for example, they are sometimes inclined towards the sea, and at others towards the mountain. Near the aqueduct at Aderno, on the southern side, I observed two sections, in quarries not far distant from each other, where beds of clay and yellow sand dipped, in one locality, at an angle of forty-five degrees to the east-south-east, and in the other at a much higher inclination in the opposite direction. These facts would be of small interest, if an attempt had not been made to represent these mixed marine and volcanic deposits which encircle part of the base of Etna, as the outer margin of a so-called 'elevation crater *'.

Near Catania the marine formation, consisting chiefly of volcanic tuff thinly laminated, terminates in a steep inland cliff, or escarpment, which is from six hundred to eight hundred feet in height. A low flat, composed of recent lava and volcanic sand, intervenes between the sea and the base of this escarpment, which may be well seen at Fasano. (f, diagram No. 11.)

Eastern side of Etna—Bay of Trezza.—Proceeding northwards from Catania, we have opportunities of examining the same sub-Etnean formations laid open more distinctly in the modern sea-cliffs, especially in the Bay of Trezza and in the Cyclopian islands (Dei Faraglioni), which may be regarded as the extremity of a promontory severed from the main land. Numerous are the proofs of submarine eruptions of high antiquity in this spot, where the argillaceous and sandy beds have been invaded and intersected by lava, and where those peculiar tufaceous breccias occur which result from ejections of fragmentary matter, projected from a volcanic vent. I observed many angular and hardened fragments of laminated clay (creta), in different states of alteration, between La Trezza and Nizzita, and in the hills above Aci Castello, a town on the main land contiguous to the Cyclopian isles, which could not be mistaken

* See vol. i. chap. xxii.

by one familiar with Somma and the minor cones of Ischia, for anything but masses thrown out by volcanic explosions. From the tuffs and marls of this district I collected a great variety of marine shells *, almost all of which have been identified with species now inhabiting the Mediterranean, and, for the most part, now frequent on the coast immediately adjacent. Some few of these fossil shells retain part of their colour, which is the same as in their living analogues.

The largest of the Cyclopian islets, or rather rocks, is distant two hundred yards from the land, and is only three hundred yards in circumference, and about two hundred feet in height. The summit and northern sides are formed of a mass of stratified marl (creta), the laminæ of which are occasionally subdivided by thin arenaceous layers. These strata rest on a mass of columnar lava (see wood-cut, No. 14) †, which appears to have forced itself into, and to have heaved up the stratified mass.

No. 14.

View of the Isle of Cyclops in the Bay of Trezza.

* See, in Appendix No. II., a list, by M. Deshayes, of sixty-five species, which I procured from the hills called Monte Cavalaccio, Rocca di Ferro, and Rocca di Bumpolere (or Borgia).
† This cut is from an original drawing by my friend Capt. W. H. Smyth, R. N.

This theory of the intrusion of the basalt is confirmed by the fact, that in some places the clay has been greatly altered, and hardened by the action of heat, and occasionally contorted in the most extraordinary manner, the lamination not having been obliterated, but, on the contrary, rendered much more conspicuous by the indurating process.

The annexed wood-cut (No. 15) is a careful representation of a portion of the altered rock, a few feet square, where the alternate thin laminæ of sand and clay have put on the appearance which we often observe in some of the most contorted of the primary schists.

No. 15.

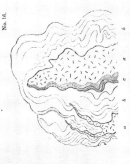

Contortions in the newer Pliocene strata. Isle of Cyclops.

A great fissure, running from east to west, nearly divides the island into two parts, and lays open its internal structure. In the section thus exhibited, a dike of lava is seen, first cutting through an older mass of lava, and then penetrating the superincumbent tertiary strata. In one locality, the lava ramifies and terminates in thin veins, from a few feet to a few inches in thickness (see diagram No. 16).

No. 16.

Newer Pliocene strata invaded by lava, Isle of Cyclops (horizontal section).

a, Lava. b, laminated clay and sand. c, the same altered.

The arenaceous laminæ are much hardened at the point of contact, and the clays are converted into siliceous schist. In this island the altered rocks assume a honeycombed structure on their weathered surface, singularly contrasted with the smooth and even outline which the same beds present in their usual soft and yielding state.

The pores of the lava are sometimes coated, or entirely filled, with carbonate of lime, and with a zeolite resembling analcime, which has been called cyclopite. The latter mineral has also been found in small fissures traversing the altered marl, showing that the same cause which introduced the minerals into the cavities of the lava, whether we suppose sublimation or aqueous infiltration, conveyed it also into the open rents of the contiguous sedimentary strata.

Lavas of the Cyclopian Isles not currents from Etna.—The phenomena of the Bay of Trezza are very important, for it is evident that the submarine lavas were produced by eruptions on the spot, an inference which follows not only from the presence of dikes and veins, but from those tuffs above Castello d'Aci, which contain angular fragments of hardened marl, evidently thrown up, together with the sand and scorie, by volcanic

Vol. III.   G

here and there escaped the burning lavas, serve, by contrast, to heighten the desolation of the scene. When I visited the valley, nine years after the eruption of 1819, I saw hundreds of trees, or rather the white skeletons of trees, on the borders of the black lava, the trunks and branches being all leafless, and deprived of their bark by the scorching heat emitted from the melted rock; an image recalling those beautiful lines—

> ' As when heaven's fire
> Hath scath'd the forest oaks, or mountain pines,
> With singed top their stately growth, though bare,
> Stands on the blasted heath.'

Form, composition, and origin of the Dikes.—But without indulging the imagination any longer in descriptions of scenery, we may observe, that the dikes before mentioned form unquestionably the most interesting geological phenomenon in the Val del Bove.

No. 19.

Dikes at the base of the Serre del Solfizio, Etna.

blue basalt with olivine. They vary in breadth from two to twenty feet and upwards, and usually project from the face of the cliffs, as represented in the annexed drawing (No. 19). They consist of harder materials than the strata which they traverse, and therefore waste away less rapidly under the influence of that repeated congelation and thawing to which the rocks in this zone of Etna are exposed. The dikes are, for the most part, vertical, but sometimes they run in a tortuous course through the tuffs and breccias, as represented in diagram, No. 20. In the escarpment of Somma where, as we be-

No. 20.

Veins of Lava.   Punto di Guaitento.

fore observed, similar walls of lava cut through alternating beds of sand and scoriæ, a coating of coal-black rock, approaching in its nature and appearance to pitch-stone, is seen at the contact of the dike with the intersected beds. I did not observe such parting layers at the junction of the Etnean dikes which I examined, but they may perhaps be discoverable.

The geographical position of these dikes is most interesting, as they occur in that zone of the mountain where lateral eruptions are frequent; whereas, in the valley of Calanna, which is below that parallel, and in a region where lateral eruptions are extremely rare, scarcely any dikes are seen, and none whatever still lower in the valley of St. Giacomo. This is precisely what we should have expected, if we consider the vertical fissures now filled with rock to have been the feeders of lateral

11 JOHN RUSKIN, Early Geology, 1830s

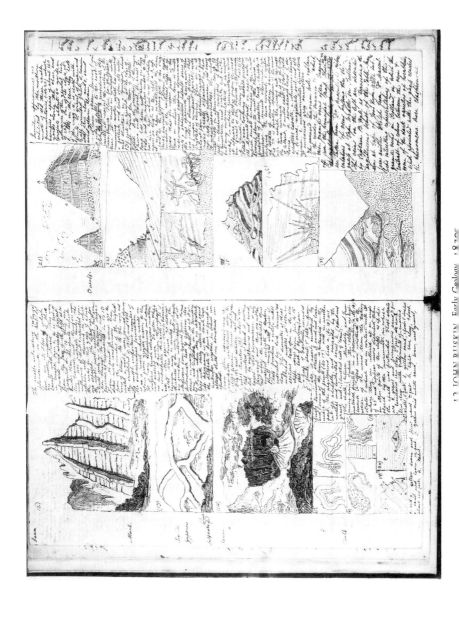

13 JOHN RUSKIN, *Traceries from Caen, Bayeux, Rouen, and Beauvais*, 1849

Theuth's Earliest Lesson

14 Lily Severn's "picture writing," 1884

PART TWO

LOOKING BACK

The gratifications of continuity depend upon the discipline of leaving things out. This dependency itself becomes one of the continuities between Ruskin's early writing and his sensations in looking back upon it – as in the autobiography he enjoyed because it "pass[es] in total silence things which I have no pleasure in reviewing" (35.11). In 1881, four years before he wrote the preface to *Praeterita* in which this clause appears, Ruskin drafted another preface (this time for *Proserpina*) that also involves principles of exclusion. "I hear it often said by my friends that my writings are transparent, so that I may myself be clearly seen through them. They are so . . . yet I know no other author of candour who has given so partial, so disproportioned, so steadily reserved a view of his personality."

Who could tell from my books, for instance, except in the course and common event of the abandonment of a sectarian doctrine, what has been the course of religious effort and speculation in me? Who could learn anything of my friendships or loves, and the help or harm they have done me? Who could find the roots of my personal angers? or see the dark sprays of them in the sky? The only parts of me that my readers know, even if they have common-sense, are, first, my love of material as well as of human beauty (so that when another man, reduced to despair, suppose, by a cruel shepherdess, would go miauling and howling about the vale and the valleys, I can climb the nearest crag, and silence, if not solace, myself in the study of granite, as uncomplainingly and irrefragably cleft) . . .   (35.628)

"Who could tell," "Who could learn," "Who could find" what Ruskin has left in silence? In fact the "view" that he gives of himself is most tellingly expressive where it takes in what is most "steadily reserved": his "friendships or loves" and "angers," rather than the religion about which he makes a large exception. Thus his remoteness becomes as "legible" as his description of the nearest rock, for the space between its cloven sides is as full of his emotions as are the parentheses within which he sets himself off from another man's "miauling and howling."

Ruskin bestows no illustrative imagery on the next two "parts of me that my readers know," his "love of justice and hatred of thieves" and his "general wish to make all honestly living creatures happy." The last and perhaps "chief" among the "characteristics legible of me," the "instinct for Teaching," is not illustrated either, or at least not insofar as it "resolves itself . . . partly into an extreme dislike of folly absolute." But images abound when he turns to "the rest" of his "instinct for Teaching," the part that "resolves itself" into

an almost inexplicable but strongly instinctive pleasure in the filling of empty heads and hearts, as if they were so many bottles, like to be broken for having nothing inside, or cells of honeycomb too hollowly fragile. And under the growling of this indignation at public folly and the minor buzzing and murmuring of the hymenopterous instinct for pouring good conserve of eternal fact, sweet in the taste and nourishing in the substance, into every cell of human soul that will let it in, I have gone on throughout my life, printing everything I could discover of such fact as fast as I could, and snarling at foolish things and people as hard as I could; but

often with no more sense of duty than the tide has in filling
sandpits, or a stone in rolling down hill.   (35.628–29)

When he writes of what is most nearly senseless and
inexplicable, sensations and explanations most nearly take
shape. Given the shapes in which Ruskin reads and rereads his
"characteristics," a potential explanation of the ten-year-
old's "cramming and ramming and wishing days were
longer and sheets of paper broader" (RFL, 200) might be
located in his latter-day account of "an almost inexplicable
but strongly instinctive pleasure in the filling of empty heads
and hearts, as if they were so many bottles." The old man's
provocative assertion that he has often acted "with no more
sense of duty than . . . a stone in rolling down hill" might
likewise provoke a reader familiar with his juvenilia to make
more sense, not less, of the fourteen-year-old's declaration
that "I roll on like a ball" (RFL, 274).

And if Ruskin's writing has filled what was "empty" and
fortified what was "like to be broken," then the kinds of
continuity I have been tracing may depend no more on the
discipline of leaving things out than on a compelling
experience of things and of people that were already found
wanting – or already left out. This possibility is as pertinent to
his first works as it is to his last. The manuscript of Proserpina
returns the reader to Ruskin's beginnings, and promises that
something wanting or left out will appear in the very
passages that seem the most replete. For the best of Ruskin's
early writing not only counters his claims that he was not
inventive but also reveals the links between a recollected
emptiness and the evidence of fulfillment.

The emphases that emerged in the first four chapters of this
book must therefore persist even as they are reformed and
renamed in each of the second four. In the second part I will

begin by looking back at passages which show the effects of Ruskin's earliest "friendships or loves," of his "personal angers" and "hymenopterous" pleasures, and then follow as – in sharply selective revisions – he himself looks back at the life of his writing.

CHAPTER 5

SEPARATIONS
(1829–49)

In contrast to the secure connections so prevalent in the prose and verse where he speaks as the son of his parents, the works that assume other personae are often marked by a dread of loss, violence, and death. As the omniscient author of "Love," the eleven-year-old Ruskin details the unaccountable death of a child ("The babe knew nought but joy / For what should trouble him / But something stole upon the babe"), the drawn-out agony of a mother driven mad by the separation, and the final reunion of the pair "in the grave": "They now shall part no more."[1] Five years later in "The Avalanche," Ruskin turns a well-documented account of two deaths on Mont Blanc into the lament of a widow for her lost "child," and of a "bride" and her son for their husband and father: "His boy, in undefinèd fright, / Stood shivering at her knee; / 'The wind is cold, the moon is white, / Where can my father be?'" (2.8). The plots of these and many other poems ("Revenge," for example, and "Despair") might make it seem simple to tie Ruskin's gloom and gore to the literary fashions of the period, and simple to separate them all from his brilliantly hearty letters and geological prose. But the simplicity in this case would be the reader's – not the writer's who, even as a ten-year-old, was carefully positioning his horrific verses about a shipwreck within two raucously jolly letters to his father: "Now papa if my rhyme has the power, I intend to keep you wishing and wishing for my next letter so will give you only two stanzas at a time of a poem that I have composed for the letters which I shall send to you" (RFL, 174–80). By the time the writer announces that he will "end [his] tragic song," the reader – the father who was held in suspense and was himself taking the risks of

travelling by water – may be the one who is saying
"farewell": "And now I'll end my tragic song / So reader say
farewell / I hope it has not been too long / Farewell farewell
farewell" (RFL, 181–82, 184–85).

In fact, Ruskin's father was always expecting to say
"farewell": "If the Almighty preserves the Boy to me, I am
richly blessed but I always feel as if I *ought* to lose him & all I
have" (RFL, 276); "In the midst of Life we are in death . . .
Our Blessings are so great that their very possession gives
fear, & as people get up in years, they seem to have so slender
a hold & so short a lease of Life that a fearful uncertainty
seems to hang over all" (RFL, 556–57). Every displacement
was a revival of the painful history of separations – from their
relations, from their class and social backgrounds, from each
other – that was suffered with extraordinary acuteness by
each of Ruskin's parents.[2] The wife's alarm about partings –
"I would not be separated from you for worlds" (RFL, 371),
although she separated herself to be with their son at Oxford
– was sharpened by the husband's concern for himself: "The
crook in my Lot is absence from you & a total Incapacity to fill
up the void in my Empyrean occasioned by family Separation" (RFL, 402). He went further: "I am when away from
my family the most lone Creature on the face of the Earth for
the Wandering Beggar holds a sort of communication with
the world amounting to more than mine" (RFL, 375).

In a different way for each of his parents, John Ruskin
became "a sort of communication" – with oneself, with each
other, with the rest of "the world." While he was still an
infant, his mother had grasped her son's potential as a means
of self-expression (e.g., RFL, 116). On her twenty-first
anniversary, she wrote from Oxford to her husband in
Chester: "What infinite gratitude do I owe to the Almighty,
for preserving to me your affection, for Making me the
Mother of a child so capable of gratifying all your kindest, as

well as your most aspiring feelings . . .'' (RFL, 583). By return mail, John James also expressed his feelings through his son: "It is strange that in thinking of getting home for Johns Birthday I never thought of Marriage day. I never know which was our marriage day – but if we may take it for 2d it is very appropriate that it was marked by an eulogium on our Sons talents in the public press of that day'' (RFL, 588).

Nothing could have been much commoner in the nineteenth century, or in this, than for parents to express themselves in terms of their children, or for children's sense of themselves to develop in terms of their parents. But the intervolvement of John James, Margaret, and John Ruskin was uncommon in its discreteness from their other relations, in its self-consciousness, in its being so fully recorded. The record shows that the connection between extremes of isolation and interdependence could be perceived by John James with some bitterness:

Unless we love our Species, it will avenge the neglect & turn this lovely world into a Solitude as dreary as an uninhabited Island. I have shut myself up with my family till the world Knows me not & little am I likely to care for the world whilst I have my family to receive me . . . I cannot say my happiness lessens as my wealth increases but I think such would be the case but for the Love of you & John & I may almost say b < ut fo > r yours for even John's I dont depend < on > for a constant & unchangeab < le > affection. Other & dearer objects must take his thoughts & a part of his Love from me . . .   (RFL, 375; Burd's interpolations)

Few wives can have worked harder to anticipate and discourage such fears. Five days before her husband wrote the letter just quoted, she addressed this to him in Yarmouth: "I think Johns love for you is innate and no circumstance nor person will make it less perfect'' (RFL, 371). The year before, in 1835, she wrote that if John "is thoughtful for any one he must be so for you for he certainly loves you better than the whole of the rest of mankind put together'' (RFL, 301–02). It is not unusual for children to work hard to prove such assertions are true, but few can have worked harder than Ruskin did to imagine his father's imagination of him, or to make that process seem fearless. The pressure to perform in writing never seems to exceed his desire; no resistance ever rises to meet his mother's commands – ''(never were commands more unnecessary)'' – that he ''exert my utmost powers of rhetoric to persuade'' his ''much revered much honoured much loved much wished for and much missed'' father to come home (RFL, 346, 247). The record shows that it was not just the conventions of the larger literary world, or of religion, that led him to play with the Gothic, or that crowded his poems with disasters: ''I say how could you be so unguarded so forgetful of all mamma's lectures and sermons upon the never ending subject of your forgetfulness of them as to go over gloomy rainy lonely darkling heathy barren starless moonless but not coldless Shapfells at the ghostical terrorfraught hour (to all little children who have frightening storytelling nurses)'' (RFL, 247–48).

As a child, Ruskin's deliberate expressions of worry can be so rhetorical yet so spectral – so high-spirited on the subject of spirits – that it is easy not to see fear at all. *Praeterita* says that there was none: he had absolutely ''nothing to love,'' ''nothing to endure'' and nothing to make him imagine his parents might vanish (35.44–45). But the insecurity is there in his securest productions. As we saw in the second chapter of this book, the letter which expresses Ruskin's supreme confidence in the connectedness of the English language is the one on which he casts shadows with images from Gray's ''Elegy'' and *Hamlet*, and he deepens these shadows with pictures of his father's ''melancholy'' when picturing his family without him (see above, pp. 47–48). The letter which says he ''roll[s] on like a ball'' is at once his profoundest expression of his own compositional principles and his profoundest expression of emotional principles which gave shape to his life at the time: the paradoxical interdependence of "vacancy" and "presence," of "minus & plus," "division" and "concentrat[ion]," "withdraw[al]" and "pressure" (RFL, 274–75; and see above, pp. 49–55). Ruskin's feeling "forced to cram and cram and cram and leave out what [he] cant put in" (as he puts it just before saying he will dole out "The Shipwreck" in pieces [RFL, 175]); his feeling (as in a birthday letter to his father) that their happiness is interdependent, and that he is happiest when "I have had more to do than I could do without all possible cramming and ramming and wishing days were longer and sheets of paper broader, though that is a wish which has nothing to do with time" (RFL, 199–200): these feelings are expressed in language which suggests that Ruskin's drive to close gaps, to occupy every blank space on each page, is a solution to problems posed by the first of the separations registered in his writing. It is not enough to say of separation that it spurred him to tighten connections, or that he knew how to make the one give poignance and drama to the other. For he grasped the fact that separation is always implicit in interrelation – grasped it in the realm of the emotions as, and as deeply as, he grasped the logic of a letter or a painting or a landscape. Because the same principles govern a multitude of phenomena – whether psychological or social, natural, visual or verbal – a problem in any given medium might be solved in terms of another. The "laws of motion" (RFL, 274) might become the composition of emotion. So feelings can be disguised even as they are being worked out. And a mastery of interrelations can as readily cover the distance between members of a single family as between separate scenes in the Alps.

.   .   .

A mastery of interrelations might also expand the distance between things or people. By 1881, when he drafted the preface for *Proserpina* quoted above (pp. 129–31), many readers could recognize a divisive aggression in his "strongly instinctive pleasure in the filling of empty heads and hearts, as if they were so many bottles, like to be broken for having nothing inside, or cells of honeycomb too hollowly fragile" (35.629). In the light of psychoanalysis, these images suggest a conventionally phallic sexuality, a design upon or a competition over spaces conventionally regarded as female. It is not, of course, a deterrent to such a reading that the language of the man (no less than the boy's about "cramming and ramming") is without conscious sexual innuendo. What *does* complicate a traditional psychoanalytic reading is that Ruskin's earliest expressions of "instinctive pleasure" are so consciously and gratifyingly focussed on his father. As we have already seen, it is not an obstacle to such pleasure but part of its fulfillment that his mother repeatedly tells him (as he reports, for instance, in the paragraph about "cramming and ramming") that he should not go on at such length in his compositions (RFL, 200). So long as John James avoids his wife's requests that he discipline Ruskin's writing (RFL, 187, 190), the course of communication runs smooth between father and son.

Such roughness as at first appears is reserved for Ruskin's mother, to whom he does not write, or his cousin Mary Richardson. Among numerous examples the best to begin with is a poem of 1831 known as "[Bed-Time]," for this (no less than Proust's drastically different description of going to bed at the start of *A la recherche du temps perdu*) presents a paradigmatic scene of the writer's development.

> "Now go, my dear. 'Tis time to go to bed."
> Oh, direful sentence; all so full of woe!

Oh dear! how mournfully those words are said,
  – So contradictory, – "*Come, dear, and go!*"
When anything had come into my head
  To all composing 'tis the fiercest foe.
I wish Mamma a little less would load us
With so much of *imperativus modus*.   (2.326)

In a poem written before this one, the "foe" of composition is likewise the foe of physical intimacy. "Oh dear the feminine gender" (the title is also the thrice-repeated refrain) parodies the contradictory way in which women rebuff men with the same luxurious garments that are designed to attract them: "With the silk and the satin / The blond and the bonnet / Keep love at a distance / Whenever they don it."[3] Nor is the frivolity of female obstructiveness confined to the home: Ruskin's fluency depends upon it at critical turns when he takes to the road in *Iteriad* (1830–32), the verse account of his tour in the Lake District with his parents and Mary Richardson. The poem begins with an anticipation of pleasure "unmingled with gall" (27), and it is with an air of great good humor that the eleven- or twelve-year-old poet punctuates his 2,310 lines with jibes against females – whether against the women "Disfiguring the Derwent" by doing their laundry on its shore (with no intervention from Jupiter, who is blinded by age or "the scolds of thy crabbèd old wife") (52); or against the "ladies" (that is, his mother and cousin) who fuss about their clothing and their comfort yet are ungrateful to the gentlemen who protect them (getting spattered annoys men too, but only when they are "soundly bemired") (59–66, 82–83); or against "the draggle-tailed, blue-stocking, curlpaper pate" of a landlady to whom the speaker, "confident in our gentility" by comparison, devotes a great deal of space, even as he (rather vulgarly) complains that "her fat-butter personage, stopped up the way!" (103–07).

The reader has long since been given to know that such comical-epical tirades are not interruptions, but the chosen medium of a speaker who wishes to avoid competition with the Lake Poets. Nonetheless, cockneys and girls help to validate this choice:

> No cockneys could find in its dread rocks so antique
> The fair picturesque or the rural romantic;
> No silly school-bred miss just turned seventeen
> Can affectedly say of 't – "How charming a scene!!!"
> But above any misses, Oh my admiration! –
> Dark Honister Crag rears his stern elevation, –
> Makes one silent in wonder and dread altogether,
> As feeling description a fruitless endeavour.   (65)

It is so frequently, and with such asperity, that young female authors and audiences are put in their place that Ruskin begins to sound uneasy about his own. Yet this uneasiness is dispelled, even as it is expressed, by his obeisance to the highest phenomena (whether masculine or feminine), and by his denigration of the lowest (here, predominantly feminine). Consider a bit more of the passage quoted above (pp. 106–07) in which Ruskin acknowledges that he is not "a proper lake-poet":

> Spite of all the endeavour by poor me that made is,
> I shall miss the applause of the misses and ladies.
> Far contrary unto the laws that are writ
> In natures own code, every miss makes a hit,
> At poor me and my rhymes, for they're not sentimental,
> And so to the – stop – to oblivion they're sent all.
> But the poets forget, when they praise solitude,
> That by rights upon her they should never intrude;
> And therefore, if truly and rightly 'twere known,
> They praise her the best when they let her alone.
> But I am digressive! Oh, pray, do not blame me!
> In description I know it would go on but lamely.

You know that description alone, it would be, sir,
A tedious thing that would tire you and me, sir.

. . .

Let every pert miss interrupt me in middle,
With a proper, school-bred, and genteel kind of giggle –
"I, I," – oh, dear me! – But I'll make a confession –
I'm digressive when I do but talk of digression.   (98–99)

Far from inhibiting the racily masculinist rhetoric of mock epic, the obstructive female is essential to its success. In getting where he wants to go, Ruskin depends no less on the interruptions of "every pert miss" than on the fellow feeling of "good Mr Reader" (112).

Texts like these allow us to turn back from the anachronisms of Ruskin's adult retrospection, and from our own, to contemporary evidence of the roles of the mother and the father, the feminine and the masculine, in the development of verbal signification. Turning back to Wordsworth's reconstructions of childhood, Margaret Homans has developed a model in which the absence or suppression of a mother identified with nature – and the absence or suppression of beloved female objects who are figurative substitutes for the mother – are originary and essential spurs to the writing of romantic poetry.[4] In the mid- and late 1830s Ruskin studied some of the works on which Homans bases her argument, and spun out his own plots in which the feminine object is identified with nature and forever out of reach. But prior to this scenario in Ruskin's writing is another in which, as we have seen, it is the absence of the father, not the mother, which is the provocation to writing – a scenario in which the father who provides an emotional and monetary motive is associated with a choice of subjects, with starting and moving and being unable to stop, while the mother is identified as a stationary curb to composition, with the limitation of time and materials. It is important to remember, in addition, that literary paradigms of the feminine and masculine were first presented to Ruskin in the reading voice of his mother and – when it came to Milton, Pope, Scott, and especially the bisexual Byron – of his father. The evidence that remains gives us no way of knowing for certain whether Margaret Ruskin somehow directed her son's expressions of love away from herself, or whether his greater expressiveness about his father bespoke a love that was, as she called it, "innate" (RFL, 371). What we can know for certain is that there were differences between Ruskin's parents in matters of social class, cultural orientation, their own writing, and the writing of a son who took in all of these differences and more – particularly when his father deputed his mother to discipline the profusion he was rewarding. But to read his parents' letters together with Ruskin's is to see that he exaggerated the relatively short distances that existed between this exceptionally close couple.

Far from beginning in adulthood, in *Fors Clavigera* or *Praeterita* where readers have always noticed it, this exaggeration is crucial to the earliest development of Ruskin's artistic identity, for he transposed his experience of his parents' separateness into the vexatious cross-purposes of writing. These purposes are made graphic in letters to the father, in which the mother's faintly pencilled, partly illegible lines are cross-written in the spaces left between those which the son has carefully set down in ink. Here is the one appended to the verses quoted above (p. 56) in which Ruskin goes on about being unable to stop:

How glad I am this is the last letter I shall have an opportunity of writing you, Papa; What a woeful time you have been away, you have absolutely let me send you 9 sheets, and without any answer. And now having concluded mine epistle, I intend to leave poor Mamma a small space of plain paper, whereon she may fairly and

distinctly set down what she has to say, for she seems always to have
something which she wishes to tell you, and for the reception of
which she is forced to find fragments of room, writing cross, and
topsy turvy and any way, so that I should be much afraid that you
and she would be at cross purposes, or at least you must be very
patient and dextrous in deciphering, if you join all the detached
pieces correctly together and no mistake; therefore in order to
obviate the necessity of so much invention on her part, and patience
on yours, I am content, without further circumlocution, to leave
her this little bit of paper at bottom and to sign myself . . .

John Ruskin
(RFL, 362-63)

No description of his parents could more succinctly spell out
a definition of their son as a writer, with his awareness that a
"woeful" absence is an "opportunity" for composition,
with his ambition to make his marks "fairly and distinctly"
on the page, always to have something "to say," to "find"
out and fill up every "fragment[ ] of room," to be "dextrous
in deciphering" and "join[ing] all the detached pieces
correctly together" – in short to be, via "circumlocution," at
once willful and polite, "inventi[ve]" and "patient." It
comes as no surprise that after all this, Margaret Ruskin's
postscript is just twelve lines long, all of them loving and
gracious, and two of them expressing the hope that her
husband received "the Nottingham letter because it was one
of Johns which I think would please you" (RFL, 363–64).

. . .

When Ruskin left his mother a bit of paper at the bottom of
this page, he had recently turned seventeen and was, like
many other adolescents, both in love and enrolled in classes
outside of the home. Nine months later his father was
anticipating that "Other & dearer objects must take his
thoughts & a part of his Love from me" (RFL, 375): even in a

close-knit Victorian family it was recognized that between their later teens and twenties children would probably separate themselves in some significant way. But for prodigies this process very often meant, and means, a turning away from their giftedness too. For the success of those gifts always depends upon a bond to a mentor who is very often a devoted mother or father.[5] Ruskin's passage through this period was fraught with trying separations: his enrollment at King's College was preliminary to his moving to Oxford (with his mother but without his father), and the unresponsiveness of Adèle-Clotilde Domecq (the daughter of his father's business partner)[6] was preliminary to her marriage to a Frenchman, which devastated Ruskin and disrupted his family's plans. But the purposes and cross-purposes already in place before Ruskin entered adolescence were not erased between 1836 and his emergence as an adult with a public career. They were deepened, disguised, and more fully pronounced.

The love poetry Ruskin wrote in 1836 suggests how closely these social and emotional patterns are related to those that define his grasp of the materiality of nature, the visual arts, and literature. In "On Adèle, By Moonlight" and "[On Adèle]," the speaker is enthralled by fluctuations that are like nature's own: the face of the beloved is not just seen by moonlight or sunset but is seen to possess the changefulness of its lights and colors. It is announced as early as the titles – "The Last Smile," "Remembrance" (1837) – that such a presence cannot last. Yet the passing of Adèle's animation allows the poet to evoke it again, in imagination. "[A]s evanescent" rhymes with "as pleasant" (2.463): the poet ends deprived of his beloved and in full possession of his power of memory. The implication is literalized in "Evening in Company – May 18" and "[A Moment's Falter]," when Adèle is described as a "word," a "name" which precipitates poetry when she is not there (2.461, 465). The irony that the "master-spell" must be cast from without and yet is his own, that the "word of power" must be sounded "in Company" yet to him alone (2.461), is drawn out in "The Name," a poem of 1838 which self-consciously compacts the lover into one of whom "This only is remembered still: / He loved a name," and the beloved into the one "sound he fancied all his own" – which is to others "A name of nothing." The metaphorical transmutation of lover and beloved into language becomes palpable in a final scene in which all that remains of the woman is a name on a tombstone, and all that remains of the lover is this poem. As in *Alastor* on which it seems based, a speaker lives on to tell the tale, a speaker who knows at the outset that the lover's "mind was made / Half of vision, half of truth" (2.81–82). Many years later that speaker will look back on the era in which Adèle was raptly described as a word, a name, and declare that it was he who gave it to her, "because it rhymed to shell, spell, and knell" (*Praeterita*, 35.180). The boy's self-affirming hints that a doomed love is necessary to the making of poetry, that he is partially inventing this love – that the writing of love expresses the love of writing – become the man's self-ridicule for the failure to behave in accordance with what "I perfectly well saw and admitted . . . having never at any time been in the slightest degree blinded by love, as I perceive other men are, out of my critic nature" (*Praeterita*, 35.229).

Back in the 1830s, the "critic nature" and the poetic nature went on collaborating in a remarkably self-affirming way. The poem about "The Mirror" (1837), whose emptiness of the beloved allows the speaker to fill it with his own imaginings, is itself mirrored in Ruskin's saying (in resistance to editorial advice from W. H. Harrison) that any number of phrases might be substituted for the one describing the "vision" of Adèle, "for a blank like this may be filled up hundreds of ways" (2.19–22). Ruskin was just as jaunty in protesting Harrison's cuts in the manuscript of his prose tale, "Leoni." In *Praeterita* Ruskin mocks this "story about Naples" in which "'the Maiden Giuletta'" [sic] embodies "all the perfections" of Adèle Domecq, and "'the Bandit Leoni'" (disguised, for the purposes of wooing, as "Francesco") stands for "what my own sanguinary and adventurous disposition would have been had I been brought up a bandit." But the ridiculous premise of swashbuckling bravery is touched with pathos once Ruskin says he "bore the pain bravely" when the beloved inspirer of "Leoni" "laughed over it in rippling ecstasies of derision" (35.180). Given this introduction – which is most people's to a reading of "Leoni" (1.xlvii–xlviii) – it is surprising to find Ruskin already mocking in 1836, as he brings the frantic lover and the calculating critic face to face in a letter to Harrison:

But I think the only thing a bandit can do to ingratiate himself with a lady is to be desperately over head and ears in love. I have therefore spouted some nonsense about morning on dark mountains . . . [Leoni] ought to be as mad as a March hare . . . it seems to me quite as dangerous to make a lady much in love as a gentleman little . . . If . . . he be properly in love, he cannot talk too great a quantity of nonsense, or come over her with too much gammon.

(1.303–04)

By the end of the story, Giulietta, her father and brother have died and Leoni has gone mad in earnest. But taken together with Ruskin's comments, the poet/lover beside himself – "Oh, how I love the love of thee!" (1.295 n.1) – reads as a poet with a critic beside him who measures the use of emotion.

Ruskin's position is equally complicated when it comes to the effects of love on the physical world. The one-upmanship of *Iteriad* (which scolds the Lake Poets for invading nature's solitude) and the moralizing of "The Crystal-Hunter"

(1834) (which warns that the seer of nature's fastnesses will loose what he beholds when he publishes it to the world) yield to the imagery of "[Nature Untenanted]" (1836), in which the absence of Adèle shows him the face of his loneliness in the landscape. *Praeterita* says that "the newly revealed miracle of human love . . . exalt[ed] . . . the physical beauty of the world I had till then sought by its own light alone" (35.181). But in the 1830s the landscape was not so much exalted as ingested, and thereby viewable in the light of his love. His sense of beauty was sharpened by his sense of its fading, which gave way to barrenness or to an eerie ghastliness when he realized, as in "Farewell" (1840), that Adèle could never return. The "lifelike undulation" in a medium that is horribly not alive brings on the image of a "water-snake" and of a deadly serpentine – of "clasped contortions" and "intertangled fold[s]" – that recall and reverse the mood in which Ruskin had pursued a "winding way" in his earliest poems and letters to his father (2.195–96). Even at the start of his love for Adèle, when he could not be sure of his failure, the figure of the serpent is already eating at the heart of a landscape that is blooming with hope (2.124–25, 465). When all mental and emotional movement is the poet's, unreceived, unreciprocated, the animation of the physical world – the "blue hills ris[ing] upon the sight" in the 1833 "Song" (2.3–4); the movement and fixity, the flux and form of the 1835 diary – is replaced by a kind of haunting, a life-in-death and death-in-life. The contrast between reverie and reality which inspirits Chamouni in his "Account of a Tour on the Continent" (1833–34) has become an anticipation which imbues the landscape with a ghastly phosphorescence – a "strange and lifeless light, / Veiled with worse horror by the quivering ray, / Like dead things lighted by their own decay" ("Farewell," 2.201).

147

As these quotations make clear, Ruskin's love poetry bears the impress of "The Night-mare *Life-in-Death*" in *The Rime of the Ancient Mariner*; of the snake already coiled within the glance of the virgin Haidee in *Don Juan*; of the mortifying dreamscapes of *Alastor*. Ruskin mocks this derivativeness in *Praeterita*, and most readers rush past his love poems because of it, missing the fact that the young Ruskin grasped not just the scenic plots of his models but grasped – more fully than any other Victorian reader – the relationship between the philosophical argument that the mind creates its own reality, and the practical articulation of that argument in figures of speech.[7] Certainly the most complicated of these romantic arguments and articulations were Percy Shelley's; and for all of Ruskin's emotional inexperience, his verses show an exceptional fluency with Shelley's logic of self-referentiality, and an exceptional sophistication in the handling of images "drawn" (as they are in *Prometheus Unbound*) "from the operations of the human mind."[8] "Far and more far the lines of azure sweep, / Faint as our thoughts when fading into sleep; / When pale and paler on the brain defined, / The distant dreamings die upon the mind" ("[Nature Untenanted]," 1836, 2.466). Ruskin says that in 1836 he got great good and "no harm" from studying Byron, but that he "wasted much time" and "took a good deal of harm" from Shelley, "in trying to write lines like 'prickly and pulpous and blistered and blue' . . ." (*Praeterita*, 35.183). Although he acknowledges that *Prometheus Unbound* "really made me understand something of Aeschylus," he insists that "With Shelley, I loved blue sky and blue eyes, but never in the least confused the heavens with my own poor little Psychidion" (*Praeterita*, 35.220). Yet he chose for the epigraph of his *Alastor*-like "Farewell" some lines from the *Agamemnon* which lay out the confusing continuum of self-projection: "for scarce the sleeping sight / Has seen its own delight, / When thro' the grasps of love that bid it stay / It vanishes away / On silent wings that roam adown the ways of sleep'' (2.xxii). The affinity between *Alastor* and the imagery of Aeschylus has only recently been noted in criticism,[9] but Ruskin had caught it by 1840. Unlike that of most other readers, whether in the nineteenth century or in this, Ruskin's understanding of Shelley was always imbued with a sense of the instability and ephemerality of the world created in language by "the human mind's imaginings" (*Mont Blanc*, line 143). It is a mark of Ruskin's astonishing linguistic discernment that his sense of these limitations comes through the language of Shelley himself.

John James Ruskin, for his part, was persuaded that his son was a romantic poet: "Memory" and "The Name" are, he exults, "truly Byron & better than Byron by far at it" (RFL, 587). Ruskin, in the meantime, gained not only his father's approval but also some of what the romantics had gained by writing as they did. If we stop with what is obvious – that love is always thwarted in romantic poetry – we will fail to see its implications for Ruskin's development as a writer. It was not just that questing after an unattainable object certified his membership in the brotherhood of poets,[10] but that he saw how the linguistic patterns of reflexivity and self-projection would allow him to express the strongest yearning for communion and community, while guaranteeing him the completest isolation from it – would allow him to express the deepest desire for mingling and consummation, while keeping him impenetrable. The dynamics of self-projection, Ruskin saw, would allow for the greatest vigor of "cramming and ramming," while insuring him an endless supply of vacancy. Fortified with this linguistic expertise, he could express his will to communicate even as he acted out a resistance or antagonism to his fellow writers and readers (including the beloved): a competition even within the society he sought by his writing to join.

Ruskin's early Gothic pieces, so often dismissed as embarrassing dead ends, likewise reveal a remarkably perceptive apprehension of the conventional. Again it is not simply that the Gothic gave him access to terrain forbidden to him in broad daylight, but that he pursued his plots with a relentless self-referentiality that points to the terrain of his writing. The very title of *Velasquez, The Novice* (1835–36) at once suggests an as yet uncommitted outsider and Ruskin's own novitiate in the genre and in love. The grouping of anonymous Venetians which replicates that of the respectable English family (1.538, 545) poses a question about what the techniques of the Gothic might have to do with the respectable English author of *Velasquez*, and a question about why he takes as his heroine an English virgin who wants to be part of the reflexive medium itself: "'Now I could wish myself a wave'" of Venetian water, says Ada (whose name was originally Adèle); "'Do they not seem as if they saw, and felt, and rejoiced in the light of their own loveliness?'" (1.544). To answer these questions it is necessary to consider that *Velasquez*, itself a fragment, portrays a fragmented world in which death is a foregone conclusion. But if the future is certain, the past is certainly not. To see the statuesque figure of Velasquez (named for a painter who himself painted statuesque figures [1.276]), or the Venetians who people the canals, or the antiquated manuscript which describes them, is to speculate upon their previous lives, to wonder how they came to look the way they do. As when Ruskin regards geological or architectural formations, the present and even the future are readily accessible to the eyes; what is less apparent, what must – most rewardingly – be imagined, is the past. It is in overlooked pieces like *Velasquez* that Ruskin first forges a connection that will obtain between the conventions of Gothic literature and his analysis of architectural Gothic, for in both cases the writer makes out an animation hidden within fatefully fixed or stonily stoical forms, and in both cases his imaginative movement back and forth between them gives an animation to his account of the object. The idea of the self as a Gothic ruin was as familiar to Ruskin as Childe Harold; but no romantic writer ever fashioned such creative analogies between the haunting of human lives, and the past astir in the stone and the landscape.

Ruskin gave to *Marcolini* (1836) the same setting as *Velasquez* and he likewise left it unfinished, but this play in verse goes much farther in reticulating genealogies that exist in the air and the blood. In *Marcolini*, the mysterious circumambience of Venice is as palpable as a family tree. For the several males in the dramatis personae are entangled not simply in plots about women but through the sins of the murdered or murderous fathers. The patterns of guilt and dread are difficult to read not only because the characters are self-divided and duplicitous,[11] but also because of their wholehearted commitment to a Shelleyan concept of love: "a going out of our own nature," Shelley calls it in *A Defence of Poetry*, "an identification of ourselves with the beautiful which exists in thought, action, or person, not our own" (487–88). The greatest human attempt to reach out to another is always a projection of self. The heroine Bianca Carrara describes her beloved Marcolini – "his thoughts / Go forth to judge the minds of other men / All dazzled by the light of his own love" (2.487) – in the same reflexive terms she uses to describe the emasculating force of love: "Nay, it will curb the heart / To such an impotent subjection / That, even reft of hope, it shall continue / To feed on its own fire" (2.488). And love, which is once again a "name" (2.507), is hard to separate from the "word," the "name" that signifies death (2.482), for both

of them move through the syntax of self-projection, and self-
nourishment, and self-consumption (2.505–06). The lover
projects his desire for his beloved in the same terms he uses to
project his plan to murder his rival in love (2.494). And if the
imagination of marriage is the imagination of death, as it is in
the hero's mixed "ditty" (2.493), then it makes sense that
the lovers' first scene together evokes the "twilight time, /
That 'twixt the day of life and night of death / Spreads its
uncertain horror" (2.501–02). But the fate of the lovers
would be the same even were they never to meet. For if one's
projection meets with no return, no reciprocity, the result is a
nightmarish self-entrapment:

> thy soul
> Recoiling from the contact of all life,
> To trust and lean upon its own despair,
> And mock at its own misery, till the heart
> Be numb and feelingless, in a living death;
> When thou shalt be as I, thou'lt feel with me
> That life is full of names for what is not,
>
> (2.496)

In the end, the linguistic patterns of heterosexual love and
homosocial competition are fused with the patterns of
genealogy, for they are identified with a parent's projections
onto a child. But the parents who provoke the self-projective
loves of their children are the very ones who stand in their
way:

> you filled
> My heart with such emotions as, I feel,
> Awake like soundings in the hollow shell
> In sympathy most sweet with what is pure
> Or beautiful in others. And it seemed
> As if I had found all which you had taught me
> To think was noble, in his thoughts, whom now
> You bid me hold no farther commune with.
>
> (2.516)

In a play where the sins of the fathers loom so large, it is striking that the parent in question here is the mother. Lord Carrara voices "No paternal threat, / Nor anger of authoritative counsel" (2.514). Yet the woman whom Bianca calls "Dear mother," "Sweet mother" (2.515) is the only one of the family who speaks with a venom. What exactly has provoked her? The lovers' suit was already doomed from the start; it needed no further obstruction. Yet Lady Carrara is determined to have the last word, and Ruskin gives it to her when he drops his play just after she speaks, making it look like what comes between lovers is mothers (of whom there were none to intervene in *Velasquez* and "Leoni") and not the reflexive structures of rivalry and desire. Or rather, the daughter's saying that she inherited these structures suggests that a woman is their author after all. Or women: much as Lady Carrara curtails her daughter's speech, so Bianca threatens to "curtail [the] tale" of Marcolini (2.503) – allowing Ruskin in each case to curtail, after approximately two pages, the only direct confrontations between the pair and within the family. Like Adèle in his love poems, Bianca at once casts a "spell," sounds a "knell," and recalls a "shell" (which is of course one of Shelley's own favorite self-significations): she is both a curb to writing and a spur that persists so long as the love that fills an emptiness can never end in fulfillment.[12]

Regarded from this point of view both Bianca and Lady Carrara merely serve the needs of the author, much as they serve the plots of the men in the play. But from another point of view, Bianca speaks for Ruskin far more meaningfully than do any of the men. As the female, the virgin, the vulnerable one, Bianca, like Ada in *Velasquez* and Giulietta in "Leoni," is naturally the object of love. But she also acts out a subjective experience of its consequences: the potential confrontations with parents, the necessary departure from home, the genuine danger of loss. The outcomes of love in Ruskin's fiction – the death of Giulietta's father, the cruelty of Bianca's mother – may seem too extreme to take seriously. But, once again, the conventionality of Ruskin's plots obscures the singularity of his response to distances within his own family, a response which might well have made him imagine *any* separation as violent.[13] Dutifulness was no guarantee against the risks of love. Although sportive enough with others, all three of the young women Ruskin creates are sweetly faithful and reverent daughters: it is their very fidelity, rather than any defiance, which promises to put them at odds with their parents. The leap it requires to see Ruskin's own situation in that of his heroines is no greater than the leap we will later see him take in *Fors Clavigera*, when he identifies with the martyred Rose La Touche and Lady Jane Grey (28.342–57; and see below, pp. 219–21), or in remarks he made in 1864, in which he is Cordelia to his father's King Lear. "[P]rovoked" a few days after his father's death by Henry Acland's "supposing that I ever spoke so as to cause my father much sorrow," Ruskin retorted that

you never have had – nor with all your medical experience have you ever, probably, seen – the loss of a father who would have sacrificed his life for his son, and yet forced his son to sacrifice his life to him, and sacrifice it in vain. It is an exquisite piece of tragedy altogether – very much like Lear, in a ludicrous commercial way – Cordelia remaining unchanged and her friends writing to her afterwards – wasn't she sorry for the pain she had given her father by not speaking when she should? (36.468–71; see also 13.481)

Even when they are not explicit, identifications across gender can exact a high price. Bianca seems to speak for her wooer when she declares that to be in the grip of love (or, by the analogy in *Marcolini*, in the grip of inherited patterns) is to be in "an impotent subjection" (2.488). In *Praeterita* Ruskin implies that his wooing females by writing in their favorite

genres made him seem more foolish than a girl (35.179–82).
As we have already seen, Ruskin was defending himself from
this possibility in the 1830s, repeating the ways men had
previously fought back against "an impotent subjection" in
love and in literature. He seems to have been as aware as any
twentieth-century feminist critic that women were entering
the literary market place in unprecedented numbers; that
they were strongly associated – both as authors and as
subjects – with sentimental writing and the Gothic; that
prominent male writers used their rivalries with women to
cover or make clear their relations to each other; that they
claimed new spaces for themselves by charging that the old
ones were devalued – and by strewing them, in proof, with
images of feminized men and fallen women.[14] Thus in *Iteriad*
Ruskin contends with uneasiness about predecessors by
dismissing rivals and readers as feminine. Once he has soured
on his earlier efforts, he scoffs at the "*very* young ladies" who
write for fashionable annuals and at the relatives who buy up
their productions – though his father's connections with
editors had made it possible for him to appear in just such
publications when he himself was young.[15] And after the
conventions of Gothic have helped him make out the
"impotent subjection" not only of women but of men who
love and who sing, Ruskin uses the speech of a woman to
bring what he sees to an end. "I might have seen to this
before," says Lady Carrara; "but yet, / It shall not be too late
to remedy" (2.516).

. . .

Unlike Leoni, Velasquez, and Marcolini, who have no parents
to be seen, Ruskin wrote frequently to his father during the
course of his own romance. The bond between father and son
is recorded not simply in their sharing a masculine point of
view, or in their sharing a desire that Ruskin sound like a

romantic poet, but – more complexly and remarkably – in Ruskin's giving his father and beloved the same language to share. In a verse letter written to John James in the winter after *Marcolini*, Ruskin expresses his desire to communicate with his father in the very terms in which he reaches out to Adèle: he conjures up words that "burn[ ]" with the "eloquent lightning" that "skips / About the openings of kindled lips"; and a voice as "thrilling" as that of "a deep loving eye / Whose night is like a soul with which we try / To mingle" (RFL, 397–400). The anxiety expressed in this letter ("For we are hurried ever on, as hanging / Between the wings of some wild bird") is occasioned not just by his unspoken suspense about Adèle, but also by his immanent departure for university and by "some mail delay" that might separate him from his father even sooner. Once he is in residence at Oxford, his poems continue to be marked by that confounding of intellectual and amorous ambitions which he satirizes in *Praeterita* (35.180,222). Pieces like "Christ Church, Oxford" and "The Gipsies" (both 1837) predict a horribly reflexive doom for youth's "yearnings" for love and glory (2.26, 29–31); while the "home" left behind remains "all" (2.36).

The connections between inner and outer, and among parent and lover and son, are still more remarkable in "The Tears of Psammenitus" (1839?), a violent account of masculine enmity which Ruskin based on a passage in Herodotus (2.185 n.1). He told his college friend Edward Clayton that he wrote the poem "as a relief from strong and painful excitement" – which was probably the news of Adèle's marriage in the spring of 1840 (2.185). If this is so, then "The Tears of Psammenitus" indirectly dramatizes the very pain it was meant to relieve; for it projects his emotion about losing Adèle as the agony of a father who has lost his sons. Or perhaps the analogy is more exact than that, for what

Ruskin has lost is not Adèle but a vision of her, and what drives Psammenitus mad after his sons are killed is the "vision passing, never past, / . . . that cast / Cold, quivering shadows of keen pain, / In bars of darkness, o'er my brain" (2.186–87). In defending these and other lines from Clayton's criticisms in 1841, Ruskin takes up positions with which we are already familiar: he scorns the praise of "ladies – who never read, and couldn't have understood, a word of" his poems; he insists that "Psammenitus" is "throughout a *speech*, a dramatic piece – not a poem in which the *author* professes to be speaking." Some bantering self-mockery follows, but Ruskin is utterly serious about how an emotion composes a vision, and about how an author composes that vision in poetic speech (1.436–44). In a letter written nine months later to W. L. Brown, his tutor at Christ Church, Ruskin is more formal in distancing himself from the subject matter of the poem, and more explicit about the composition of emotion:

As far as I have had any experience of mental pain, I think its tendency is to render intellectual impressions at once rapid, distinct, *material*, and *involuntary*; . . . while the outward senses and inward emotions seem to change places with each other – all emotions becoming material and suggesting material impressions of darkness or weight or sound, and all external impressions mixing with these and becoming mistaken for them, and adding to their cause – all inanimate objects becoming endowed with a strange sympathy, and having influence like living things. This strange confusion of the functions of the intellect and senses I particularly aimed at giving in the "Psammenitus." (36.27–28)

The vision of Psammenitus expresses the horror that materialized before Ruskin's eyes when Adèle Domecq gave him a vision of absolute separation. The romantic idiom of self-projection is now theorized as the consequence of "mental pain" – as it will be in his examples of the pathetic fallacy – not of pleasure or bittersweet frustration.

The compositional process he describes to Brown is grotesquely literalized in a Herodotean poem he wrote within two months of the death (by a gruesome accident) of the father of Adèle Domecq (RFL, 593 n.1). In "The Scythian Guest" (1839), as it is called, a corpse visibly phosphoresces into an amalgam of "fear" and "atmosphere" – "Something half substance and half thought" (2.106). So that the dead object on which the living gaze takes on the medium of their own subjective emotion. Something comparable happens in "A Scythian Banquet Song" (1838) whose speaker, Ruskin tells the editor Harrison, has "Not only . . . been brought up in the school of Scythian horror, but in a far severer one – that of his own agony . . . I know it is horrible; it ought to be so – the man is seeking for something more horrible than his own thoughts" (2.69–70). The poem is one long, autobiographical "Banquet Song," sung by a man orphaned when his family was slaughtered, then crazed when his beloved was killed by the foe whose skull has become the drinking cup he now raises. In the last stanzas, the dead woman no longer comes between the living and dead men who now meet "in love": "Kiss me, mine enemy!" the singer twice repeats; "Lo! how it slips, / The rich red wine through his skeleton lips" (2.69).[16] John James Ruskin drew the line here. He wrote to Harrison, whose opinion he had sought,

The points you note render the poem to me most appalling and disgusting . . . There is to me a double dose of Disgust in Kiss Me mine Enemy – the Living enemy being a man – . . . I cannot understand why the young students are kept so long on these subjects in Herodotus or how John . . . lets his mind dwell on these dark pages . . . I hope he may alter his poem for he wrote it in a day . . . The unwillingness to rewrite or compress will be fatal to all his Oxford poems . . .

Although wishing to eliminate the phrase about men kissing, John James declared himself able to "endure" the "other Horrors" once he took in his son's impassioned defense of them to Harrison (RFL, 532, and quoted above). A few weeks later, he was not only calling "A Scythian Banquet Song" "by far the best of John's doings," but praising it particularly in point of manliness: "There is a healthy, manly tone about it; a nerve and power and originality that give promise of poetry worth reading" (2.57 n.1).

The shift in John James's position suggests his responsiveness to the positioning of his son. This responsiveness could be both empathic and judgmental; he was well aware that the intensity of his feelings meant he must try to see his son's work from a distance (RFL, 618–19). What did not shift was his belief that if a young man were to win celebrity while at Oxford – and John James did everything he could to realize that goal, including research for the poems and editing and urging Harrison to edit them further – then he would have to play by the rules. In the view of John James, these rules took in matters of diction, genre, and publicity as well as of academic and social tradition. Each of these matters existed for him in remarkable proximity to one another, as they do in a letter he wrote to his wife in March 1840, just days before the marriage of Adèle Domecq and weeks before the health of his son would break down:

I mind nothing so much as Johns continuing a member of Ch[rist] Church & terminating Studies there with Credit. . . . I am sorry for anything being done even by ignorance or omission against College rules. I am greatly obliged by so rigid an Enforcer of rules as the Dean treating my Son with lenity & consideration.

Please tell me if I am right in giving line

> And when the heart must bear the weight
> Of its own Love alone

Own is not written plain. John must adopt some pretty & uncommon Signature for these poems which are too valuable to be let pass for anyones & yet scarcely such as can from the Subject be sent out by J. R. The Revd. of Ch[rist] Ch[urch] the Dean may smuggle *Love* in *Prose* into his College but will not patronize an open trade of *Love* in *Verse* going out of it. (RFL, 660–61)

The bit of verse that he quotes is from Ruskin's "Agonia," the last of the poems that focus on his relationship to Adèle. About the subject of his agonized and carefully formulated lines, as opposed to literary questions about their interpretation, nothing is said in the family correspondence, although Margaret probably copied them out and John James said he knew the "little *gem* . . . by heart" (RFL, 658, 662–63). Two weeks earlier he was asking his wife how their son "is prepared to hear of *A's* marriage. I am anxious about him – because I do not know the depth of the Impression" (RFL, 648). That so passionate a poem as "Agonia" did not answer the personal question was owing not simply to the ways in which the father read the son but also to the ways in which the son learned to write for the father. The transmutation into print of Ruskin's early emotional and academic life is behind his affirmation, in the 1881 manuscript quoted above (pp. 129–31), that his works are at once "transparent" and "reserved," as it is behind his lifelong habit of writing at large as he would at home, and behind the startling and deliberate variations he repeatedly plays on the conventions of privacy and publicity (e.g. 14.462, 17.478 n.1, 28.449).

. . .

Ruskin's self-assertiveness in and about his writing between 1836 and the early 1840s suggests the simultaneous force of his feelings about himself as a lover and critic, and about any man's standing in the way of his chosen self-expression. The will to justify his self-expression becomes more impersonal and more aggressive when he turns, during these years, from making poems to making commentaries in prose on other men's work. With the pursuit of mastery in critical prose his pursuit of a female becomes relatively covert, but his competition with other males – not so much the students of his own age, who presented little challenge, but teachers and examiners and reviewers[17] – moves further into the open. The genre of non-fiction prose may itself have had something to do with his altered demeanor; for, more than poetry and Gothic fiction, it was not devalued by association with women, and retained an authority that was decidedly masculine.[18] In Ruskin's hands non-fiction shares some of the preoccupations and techniques of his work in other genres, much as science, the visual arts, and literature were seen to interact in the chapter on "Disciplines" in the first part of this book. But as of 1836, Ruskin's non-fiction shows him more determined to be a disciplinarian, to discipline the resistant or ignorant reader.

His two unpublished essays of 1836 are keenly adversarial, staging contests among disciplines and their exponents. "A Reply to 'Blackwood's' Criticism of Turner" pits Turner's painting, particularly *Juliet and her Nurse*, and the poetry of Shakespeare, Coleridge, and Shelley, against the prose criticism of a periodical reviewer. As was noted in the introduction (see above, pp. 6–8) Ruskin's imagery suggests an erotic plot which involves the defiling rivalry of men, a fallen female figure, and a transcendent virgin or two, for Turner is like the female moon who will not "bate of her brightness, or aberrate from the majesty of her path" (3.640). "The brightness of Juliet" was, according to *Praeterita*, one of Ruskin's models for Bianca in the closely contemporary *Marcolini* (35.182); and as in that play, the writing in "A Reply to 'Blackwood's'" suggests that romantic aesthetics bring with them a plot about gender and sexuality.

While in this piece it is Turner who, "In a wildly magnificent enthusiasm, . . . rushes through the aetherial dominions of the world of his own mind, – a place inhabited by the spirits of things" (3.639), in the "Essay on Literature" it is the novelist Bulwer who "floats on amidst the calm but beaming aether of his own imagination," giving "Nature a spirit that she had not before" (1.370).[19] Although the terms of Ruskin's praise bring prose and poetry (and visual art) close together, he introduces a distinction in this essay which gives prestige to the medium in which he writes it. Poetry is "most inspiring," but prose is "more refined":

It might be thought that what we have been saying of Bulwer's works might have been said of all poetry, but this is not the case; it could only have been said of poetical prose, and we will let him tell the reason in his own words. "Verse cannot contain the refining and subtle thoughts which a great prose writer embodies: the rhyme eternally cripples it; it properly deals with the common problems of human nature which are now hackneyed, and not with the nice and philosophising corolleries which may be drawn from them: thus, though it would seem at first a paradox, commonplace is more the element of poetry than of prose." (1.371–72)

Is it because Ruskin has been freed by the medium of prose that he can develop another new argument in the "Essay," according to which it is not only the writer and his subject, the mind and its object, which intermingle, but also the reader who is entangled in great art? Paradoxically, the most self-reflexive, self-projective art can take an audience outside of itself, so that we "enwreathe ourselves with the imagination of the poet, or mingle amongst the creations of the romancer" (1.359). And in art which is less imaginative but more inventive, like Scott's fiction, "selfishness is put entirely out of the question" (1.365, 371).

The mingling of writer and reader brings to mind Ruskin's

comment in *Praeterita* that he tried to woo Adèle with his writing (35.180). But the essay is also full of reminders that it was produced either as a theme set by Thomas Dale, once his schoolmaster and now his professor at King's College, or "in protest against views to which [Dale] had lent authority" (1.357 n.2).[20] The youth attempts to establish his own authority with a prolonged and rather ugly assault on "ugly" young ladies and old men and women; by the end of it he is so confident that he adds an inside joke (which only his parents would have caught) linking the laughable publications of "home-bred misses" to the pieces he wrote as a child (1.359–61). Sixteen pages into the essay, so little opposition seems left to him that Ruskin's energy begins to flag. He can arouse himself to a climactic finale only by imagining the murmur of adversaries.

We feel as if we had been beating the air – contending, but with no opponent – struggling, but with no impediment. But when we pronounce the name of "The Bride of Abydos," we feel that the case is altered. The dust and ashes of criticism become living before our eyes, and a murmur of indignation arises from the multitudes of crawling things. But the name hath touched us with its finger, and our brain is burning, our heart is quivering, our soul is full of light. (1.372)

Ruskin will always be inspired by the role of isolated champion of the isolated artist; in this "Essay on Literature," where he is still committed to romantic conventions, he derives the greatest joy from his sense of being at one with the man who was, apart from Shakespeare, "the greatest poet that ever lived, because he was perhaps the most miserable man" (1.373). The mingling of writer and reader celebrated earlier is now enacted in a romantic embrace: "we are clasped in the arms of the poetry as if borne away on the wings of an archangel." Down below, the Grub Street critics are like "dogs that bay the moon" as they did in his defense of Turner (3.640), like "foul snails that crawl on in their despicable malice, leaving their spume and filth on the fairest flowers of literature." Ruskin's "impoten[t]" competitors are stuck in their own repulsive "slime." The visionary "Essay" about the union of artists and subjects and readers ends in a vision of the triumphant extinction of "multitudes" (1.374–75).

In the spring of 1838, in his "Essay on the Relative Dignity of the Studies of Painting and Music," Ruskin again defends his chosen discipline by reworking the stereotypes of gender and sexuality. He remembers in Praeterita that the essay came out of his acquaintance with Charlotte Withers, and he makes fun of its "proposing the entire establishment of my own opinions, and the total discomfiture and overthrow of hers, according to my usual manner of paying court to my mistresses" (35.222). Yet Praeterita is silent about how his language in the "Essay" not only subordinates music by identifying it with women, and then usurps what he wants from the discipline, but also usurps his reader's own status as virgin. For the fine painter is no mere sensualist, as the musician generally is (1.279), but a gentleman: in order to paint a virgin (which is a reflexive, self-projective operation that repeats itself in its result) you must be one (1.276–77). Ruskin seeks to clinch his argument for the superiority of those who (like himself) know how to draw by quoting a dialogue between Hamlet and Gertrude, in which the son sees what the mother cannot. As if this were not enough, Ruskin proves his point by describing what the sketcher (as opposed to the non-sketcher) will make of an encounter with "an old woman in a red cloak" in a green country lane. In Ruskin's word painting the woman is obliquely subsumed into the red touches of lichen "all mellowed and mingled into a garment of beauty for the old withered branch" of a tree; if the "twisted," "snake-like coils" of the roots recall Ruskin's descriptions of Friar's Crag in *Iteriad* (see above, pp. 108–10), they also recall the more nearly contemporary *mise en scène* of his poems to Adèle, where darkness and age and the serpent all mingle with the light of romance:

Then come the cavernous trunks, and the twisted roots that grasp with their snake-like coils at the steep bank, whose turfy slope is inlaid with flowers . . . and down like a visiting angel, looks one ray of golden light, and passes over the glittering turf – kiss, – kiss, – kissing every blossom, until the laughing flowers have lighted up the lips of the grass with one bright and beautiful smile, that is seen far, far away among the shadows of the old trees, like a gleam of summer lightening along the darkness of an evening cloud.

(1.283–84)

The old woman reappears in the paragraph after next, aestheticized, as she would be by "a sketcher, – or a rhymer," into "the most insignificant circumstance" that might enhance the effect that he decides to create (2.284–85) – like the red or blue rag that the painter must choose between in the last installment of *The Poetry of Architecture*, written later the same year (1.172–73). The feminine must be metamorphosed into material about which the critical sketcher can readily adjudicate. In the meantime, the male who would become a sketcher – who would therefore "feel, on looking out upon nature, almost like a blind man who had just received his sight" – is locked in communion with the "soft blue eyes" of heaven. Once again, Ruskin's dwelling on the snake in the garden, the worm at the root of an otherwise "pure" romance, is not a depressive downturn but a self-stimulating call to arms. The readers who refuse to learn what Ruskin teaches are sharply cut off with a warning: "[T]he more fools they, – that's all!" (1.285).

The transformation of personal emotions is harder to trace in the rhetoric of *The Poetry of Architecture; or The Architecture of the*

Nations of Europe Considered in its Association with Natural Scenery and National Character, which was published serially in *The Architectural Magazine* under the name "Kata Phusin" (1837–38). Like his unpublished pieces of criticism, *The Poetry of Architecture* is concerned with theoretical and practical questions about how an individual entity should and does relate to the several factors which make up its context. Architecture should mediate between those who make, inhabit, and regard it, and it does so in the medium through which it meets the reader's eye. This is part of the single overwhelming conclusion that emerges after a hundred and eighty-two pages:

Only one general rule can be given, and that we repeat. The house must NOT be a noun substantive, it must not stand by itself, it must be part and parcel of a proportioned whole: it must not even be seen all at once; and he who sees one end should feel that, from the given data, he can arrive at no conclusion respecting the other, yet be impressed with a feeling of a universal energy, pervading with its beauty of unanimity all life and all inanimation, all forms of stillness or motion, all presence of silence or of sound.   (1.187)

Like the language of a building, *The Poetry of Architecture* is a construct which attempts to mediate between its subject, its maker, and its readers, with their natural settings and various though national characters.

But the ideal of unanimity is not fully realized in Ruskin's practice.[21] He usually describes buildings that exist in isolation from each other; where cottages do form a group, they are seen as an aesthetic unit, not a social or economic one. The distinctions that make them so incompatible with each other and so apt in their different settings become problematical when we consider that Ruskin's paradigmatic descriptions of the English cottage, the French, the Italian (and Spanish) encode the diverse propensities that exist within Ruskin himself, as well as encoding the differences between his background and that of Adèle Domecq (1.12–

30, xxvi). Then there is Ruskin's repeated condescension to domesticity in a book whose entire subject is domestic architecture, and his condescension to the wealthy when he devotes nearly two-thirds of his space to their homes. Compatibility seems to prevail when he enters into questions about how ornament assimilates a building to the man of feeling or of imagination or of intellect who inhabits it, perhaps because the association between architectural and human characteristics was already familiar in other people's work when Ruskin began to write The Poetry of Architecture,[22] and certainly because he is describing relatively compatible facets of himself when he speaks of choosing these facets of a building (1.135-38). But the survey of specific details and settings gives way to a long and vexatious struggle to set guidelines for deciding whether an entity should be designed in "contrast" or "assimilation" with its context – a struggle which ends in the declaration that the subject (like the house that cannot "be seen all at once") is too much to compass (1.171-87). Ruskin said in Praeterita that "though deformed by assumption, and shallow in contents," the essays that make up The Poetry of Architecture "are curiously right up to the points they reach" (35.225). And his insight in 1838 that the life of the Swiss mountaineer is inscribed by the work of his hand on his cottage (1.37-38) – this insight really does anticipate the pronouncement in The Stones of Venice that "All art which is worth its room in this world . . . is art which proceeds from an individual mind, working through instruments which assist, but do not supersede, the muscular action of the human hand . . ." (9.456). But in The Poetry of Architecture the Swiss cottage can have "none of the mysterious connexion with the mind of its inhabitants which is evident in all really fine edifices," because the Swiss have "no climate," "no character," "no perceptible nationality," "no language," "no peculiar turn of mind" (1.40). The papers did not continue long enough to test Ruskin's insight about handwork in the sphere of public architecture (1.xxxvii–xxxviii); but even "up to the points they reach" in examining villas, the hand of the worker is not the same as the hand of the architect, much less of the owner – whose "vanity" is the "chief enemy" of the architect (1.170–71) and the butt of jokes by the viewer. The effort made in The Poetry of Architecture to repossess private property for public viewing always bears the marks of its prepossessing and possessive young author (1.126–33).

Like his shorter critical essays, The Poetry of Architecture acts out the paradoxes of an individual will to community. In the end the ideal of "unanimity" exists in tension with the identity of the individual artist and artifact. Ruskin's drive towards interrelationships is sustained in language that declares his extreme independence from and dominion over other people, his devotion not to teachers or to previous critics but only to his subject matter. The nom de plume "Kata Phusin" – "According to Nature" – reveals his pride in himself while concealing his name, as Ruskin suggests in Praeterita (35.224). During the next fifty years, the problems that "deformed" The Poetry of Architecture will be brilliantly worked out, but they will never be solved entirely, and they will never again be so easy to see. These problems are central not only to Ruskin's work but to that of many other Victorians, for whom the conflicts between self and society were always so central a theme. The familial, sexual, social, and institutional forces and counterforces that made for Ruskin's early writing may seem idiosyncratically remote from everyone else's past. But they point to stresses that issued in the voices of other Victorian sages, with their repertories of menacing and comforting tones, their unaccompanied solos demanding that their listeners work together, their deceptive modulations of the rise to dominion.

.   .   .

John James Ruskin paid relatively little attention to these pieces in which his son first attempted to establish his masculine authority as a critic. But he was very attentive when some of the pressures reflected in them contributed to the anticlimax of Ruskin's ambitions in love and at Oxford. The records preserve the painful course of events between the autumn of 1839 and the spring of 1842: the family decision that he not take another year at Oxford but try to graduate with a first the next term; the driving intensity with which he pursued his studies; the witholding and disclosure by Ruskin's parents of information about Adèle Domecq's marriage; the physical breakdown and coughing of blood; the postponement of his examinations and the family journey to Italy in search of health; the revulsion from the landscape of Rome and from academic competition at Oxford (1.381–84); the six weeks in Leamington in the care of a physician; the doubts about whether he should enter the ministry; the Oxford examinations at last, and the decision not to go home directly, or even to describe the event at length in a letter to the father who had spurred him on, but instead to travel back to Leamington for a few days alone. During his longer stay there, in the autumn of 1841, he wrote *The King of the Golden River*, which would be his most popular work. In this fairy tale and in the poem called "Charitie" from about the same time, his earlier love seems to have died and been reborn as a savior, a savior who is at once like a pacific and desexualized version of Ruskin himself and, in many respects, like a female[23] — as if to say that a virgin led him into the labyrinth and (as with the Theseus of *Fors Clavigera*) a virgin must lead him out. Later the same year Ruskin was caught up in Samuel Richardson's saga of madness and chastity: "Read the Clementina part of *Sir Charles*

Grandison," he writes in his diary; "I never met with anything which affected me so powerfully . . . It . . . has, I think, a greater practical effect on me for good than anything I ever read in my life" (*Diaries*, 220).

John James was quick to think of publishing *The King of the Golden River* (RFL, 689 n.4, 700), but not before he had been worried enough to warn his son against some of the directions he was taking:

> . . . formed as we are half Body & half Spirit our Safety & our necessity is in the middle part . . . I believe it safer for poor weak Creatures like ourselves, to walk in the track of Men distinguished by their *half*-worldly but wholly charitable conduct than to aim at some as yet unattempted flight. Our understanding & our feelings are too weak to sustain the Load you would impose upon them. No man could live under the daily & Nightly fear of Hell fire . . . too much enthusiasm in Religion ends in Selfishness or Madness . . . I never wish nor hope to find you a better preacher than St Paul yet who was more subject to the flesh. (RFL, 680–81)

Ruskin seems to have thought that an overt commitment to chastity was the unavoidable conclusion once it was clear that his desire for Adèle Domecq could never be sanctified by church and state. "[T]o remember is to sin," he declares with finality at the end of "Agonia" (2.207). It must be borne in mind, however, that even "pure" love was tragically doomed from the outset in the earliest writing inspired by Adèle (2.124–25), not to mention the well-deserved doom he saw waiting for the corrupt and corrupting desire of nameless others. But there is a change in the fate Ruskin foresees when he starts to think more explicitly about the biological facts of sexuality. At the same time that he reimagines the life-in-death and death-in-life of the love poems in terms of cycles of reproduction and extinction in the physical world, he is also changing his position about his own acts of creation, his own self-begetting and begetting of characters in Byronic and Shelleyan language.

These changes are most revealingly laid out in the letters he wrote between 1840 and 1843 to his college friend Edward Clayton, who had since taken orders. The letters bear a characteristically mixed message about communication: on the one hand Ruskin is full of assertions of kindness and gratitude, and on the other he is vigorously and vividly patronizing, dictatorial, bullying, and mocking. His preferring to correspond on paper rather than to meet face to face recalls not only his early letters to his father but also the tactics of his romanticizing poetry (1.455–56). But Ruskin renounces his reflexive, self-projective aesthetics – or rather, he denounces them as if he had never taken them up. One letter is particularly interesting, both in its anticipation of the argument at which we will look in the "Fontainebleau" chapter of *Praeterita*, that a faithful drawing in the presence of a tree is "immeasurably better and more beautiful than the prettiest you can make out of your head" – and in its categorical reversal of the language of his 1836 "Reply to 'Blackwood's' Criticism of Turner": "I congratulate you exceedingly on your mild reception of what you supposed to be a moon shining in her own eyes – I have heard of men standing in their own light, but I should not venture even to realise that much of phenomenon in a painting. I think everything is allowable in an artist that violates no law of nature, but not a step further" (1842/43? 1.497).

In a letter to Clayton written within a year of this one, Ruskin draws on his study of trees to make an explicit connection between sexual reproduction and death.[24] A tree, Ruskin says, is "a growing, changing, and preparing thing"; because of the limited supply of nourishment, "When you say a growing thing . . . you mean something advancing to death.''

Neither can the new tree and the old tree exist together. One must perish to make room for the other. Therefore, every bud and blossom of the parent tree implies and necessitates its destruction . . . That which has not in it the beginning and germ of death, is not a tree. Consequently, if there were trees in the Garden of Eden there was death . . . (1.476)

Ruskin's scientific argument about trees leads him to the idea of competition in the family tree and thence back to Adam's tree in the Garden. This circuit is enforced linguistically as well, for Ruskin's scientific argument by design is based upon an Adamic view of language: the names of things accurately signify their functions, for Adam had "knowledge of their nature" (1.477). In defense of his views Ruskin produced an essay – "Was There Death Before Adam Fell, In Other Parts of Creation?" – whose argument about bearing seed is all the more telling because it is explicitly and sarcastically directed not only against Clayton but also against a woman who will presumably bear young herself, Clayton's sister. Ruskin spells out the connections:

. . . the moment we hear of [a tree's] bearing seed, that moment we know that it must perish. Its seed implies that God has willed it to have a successor. Its successor cannot rise but out of its decay . . . each species of existence furnishes in its death food to the other, and the nourishment of one implies the simultaneous dying of the other . . . Hence a balance must be kept between them . . . the inorganic constituents of the earth are left in a state of perpetual circulation from death to life, and *vice versa*. Hence, whenever we talk of life, nourishment, or increase, we talk in the same breath of a supplementary death and diminution. (1.482–83)

The result would be still more disturbing were there unlimited nourishment for every plant and animal, and never any death:

In two centuries after the creation the earth would have been packed tight with animals, and the only question remaining for determination would have been — which should be uppermost. Long before the flood the sea would have been one solid mass of potted fish, the air of wedged birds, and the earth of impenetrable foliage.

(1.484)

Ruskin's earlier comments about cannibalism and the war for food between rich and poor would make the human reference of his essay inescapable, if that were not already the case (1.408-09). Familiar though his Malthusian premise may be to any reader of standard Victorian texts, the terms in which he reasons on that premise are startling: sexual penetration would create an impenetrable world, if the laws governing Eden were revoked. Procreation would leave the creative no room.

Ruskin's vision of a terrible contiguity is not a simple rejection of Adèle Domecq or of the competitions he went through at Oxford. It is rather a nightmarish culmination of that compulsion for interrelationship which antedated them both, and which they both affected in turn. This culmination casts light on the imagery of interconnection – whether blessed or ghastly – that abounds in the work of other nineteenth-century writers, suggesting that one of its origins might be found in the intricate pattern of ties in earliest family life. In Ruskin's case, it is possible to see that in the beginning, the need for connection drove him to close up every distance; but the consequent closeness may have driven him to cut himself or his surrogates off. His fictions of surveillance, exile, and madness – of patricides, fratricides, suicides – all come of having gotten too close.[25] And the impulse to narrow a gap can widen it in a different sphere, as when connections on paper add up to an independent career that separates writer from writer, reader from writer, father from son. By the time that happens in Ruskin's writing, the closeness or division is less effectively covered by the figure of an obstructive female than by the feminized versions of himself we have seen.

The situation I am describing points beyond the frequently debated question about why Ruskin ceased to write poetry,[26] to broader issues suggested by his turning away from creative fictions altogether, in prose as well as verse. His statement in *Praeterita* that, after his poems of 1845, "I perceived finally that I could express nothing I had to say, rightly, in that manner" is intended to end all debate in the "extremely wholesome conclusion" that he was not a creator (35.344). But the segregation of Ruskin's poetry from his prose fiction and letters tends to conceal the complex interaction of literary and personal experience which shaped his identity as a writer. Commentators interested in that identity have attended to Ruskin's observing, on several occasions, that his father was sadly disappointed by his decision. But John James's disappointment that there were to be no more poems "as good as Byron's, only pious" (35.185), no more "Herodotus pieces" that "show real power – & have a spice of the Devil in them,"[27] can obscure his son's exploration of matters that he might have found more devilish if he had read them differently. The romantic ideal which made him feel close to his son also made such a reading unlikely. It was all too easy to take for granted the Byronic convention that artistic identity is fused and often confused with the identity of the isolated and transgressive adult. In Wordsworth, Coleridge, Byron, and Shelley – as in *Paradise Lost* and the bible before them – artistic power is often represented as guilty, as a sin against the fathers or Father. But the fathers of

Wordsworth, Coleridge, and the anti-patriarchal Byron died when their sons were quite young, and the anti-patriarchal Shelley orphaned himself. So there could be no face-to-face confrontation over the fact that the sin through which the sense of power emerges in their writing is often implicitly sexual. To look at Ruskin's fictions in poetry and prose is to see that his attempts to formulate an artistic persona were involved in his attempts to formulate one as a dominatingly masculine, sexual adult. And vice versa: his sexual identity is aestheticized and borne out in aesthetic theory; his artistic identity is eroticized in pieces like "Leoni" and *Marcolini*, where love is the love of writing, and both are linked to homicidally rivalrous ambition. The distance between these identifications and Ruskin's day-to-day life is the occasion of a tragi-comical self-portrait in *Praeterita*, with pendants of Byron and Shelley. As we have already seen, the latter is faulted for his language, and the former is defended from other people's assumption that Ruskin's fault might be owing to him (35.179–84). There is no acknowledgment in *Praeterita* that any of them had anything to do with the links between artistic and sexual life lived in resistance to parents. And there is no acknowledgment that his entangled creative and sexual roles had to go as they came: together.

Without returning to the fictions Ruskin wrote between 1836 and 1840 it would be difficult to see the full significance of his claim in *Praeterita* that (like himself) the heroically truthful Byron had "scarcely any" invention, and no sexuality of a kind to cause "the slightest harm" to the reader (35.148, 142–43, 183); and it would be difficult to see why Ruskin's account of his own romance must end in such vehement self-abuse. His presumption in love is linked to his presumption in art by the disobedience he discovers in both. So this part of his past is consigned to "the Dustman Oblivion":

With this one general note, concerning children's conduct to their parents, that a great quantity of external and irksome obedience may be shown them, which virtually is no obedience, because it is not cheerful and total. The wish to disobey is already disobedience; and although at this time I was really doing a great many things I did not like, to please my parents, I have not now one self-approving thought or consolation in having done so, so much did its sullenness and maimedness pollute the meagre sacrifice. (35.229)

To most of Ruskin's readers, the sacrifice of his poems and fictions would not be much of a loss. After all, 1836 was not the beginning (as it would not be the end) of his erotic life: like other children, he was full of sensuality from very early on. But the "passion" he acknowledges in Praeterita (35.219) and that we have seen in the first part of this book is not the would-be interpersonal thing that it becomes in the later 1830s. Nor, before that period, did his self-affirming creativity undergo a challenge from outside of the family. Although Ruskin achieved neither physical contact with a woman nor an indubitably great piece of poetry, his sense of himself as a sexual and creative person was irreversibly altered by his attempts. By 1845 he is responding to his father's wish for more poems like "A Scythian Banquet Song" with the claim that he no longer has the "living passion" it would require. While he implicitly blames his father (whose wealth ensures the bodily gratification and aesthetic detachment that make good poems "[im]possible"), he is explicitly satisfied that his mind has improved: "were [I] again under such morbid excitement, I might write as strongly, but with more manly meaning."[28] His idea of manliness is more Victorian, less romantic, now. In the laws of composition he will passionately lay down in Modern Painters II and V and The Elements of Drawing, the desire to possess and to dominate are drawn into ideals of harmony and reciprocity. It is well to remember not only that his exemplary designs –

as of movement within fixity, of freedom within restraint – grew out of his childhood writing, but also that his will to compose willfullness into theories of art was first tested in the late 1830s. Yet his experience between 1836 and 1842 eventually led him to purge the works he wrote then, and to devalue the works that had come before. Unlike many prodigies, Ruskin did not separate himself from either his great giftedness or from his parents when he passed through adolescence. But he could do this only by burying vital parts of himself.

.   .   .

What Ruskin buries he buries alive. This is discernible even, or especially, in his moments of greatest self-containment. The most pertinent example comes in The Seven Lamps of Architecture (1849), where Ruskin's account of the development of Gothic architecture itself develops in the chapter called "The Lamp of Truth." As elsewhere in Ruskin's analyses of art and nature, these are developments backward in time as well as forward. For Ruskin's first extended history of Gothic is, among other things, a retrospect on the transition from his childhood fascination with relations between organic movement and fixed form, to his later fascination with Adèle Domecq, whom he initially apprehended in terms of the changefulness he was drawn to in nature. As we have seen, Ruskin wrote a series of poems in which his idiosyncratic language for natural change is replaced by Gothic literary conventions for expressing life in death and death in life. Ruskin was attacking these conventions by the early 1840s, but they again come into touch with his boyhood geology in "The Lamp of Truth," making it a Gothic narrative as well as a narrative about the Gothic. For the "wrecks and remnants" in this second chapter of The Seven Lamps lead Ruskin back to the moment when vigorous youth yielded to the machinery of the Gothic – when, as he puts it in a note, there was a "wasting of the voice into a skeleton of sound," bespeaking "sickly phantoms and mockeries of things that were" (8.97, 66 n.2, 65). As in the geological studies he had read and written, the present is the clue to the past, and the past is the explanation of the present aspect of things. Gothic remains announce a terrible death early in the chapter; Ruskin's reconstruction of the emaciated "skeleton" brings him, in the end, to see that death as a suicide.

His way to this discovery is lit by the image of "the enlightenment of the globe" with which he begins "The Lamp of Truth." The "essential separation" between virtue and its variants is as "marked" as that between daylight and darkness, although there are what he calls "gradations" between the two, a "strange twilight of the virtues," a "dusky debateable land." But Truth, the central virtue of them all – their "very equator and girdle" – is the least tolerant of gradation and the most vulnerable to it (8.54–55). Ruskin calls upon "manly" "chivalry" to protect Truth from being "mingled" with anything else, from being defiled "in the acts and pleasures of men" – particularly of architects whose "direct falsity of assertion" "violat[es] . . . the nature of [their] material" (8.86, 57, 56, 59). Ruskin's gendered language here and later[29] – as when the "masculine" emphasis on architectural "mass" degenerates into an effeminate focus on the undulations of "line" (8.90) – is of course a reminder that he began writing *The Seven Lamps* during the first year of his unconsummated marriage. This reminder is strengthened in the manuscript version of the opening of the chapter, which lays out the ethics of chivalry: "The love is the virtue, not the act or exhibition of love . . . And the love is as much a virtue when it is fruitless as when it is effectual" (8.283).

The sexual drama of Ruskin's language suggests not only

his life at home but also his response to evolutionary readings in the public domain. For "The Lamp of Truth" is a retrospect that anticipates horrifying results when different entities "gradate" towards and "mingle" with one another. Ruskin likens Gothic architecture not simply to the organic form of vegetation but also to the architecture of vertebrate anatomy: "the architecture of animals . . . is . . . a marble architecture, not a flint nor adamant architecture . . . The jaw of the ichthyosaurus is pieced and riveted, the leg of the megatherium is a foot thick, and the head of the mylodon has a double skull . . ." (8.71–72). What the "manly and unaffected spirit" must be especially "watchful[ ] for" – and we too should watch for anticipations of Darwin – are those dextrous forms of "over-reaching" which end in "total paralysis or extinction" (8.86–87). In architecture as in animal development, this "extinction" is the culmination of "the natural progress" which Ruskin pursues by extending the image of "enlightenment" which opens the chapter. Now light is visualized as a shining silver "zone" it is perilous to follow (8.89–90). For its route leads down into the dark mingling of things that ought to be kept separate.

In Ruskin's narrative, the moment the architect took his eye off the "penetrating shape" of light in the windows, and focussed instead on the material through which it passed, the tracery "lost its essence as a structure of stone." The movement of the eye from the light to the human design is a "consummat[ion]" which eventually issues in "an independent form." In its flexibility this "ignoble" form could be beautiful, but not in its penetrability (8.91–93). Ruskin's account of the intersection of mouldings in later Gothic architecture is a history of violence. During what he calls "the great periods," mouldings sometimes "melt[ ] into each other," but they are "similar mouldings," and they "became one at the point of crossing or of contact." But in the subsequent time, "two different mouldings meet each other," are in fact "studiously associated, in order to obtain *variety* of intersectional line" (8.93–94; italics mine). After their conjunction, the two reemerge, and "preserve an independent existence" (8.94). This interpenetration of two essentially different forms is the "abuse" by which "caricatures of form" are proliferated, those "multitudinous forms" – "flattened," "shrunken," "distorted," "extravagant" – of "disease and decrepitude." The process of its extinction can be read in "those rent skeletons of pierced wall, through which our sea-winds moan and murmur, strewing them joint by joint, and bone by bone, along . . . bleak promontories . . ." The remains say that this architecture died by its own hand, having "violated" its own essential truth. Ruskin insists that Gothic was not destroyed by penetration from without – as by the "torrent of the Renaissance" – but by interpenetrations within (8.97–99). The verdict of suicide allows Ruskin to affirm the singularity of developmental form: the very death of the Gothic is made to be an assertion of the essentialism on which its life depends.

The words "moaning," "melting," and "penetration" suggest not only his passion for buildings beloved as a body, but also his fear on behalf of his own body. The fear was most intense when this son of first cousins contemplated both *The Seven Lamps of Architecture* and his marriage to his own distant cousin in the house where his grandfather had killed himself. If we read it only for the plot, "The Lamp of Truth" would seem to be a cryptogram of this ending, or just another mid-century nightmare of a Darwinian future. But it in fact contains some of the most exhilarating pages in all of Ruskin's prose – and among the very few that Ruskin himself admired in the book he later dismissed as "the most useless I ever wrote" (8.15). In "The Lamp of Truth," Ruskin's resistance to one process is the consummation of his involvement in another. His vision of the shifting focus of Gothic structures the development of one of his greatest rhetorical achievements, the production of those drawn out and compacted historical dramas in which, through time and across space, one thing (such as a mass) changes into another (such as a line), while the two are seen, together, at once: both the form, and the growth or force expressed in the form, as he said in the diary that records research towards *The Seven Lamps* (see above, p. 120). Ruskin introduces this vision in the shape of a single illustrative plate, which arranges six instances of architectural form in chronological sequence, on three levels, which have both an immediate effect and also a rhythmic movement, from right to left, from lower to higher, from past towards present [Illus. 13]. ''I have drawn,'' Ruskin says

all these traceries as seen from within, in order to show the effect of the light thus treated, at first in far off and separate stars, and then gradually enlarging, approaching, until they come and stand over us, . . . filling the whole space with their effulgence. And it is in this pause of the star, that we have the great, pure, and perfect form of French Gothic . . .   (8.89)

The movement contained in the plate rehearses the experience, laid out two pages later, of the evolution of perception:

. . . the traceries had *caught the eye* of the architect. Up to that time, up to the very last instant in which the reduction and thinning of the intervening stone was consummated, his eye had been on the openings only, on the stars of light. He did not care about the stone; a rude border of moulding was all he needed, it was the penetrating shape which he was watching. But when that shape had received its last possible expansion, and when the stone-work became an arrangement of graceful and parallel lines, that arrangement, like some form in a picture, unseen and accidentally developed, struck

181

suddenly, inevitably, on the sight. It had literally not been seen before. It flashed out in an instant, as an independent form.

(8.90–91)

This form which contains the seeds of its own violation is the same form that sets Ruskin's history of stone most thrillingly in motion. The yielding of its "stiff[ness]" to "ductility" is a violation of the essence of the stone, but it frees Ruskin to catch in language the animation of the Gothic:

At the close of the period of pause, the first sign of serious change was like a low breeze, passing through the emaciated tracery, and making it tremble. It began to undulate like the threads of a cobweb lifted by the wind. (8.91–92)

Fatal as he says they are to the Gothic, "gradations" and "mingling" and "ductility" all make for vitality in Ruskin's prose. It is in his handling of this passage of one entity into another that he looks back most fruitfully to his early study of "gradations" in art and Lyell's science, and looks ahead to Darwin. When Ruskin wants to make what is theory seem to be only the facts of the matter – as here in The Seven Lamps, where everything before the "perfect" moment was "ascent; [and] after it, all was decline" (8.89), or when the moral history of architecture emerges from a series of cornice and capital profiles in The Stones of Venice (9.359–73) – he sets a series of images into motion, like so many stills end to end in a motion picture, and declares that it has been animated not by himself but by the human energy with which the stone is imbued. So that the theory is already in the data, as it was in his earlier Lyellian prose. As for Darwin, Ruskin's insistence on tripartite divisions, whether of artists or natural history, might seem far removed from the "insensible gradations" or "transitional grades" by which a feature or "species has been perfected" in The Origin of Species.[30] But Ruskin also believes – in

182

the case of artists – that "The three classes of course pass into each other by imperceptible gradations" (*The Stones of Venice*, 10.217), and – in the case of an 1875 comment on Lyell – that the three "periods of the Earth's history" all "interlace with each other, and gradate into each other – as the periods of human life do . . ." (*Deucalion*, 26.117).

Nor can a period of his own family history be sealed off in "The Lamp of Truth." In 1869, in the dazzling lecture called "The Flamboyant Architecture of the Valley of the Somme," Ruskin again looks to France, where the Gothic "passes away in your sight," rather than to England, where it "was fastened down and helpless under stern geometrical construction, and frigid law of vertical line, so that it is walled up like a condemned nun, and you cannot see it die" (19.245). The contradistinction is continuous with the one in *The Poetry of Architecture* (1837–38) between the "finished neatness," the "firmly pegged down, and mathematically levelled" containment of the English cottage, and the French cottage's air of "having once possessed strength, which is now withered, and beauty, which is now faded" (1.12–17). More to the point, Ruskin's characterization of cottages predicts his self-representation over the years, as being both bound like a nun ("convent-bred more closely than" even the faded beauty, Adèle Domecq) and flaming out like a fallen woman (35.179).

In "The Flamboyant Architecture of the Valley of the Somme," Ruskin says that his criticism of ductility in the fallen Gothic was "in the main" correct as he had described it in *The Seven Lamps*. But he adds a crucial reminder:

[Y]ou may not have considered, – that, disguised by other and more subtle qualities, the same instinct is manifest in the living art of the whole world[,] [t]his delight in the embroidery, intricacy of involution, – the labyrinthine wanderings of a clue, continually

lost, continually recovered . . . [I]n all living art this love of involved
and recurrent line exists, – and exists *essentially* – it exists just as
much in music as in sculpture . . .   (19.258–59; italics mine)

It also exists in his prose. In manuscript passages he chose not
to print in *Praeterita*, Ruskin describes his own "invaluable
quality of ductility," and "an idiosyncrasy which extremely
wise people do not share, – my love of all sorts of filigree and
embroidery, from hoarfrost to the high clouds. The intrica-
cies of virgin silver, of arborescent gold, the weaving of
birds'-nests, the netting of lace, the basket capitals of
Byzantium, and most of all the tabernacle work of the French
flamboyant school, possessed from the first, and possess still,
a [forceful] charm for me . . ." (35.618, 157 n.3). In the
lecture on "Flamboyant Architecture," Ruskin says that if
this "instinct" is preserved in its pure essence – is kept
resilient and "elastic," rather than "loose," "weakly or
wildly undulatory," "feeble," "unbound," "licentious" – if
it is worked into stone by "a Pure people" who are clearly
"separat[e] from brutes" (as people are not in *The Origin of
Species*, which was published ten years before), then architecture can be not merely individual but collective, can be an
expression of "Common Pride" and "Common-Wealth"
(19.259–60, 264). As in *The Seven Lamps* and *The Stones of Venice*,
handwork records the world of the worker, implicitly
allowing the work of Ruskin's hand to project his individual
vision of essential form, while making it simultaneous with a
vision of communion – between artifact and worker,
between worker and worker, between worker and generations of spectators.

Thus Ruskin's pressing differences with others and within
himself are composed into recreations of material constructs
within which people have lived or ought, in his view, to live.
In his very attempts to locate in history a moment when the

flamboyant and the reflexive split themselves off from
healthy interaction, Ruskin retells the history of his own
attempts to coordinate extremes of independence and
interdependence. And so the Gothic dies once more in his
lecture of 1869, "weak with unwholesome and ominous
fire," literally "flamboyant with a fatal glow" (19.261). The
flamelike curves which give it its name have themselves gone
up in flames. A reference immediately follows to Walter
Scott's description of Gothic carving that seems to be on fire
at Roslin Chapel. Seventeen years later, in the autobiography
in which, as he said, "it becomes for me a matter of acute
Darwinian interest to trace my species from origin to
extinction," it is not only the Chapel but "all the strength and
framework of my mind" which has become "lurid" to
Ruskin, "like the vaults of Roslyn, when weird fire gleamed
on its pillars," and "'every rose-carved buttress'" "blazed"
(*Praeterita*, 35.244, 233). The same impulse which protected
the Gothic from invasion now leads Ruskin to find the flames
within his life, not outside of it – and to leave his readers with
an image of isolation ambiguously righteous and grieved and
guilty: prized for purity, lamented for selfishness, decried as
his family's fault.

The "leading lines" of the first part of this book are
continuous with the flaming lines we see now. Rather than an
absolute separation between them there is an uncountable
number of gradations, as between the vitality of some of his
prose about death, and the deathfulness of some of his
idealizations of life. In *The Ethics of the Dust* (1866), the "Old
Lecturer" who speaks for Ruskin says that life is "the power
of putting things together, or 'making' them," and death is
"the power of pushing things separate, or 'unmaking' them"
(18.344). But he also says that "Things are not either wholly
alive, or wholly dead. They are less or more alive" (18.346):

As soon as you are shut off from the rest of the universe into a Self, you begin to be alive . . . There can be no communion where there is no distinction. (18.238)

CHAPTER 6

UNLAWFUL MOTIONS
(1843–80)

The changes traced in the first five chapters of this book anticipate fluctuations in Ruskin's representation of the means of representation in the works of his prime. To begin with his most conspicuous beginning, the verbal mastery of the young writer is not at all jeopardized by the declaration in *Modern Painters* I (1843) that "art generally . . . is nothing but a noble and expressive language, invaluable as the vehicle of thought, but by itself nothing" – for at this moment Ruskin writes with confidence that such language is not "by itself" (3.87). The separation of the language from the thought is killing to a work of art: that is one way you know it is a work of art. In fact, Ruskin implies elsewhere, the inability to recognize such interconnections has led to stupid complaints about his own writing. He appends to *Modern Painters* IV (1856) a section on "Logical Education," which names as "among the most pitiable and practically hurtful weaknesses of the modern English mind, its usual inability to grasp the connection between any two ideas which have elements of opposition in them, as well as of connection." What he does not say, in reminding the reader that this judgment addresses an issue he previously raised, is that he had raised it because of charges that his prose is illogical. Rather than being helped to see beyond apparent discontinuities to the roots whereby they are interconnected – which is precisely the power Ruskin believes himself to possess – boys are taught "to *say* anything in a glib and graceful manner, –

to give an epigrammatic turn to nothing, – to quench the dim perceptions of a feeble adversary, and parry cunningly the home thrusts of a strong one, – to invent blanknesses in speech for breathing time, and slipperinesses in speech for hiding time, – to polish malice to the deadliest edge, shape profession to the seemliest shadow, and mask self-interest under the fairest pretext, – all these skills we teach definitely, as the main arts of business and life.

Can anyone entirely survive such an education? The famous ending of the piece – warning that "There is not an hour of [youth] but is trembling with destinies" – suggests not. The child on the brink of rhetorical training is like a "vase of Venice glass . . . in its transparent heat": as clear, as fresh, and as destroyable by the winds that blow (6.482–85).

However parodic, the mastery of the rhetoric that Ruskin deploys against rhetoric implies a worrisome verdict on his own recovery from an education like the one he deplores here.[1] His mastery of the rhetoric of architecture also comes in for a share of this verdict. In 1849, the reviewer for the *Dublin University Magazine* complained that in *The Seven Lamps of Architecture* "There are . . . many flamboyant and even a few *rococo* passages, where outline is lost in tracery, and projection confounded by obtrusive imagery"[2]; thirty-one years later, Ruskin found his basic argument to have been "overlaid with gilding, and overshot, too splashily and cascade-fashion, with gushing of words" (8.15). More recently, critics have returned to the links between Ruskin's analysis of the "hollow formalism" of later Gothic tracery – of "the substitution of the *line* for the *mass*, as the element of decoration" ("The Lamp of Truth," 8.90) – and his sense, articulated in his chapter on the pathetic fallacy and elsewhere, of the deceptiveness or duplicity of figurative language that corrupts the verbal work of art.[3] In judging his own indulgence in what he takes to be an abuse, it is well to remember that when the elasticity of stone gives way to "loose lines of fillets, ribands, and weakly or wildly undulatory drapery" (19.260), this is for Ruskin a mark not only of its referring reflexively to itself rather than to a stable and external "Truth," but also a mark of its reference to the metamorphosis of that "Truth." The movements of the medium will capture the destabilization of the subject matter as well as any departures from it. Where Ruskin's subject matter is precisely the breakdown of his own faith in the bond between word and thing, their movement apart is embodied not only *in* but *as* a change in the material form of language:

You speak of the Flimsiness of your own faith. Mine, which was never strong, is being beaten into mere gold leaf, and flutters in weak rags from the letter of its old forms; but the only letters it can hold by at all are the old Evangelical formulae. If only the Geologists would let me alone, I could do very well, but those dreadful Hammers! I hear the clink of them at the end of every cadence of the Bible verses –   (1851 letter to Henry Acland, 36.115)

The weakening of his belief in the literal truth of the Word is acted out in a figure of speech. Eight years later, he subordinates his figures of speech when he wants to give priority to the truth of his views:

[T]he thing so commonly said about my writings, that they are rather persuasive than just; and that though my "language" may be good, I am an unsafe guide in art criticism, is . . . not merely untrue, but precisely the reverse of the truth . . . For my "language," until within the last six or seven years, was loose, obscure, and more or less feeble; and still, though I have tried hard to mend it, the best I can do is inferior to much contemporary work. No description that I have ever given of anything is worth four lines of Tennyson; and in serious thought, my half-pages are generally only worth about as much as a single sentence either of his, or of Carlyle's. They are, I well trust, as true and necessary; but they are neither so concentrated nor so well put. But I am an entirely safe guide in art judgment . . .   (*The Two Paths*, 16.415–16)

But figurative language returns in "Of Kings' Treasuries" (1864), when he speaks on behalf of the "best wisdom" of

other men. Now gold does not "flutter[ ] in weak rags" but
lies strongly and deeply hidden, as the great writer's "mind
or meaning" is hidden in words which "are as the rock
which you have to crush and smelt in order to get at" the
precious metal (18.64). His argument that language should
be purified of corruptions recalls R. C. Trench's *On the Study of
Words* (1851); and Ruskin explicitly calls attention to F. Max
Müller's *Lectures on the Science of Language* (1861, 1864) in
support of his view that "a deep vital meaning" inheres
within each word, no matter what changes it has undergone
(18.68–69).[4] But the repeated references to buried treasure,
to his "grave subject" and to books piled "upon a
gravestone" (18.54, 98), are also reminders that John James
Ruskin died nine months before his son delivered in "Of
Kings' Treasuries" the assertions that writing allows us to
commune with the absent dead, that the best words are
perpetually loyal to their honorable sources – and that words
are now dangerously destabilized, like so many subjects of a
country without a proper king or father or god. Language
that was "by itself nothing" in *Modern Painters* I is something to
worry about in "Of Kings' Treasuries":

... words, if they are not watched, will do deadly work sometimes.
There are masked words droning and skulking about us in Europe
just now ... such words wear chameleon cloaks – "ground-lion"
cloaks, of the colour of the ground of any man's fancy: on that
ground they lie in wait, and rend them with a spring from it. There
never were creatures of prey so mischievous, never diplomatists so
cunning, never poisoners so deadly, as these masked words; they
are the unjust stewards of all men's ideas: whatever fancy or
favourite instinct a man most cherishes, he gives to his favourite
masked word to take care of for him; the word at last comes to have
an infinite power over him, – you cannot get at him but by its
ministry.[5]   (18.66)

Like the turncoat parricides of "Leoni" and Marcolini, these "masked words" suggest a subversive potential lurking in the very language with which Ruskin urges his audience to restore their hereditary kingdom. For in giving a lecture at all, he was opposing the wishes of a father who thought "the platform" vulgar[6]; and this lecture in particular opens with a protest against pressures related to those his parents brought to bear on his education, and closes with political arguments of a kind that would have made his father uneasy (12.lxxxiv, 17.xxvi–xxvii).

.　　.　　.

Much of the complexity of Ruskin's position is lost in the long series of complaints against praise of his writing which he initiated in the 1840s and stepped up later in the century, partly in resistance to the rise of prose stylism in which he was certainly implicated.[7] His attitudes are more subtly apparent in "The Mystery of Life and its Arts," an 1868 lecture which he hoped would be heard by Rose La Touche, a young woman who had made him think yet again about education and youth. Near the beginning of his lecture, he says that the widespread valuing of his language rather than his thoughts has been his punishment for pride in his ability to write beautifully. Not the punishment but the "knack" is Ruskin's "misfortune," though it is easy to confound them, as both are "passing away from me" together. His words at once deny that he has control over his way of writing (he not only thinks with a new "earnestness" now but also "find[s]" himself "forced" to express himself plainly), and link that writing to a universal experience. Ruskin wants to identify this "cloudy life" we share, this mysterious course of human existence, with the painful fate of his thoughts, rather than with that of his language. Yet it is purportedly because of his language that he is now forced to reveal the sad mysteries of his own life, to prove to his audience that he has "real knowledge of my subject." The sadness is not mixed up in the power of his language (as it is in the poets he chooses to exemplify life's mysteries), but only in his work's having failed to change people's lives. Yet once again, his choice of words keeps suggesting a preoccupation with his manner of writing. His valediction to his "power of using such pleasant language" ushers in, a few lines later, "the third and most solemn character in which our life is like those clouds of heaven," namely in "their power." His mystified representation of the changes in his writing, as opposed to his certainty about his thoughts, is like the "mystery" that is symbolized by clouds. And his "foolish vanity" in his fine writing evokes "the vanity which we cannot grasp" in the next paragraph, the "transience" of this "'vapour that appeareth for a little time, and then vanisheth away'" (18.145–47). As he goes on to catalogue the power, the mystery, and the transience which other artists have discovered in human life, connections with his own art multiply beneath its surface. Ruskin looks to Milton and Dante for their "earnestness of thought" and "mastery of word," but discovers in the first an "artifice of invention" that is too "visibly and consciously employed." His objection that Dante's conception is only a "dream," a self-projective vision that "entranced" his soul, is immediately followed by Ruskin's effort to "strive more with this strange lethargy and trance in myself," to "awake to the meaning and power of life" (18.156–58).[8]

In his awakened responsiveness Ruskin regards the silence of all those who do the useful work of the world, and learns from them that the best artists work with "involuntary power which approximates literally to the instinct of an animal." Nor do they talk much more than animals about what they have made (18.166–67). This idea puts him in position to deliver another blow to expectations that in his present lecture he will predictably, obediently, talk as he has in the past. Instead, he so characterizes art that it becomes nearly impossible as well as inappropriate to talk about – except in the gravest ways. He thus draws attention away from his connection to artists and back to his role as the failed teacher of the lecture's opening. Only now he finds it useful to boast that "Old as I am, I could play you a tune on the harp yet, that you would dance to," because now the audience is in a position to share his sense of the triviality of such playing (18.169).[9] Ruskin's maneuver here bespeaks not simply a self-disqualification from the ranks of artists, but also an artist-like resistance to speaking of the art that he deploys; bespeaks not solely his own failure, but the acknowledgment in all beautiful art that it was made by people who erred; bespeaks not finally the lack of verbal power, but its subjection to the law that its comings and goings must be "involuntary." Nothing could be more succinctly telling than this variation on the "voluntary power" with which a peak seems to rise in the boat-stealing episode of *The Prelude* (Book I, lines 357–400). Wordworth's passage infuses the act of creation with the artist's pride and transgressive excitement; the boy's punishment is a sign of power, not of impotence. Ruskin, who understood these connections as well as Wordsworth, bends his will to breaking them apart.

The advice Ruskin ultimately gives his audience is born of his conviction of failure and success: failure to effect the results he sought, success as a word painter which "seemed to me worse than failure" (18.152). The turn from self-negation to the call for action bears comparison to the last paragraph of the "Conclusion" to *The Renaissance*, which Pater wrote in the same year – a comparison that suggests how deeply Ruskin's conclusion, like Pater's, is based on his experience of his own art, and suggests how sharply his argument is set against a belief, such as Pater's, in writing for its own sake.

> Although your days are numbered, and the following darkness sure, is it necessary that you should share the degradation of the brute, because you are condemned to its mortality; or live the life of the moth, and of the worm, because you are to companion them in the dust? Not so; we may have but a few thousands of days to spend, perhaps hundreds only – perhaps tens; nay, the longest of our time and best, looked back on, will be but as a moment, as the twinkling of an eye; still we are men, not insects; we are living spirits, not passing clouds . . . Let us do the work of men while we bear the form of them; and, as we snatch our narrow portion of time out of Eternity, snatch also our narrow inheritance of passion out of Immortality – even though our lives *be* as a vapour, that appeareth for a little time, and then vanisheth away.　　　(18.179–80)[10]

Writing does not matter unless it is a deed that conduces to life. And this is not possible so long as language is sundered from meaning, so long as the intellect of boys remains unturned "from dispute of words to discernment of things" (18.186).

Ruskin returns, in the last lines of his lecture, to his classical education because he is trying to free himself from the ordinary conditions of writing by coming to terms with their sources in his youth. "The child is the father of the man," Ruskin says. But when he says it, near the middle of the essay, his suggestion is that this fathering is done by females as well as males. Ruskin's version of Wordsworth's line becomes the moral of a dream he has recounted, in which girls and boys behave at a house party as if they were adults competing for kingdoms and wealth. In the terms that the dream introduces, Ruskin's own behavior is far more girlish than boyish, but the implication against which he wants protection is not that his dream concerns himself but that he is its dreamer: "I am no poet," he needs to insist, for by his dreaming he seems to be one (18.163, 165). He is still worrying about this implication nine years later, in a preface to *The Ethics of the Dust*:

One licence taken in this book, however, though often permitted to essay-writers for the relief of their dulness, I never mean to take more, – the relation of composed metaphor as of actual dream . . . I assumed, it is true, that in these places the supposed dream would be easily seen to be an invention; but must not any more, even under so transparent disguise, pretend to any share in the real powers of Vision possessed by great poets and true painters.

(18.206)

"The Mystery of Life and its Arts" ends with a vision that seems removed from artistic ambition, a vision in which he finds occupations which would be useful for those who, at a younger age, had hurt themselves and each other in his dream. But what serves these girls and boys also serves Ruskin's art, for his own occupation is bound up in theirs. His veiled allusions to Rose La Touche are more than long-recognized attempts to correct her mistakes. For he identifies his rescue of her with the rescue of himself – not just because he thinks she could save him once he taught her how to do it, but because he believes his writing would be saved (as girls would be) by the devotion to good work, that his writing would be led (as girls are in hill country, as Ruskin was during all his boyhood climbs in the Alps) by the watchful eye and iron arm of a guide. His fidelity to her would allow him to say of his most important meanings what he says of "the meaning of the great Book": that "no syllable" of it "was ever yet to be understood but through a deed" (18.186). Through his imagination of a youth guided by religious faith, hope, and charity, Ruskin guides himself to a hope that this writing will not have been in vain. But he does not say so in "The Mystery of Life and its Arts." For about this

195

writing, Ruskin writes as if he were – like the best artists – silent.

. . .

The cunning of the piece is in this silence, which both denies and affirms that he is an artist. While some of the ideas on which this maneuver is based are at least as old as the bible, and might be compared to the terms of Byron, Wordsworth, and Carlyle,[11] its most pertinent history is in Ruskin's juvenilia. Almost from the beginning, his writing integrated visual with verbal signification, pictorial with scriptorial signs, what is silent with what is pronounced (see above, pp. 62–67).[12] This integration is not only asserted by argument or presumption but is encoded in the image of the "winding way" of his own writing, which makes an appeal both to eye and to ear, which affirms his own achievement yet defines it as a tracing of the patterns that exist outside himself. Partly from the movements of his serpentining prose Ruskin learned to understand "a powerfully imaginative mind" which he will not acknowledge as his own in *Modern Painters* II (1846):

a powerfully imaginative mind seizes and combines at the same instant, not only two, but all the important ideas of its poem or picture; and while it works with any one of them, it is at the same instant working with and modifying all in their relations to it, never losing sight of their bearings on each other; as the motion of a snake's body goes through all parts at once, and its volition acts at the same instant in coils that go contrary ways.

This faculty is indeed something that looks as if man were made after the image of God. (4.235–36)

So that what is made after the image of God moves like what is made after the image of God's enemy. As in his image of the Gothic in *The Stones of Venice* (1853) – "subtle and flexible like a fiery serpent, but ever attentive to the voice of the charmer" (10.212) – the glory or the doom of art depends upon whether the charmer listened to God or to the voice of the snake in the Garden.[13] In *The Queen of the Air* (1869), the serpent not only has but is a tongue, an "inner language" that Ruskin deciphers:

Watch it, when it moves slowly: – A wave, but without wind! a current, but with no fall! all the body moving at the same instant, yet some of it to one side, some to another, or some forward, and the rest of the coil backwards ... Startle it; – the winding stream will become a twisted arrow; – the wave of poisoned life will lash through the grass like a cast lance.   (19.361–63)

He catches in this coil the links between the unlawful motions of the devil and the "laws of motion" he wholeheartedly endorsed as a boy – between the "winding stream" of the serpent and the "winding way" of his earliest prose: "the links between dead matter and animation drift everywhere unseen" (19.362). The involvement of the one with the other is spelled out in the disorder of language; so that language is powerless to dispel it. In *The Queen of the Air*, words designed to demystify the creature assemble a mysterious new creation instead. Representation meant to redeem the art Ruskin loves is doomed to display its own damnation.

In the Psalter of S. Louis itself, half of its letters are twisted snakes; there is scarcely a wreathed ornament, employed in Christian dress, or architecture, which cannot be traced back to the serpent's coil; and there is rarely a piece of monkish decorated writing in the world, that is not tainted with some ill-meant vileness of grotesque – nay, the very leaves of the twisted ivy-pattern of the fourteenth century can be followed back to wreaths for the foreheads of bacchanalian gods. And truly, it seems to me, as I gather in my mind the evidences of insane religion, degraded art, merciless war, sullen toil, detestable pleasure, and vain or vile hope, in which the nations of the world have lived since first they could bear record of themselves – it seems to me, I say, as if the race itself were still half-serpent, not extricated yet from its clay; a lacertine breed of bitterness – the glory of it emaciate with cruel hunger, and blotted with venomous stain: and the track of it, on the leaf a glittering slime, and in the sand a useless furrow.   (19.365)

As when artistic and sexual power are twisted together in his 1836 "Essay on Literature," the creative potency of The Queen of the Air must expend itself in an image of masturbatory sterility. The "blot[   ]," the "stain," the "track," the "useless furrow": Ruskin's words "bear record" of the very appearance of writing that does not bear fruit. What is at issue now is not the "slime" or "impotence" of "Grub Street reptiles" who "crawl[ed]" far beneath Ruskin's sphere in 1836 (1.374–75), but the art to which he is most deeply attached. And possibly not the art only. The passage quoted above contains at least one of the words which Ruskin said would be understood by Rose La Touche alone; and her marginalia do show that she recognized in the adjective "lacertine" an allusion to her mother, whom Ruskin called "Lacerta" and Lamia, and whom he believed to be traitor-ously obstructive to his love. But as Rose La Touche would not know for another two years, Ruskin was writing to their mutual friends not far from the time of The Queen of the Air, confessing that he had committed the "sexual sin" of masturbation in his youth.[14]

That his own art may be tainted, or that he may need to think so, is again suggested in his lecture on the motion of snakes called "Living Waves" (1880). He begins by making a connection between "undulatory" geological movement and his own "curiously serpentine mode of advance towards the fulfillment of my promise" – between his proposed revisions of his text and "one colubrine chain of consistent strength" (26.295–96). But the energy of this beginning winds up in a venomous passage about paternal ambition, which breaks down the will and breaks up the designs of the sons of England:

How often do I receive letters from young men of sense and genius, lamenting the loss of their strength, and waste of their time, but ending always with the same saying, "I must take as high a class [in university examinations] as I can, in order to please my father." And the fathers love the lads all the time, but yet, in every word they speak to them, prick the poison of the asp into their young blood, and sicken their eyes with blindness to all the true joys, the true aims, and the true praises of science and literature . . .   (26.329)

Ruskin derives the authority of his assault on fathers from his own superior capacity to decipher, to follow, and to reproduce the true form of geological forces, of snakes' movements, and of sons' lives. It is the congruence of these forms with each other which redeems the apparent disjunction of his writing into an approximation of organic design. In regarding these designs, Ruskin takes care to avoid the implication that he has usurped either the phallic or creative powers that are associated with the serpent; for "In the deepest and most literal sense, to those who allow the temptations of our natural passions their full sway, the curse, fabulously (if you will) spoken on the serpent, is fatally and to the full accomplished upon ourselves" (26.324).

Thus the *extremity* of his insistence in *Fors Clavigera* (1871– 84) that he utterly lacks invention:

Among other inferiorities of power, one good flow in my gifts of thought has been in some ways serviceable to me . . . I am totally destitute of invention, while I have curiously intense and long practised habits of analysis; hence I am always happy in contemplating or explaining other people's work, and have been . . . a sound interpreter of the genius of others, without being able to produce anything of the slightest value of my own. (29.539–40)

But this declaration no more protects him than do the denials in Modern Painters and The Elements of Drawing that he can explain what is most worth knowing about composition, or, in Praeterita, that he could ever compose at all. In his works of the 1860s and 1870s, nature's order is already poisoned by man's disorder, the son's authority by the father's authoritarianism. For all his buttressing of the patriarchal order of things, the aspects of "brightly serpentine perfection" can only lead Ruskin to an act of filial disobedience (26.328). And filial disobedience of an explicitly phallic kind is just what led Reuben's father to deliver upon his son the biblical curse Ruskin identifies with the blight on his writing in Fors:

It would be difficult to give more distinct evidence than is furnished by these pieces of [Ruskin's handwritten] manuscript, of the incurably desultory character which has brought on me the curse of Reuben, "Unstable as water, thou shalt not excel."   (28.275)

With the movement of these waters, we are returned to the sign of the serpent – a "winding stream," "A wave, but without wind! a current, but with no fall!" (19.362) – and to the ambivalence of that graphic imagery of writing that silences and speaks its own power, that serves the paternal commonwealth under God, while announcing an undying antagonism to the fathers.

.   .   .

Of course the dizzying sequence of issues interwoven in each of the texts I have mentioned makes it difficult to concentrate on the narrative divided among them about Ruskin's art. This difficulty is waiting for readers of everything Ruskin wrote.

What makes such a focus unlikely in his readers is the adjustment of Ruskin's own sight: first to the subjects of his criticism and thence to their interconnections across each disciplinary line which keeps them apart. Once he has pursued everything to its tangency with everything else, he backs up in admiration to exclaim one more time, at the end of his last book, "How things bind and blend themselves together!" His emphasis is always that they have done it "themselves" (*Praeterita*, 1885–89, 35.561).

So the reader who would look at the artful designs of Ruskin's prose, who would follow his first experiences of language into the forms they took in age, must make her way against Ruskin's own multifarious objections. There is no way around his will to postpone "the extremely minor question of my own work" past the middle of an autobiography undertaken because his work is not minor (35.368). But then there is no way of catching him in *Praeterita* either – not before he has altered his age and gender to avoid being taken for a man of letters. Ruskin is ready with the news that he always wrote as a girl stitches and hems her sampler; his pleasure in his results was that of a daughter who daily displays them to her parents, rather than that of a woman, a "modiste," who is rightly proud of her work in the world. The manly abandon with which a Byron or a Scott would scrap unappreciated work is diminished into his own girlish complacence. After he has taken care to repeat the word "drudgery" three times, the sweeping effect with which he dispatches his "drudgery of authorship" seems methodically domestic, especially since he has protectively dropped into a footnote the qualification that he refers only to his "*Manner* of work" here, not to its matter. In the meantime the main text proceeds to answer "the question" about how his "work is done" by changing the subject to his drawing, referring first to his inability to finish it, and then to the education he received from Shakespeare's superior art of showing that "for [the] best sort of people, everything always goes wrong." Replacing discussion of how Ruskin wrote, the reading of Shakespeare marks a new beginning in Praeterita – the beginning of a "student's life," which teaches that an earlier, more promising start to the book, though lavishly illustrated with his boyhood efforts as an author, was only a record of "mere instinct of rhythmic mimicry" (35.367–69).

"How great work is done, under what burden of sorrow, or with what expense of life, has not been told hitherto, nor is likely to be" (35.368). This, of course, is exactly what he has been attempting to tell for years. But then he has many times asserted that his is not great work. Possibly because he suspects the reader may disagree, Ruskin chooses this moment to undermine his reputation for achievement by recalling all the work he could not complete. And no one, not even Coleridge, could write more distracting and enthralling accounts of unfulfillment. Ruskin devotes none of his eloquence to the advantages he gained from overwhelming himself, from considering so many subjects and so many interrelations among them that he could not bring everything to definition. For anyone who tries to define Ruskin as a writer, the greatest paradox is not, as G. M. Young put it long ago, that "the mind of Ruskin [was] endowed with every gift except the gift to organize the others, was more tumultuous than the tumult in which it was involved."[15] The paradox is rather that the "gift" which definitively separated him from others was his mastery of interrelationships, and that it was this very mastery which he used to disguise his own art.

Not that Ruskin does not frequently celebrate himself – as when he agrees with Mazzini that his own is "'the most analytic mind in Europe'" (28.350), or tells his father that his unanalyzable instinct to draw and describe what he loves is a sign that "I have genius."[16] It is easy to find, for every lamentation that people prefer his style to his thoughts, a combative insistence on the justness of his diction or the unerringness of his rhythms. But once Ruskin's early youth has passed, and he has turned away from the entanglement of creative and sexual ambitions, it is not easy to locate overt acknowledgments that the interconnections he makes are indubitable signs of invention. Usually such acknowledgments come only indirectly, in his characterizations of the art of others ("Only another Turner could apprehend Turner" [7.453]), and in his enumerations of the principles of composition which he says he learned from their art. For with *Modern Painters* I and the beginning of his fame, the assertions of an artistic identity that were so common in his work of the 1830s have begun to be usurped by attempts to establish his authority as a critic.[17]

There are two exceptions worth pausing over. It is not coincidental that they were both provoked by his rereading of his own writing. In 1877, when the last volume of *Modern Painters* had been in print for seventeen years, Ruskin gave a course of lectures called "Readings in *Modern Painters*" before an Oxford room he was pleased to see "crowded by six hundred people, two-thirds members of the University, and with its door wedged open by those who could not get in" (22.xlii). The third lecture is devoted to an analysis of his language at different times in his life. A passage he quotes from *Unto this Last* is superior to one from *Modern Painters* I because in it "there's not any art of an impudently visible kind, and not a word which, as far as I know, you could put another for, without loss of the sense." But it could be better:

there is still affectation in the passage – the affectation of conciseness. Were I writing it now I should throw it looser, and explain here and there, getting intelligibility at the cost of concentration. Thus when I say –

"Luxury is possible in the future – innocent and exquisite – luxury for all and by the help of all" –

that's a remains of my old bad trick of putting my words in braces, like game, neck to neck, and leaving the reader to untie them. Hear how I should put the same sentence now: –

"Luxury is indeed possible in the future – innocent, because granted to the need of all; and exquisite, because perfected by the aid of all."

You see it has gained a little in melody in being put right, and gained a great deal in clearness. (22.515)

The privileged upbringing – "at once too formal and too luxurious" (35.46) – for which Ruskin blames his parents issued in a formality and luxuriance of language which he must now make accessible to all. His approval of his self-redeeming revision explains his readiness to turn to new account the compliment he used to ridicule:

The explanation of the difference [between the style in the 1840s and 1860s] is a very essential part of my work here; for the art of language is certainly one of the fine arts, and many of my readers, I observe, suppose I know no other, but at least most of them credit me with that. (22.513)

Three years later, Ruskin goes further in crediting himself with the making of art. The occasion is the republication of a hundred and fifty-two letters he had written, mainly to newspapers, over the past forty years. Alexander Wedderburn collected these into a volume Ruskin called *Arrows of the Chace*, then asked for a preface and an epilogue. In the first, Ruskin mentions things that go wrong "In the building of a large book," and commends by contrast the art of these letters. His repeated reminders that he is old now, that he is no longer so fertile in imagery or concentrated in argument, are presented in images which surpass their predecessors in dazzling suggestiveness, binding past and present in a syntax of such virtuosic agility that it gives as much pleasure as he says he takes in his old letters (34.469–71). With the cutting back of one sort of verbal luxuriance (praised as an economy that is at once literary, moral, and political in "Readings in Modern Painters"), better varieties grow up in its place; they become stronger still as he draws out their meaning. Like his preface, Ruskin's epilogue suggests that it is not only his argument but also his language that is formed by his rereading of himself. He is thinking of both parts of "the building of a large book" when he addresses to his public this conclusion from Amiens, one of his favorite architectural sites in Europe:

The multiplicity of subject, and opposite directions of investigation, which have so often been alleged against me, as if sources of weakness, are in reality, as the multiplied buttresses of the apse of Amiens, as secure in allied result as they are opposed in direction. Whatever (for instance) I have urged in economy has ten times the force when it is remembered to have been pleaded for by a man loving the splendour, and advising the luxury of ages which overlaid their towers with gold, and their walls with ivory. No man, oftener than I, has had cast in his teeth the favourite adage of the insolent and the feeble – "ne sutor [supra crepidam: let the cobbler stick to his last (sandal)]." But it has always been forgotten by the speakers that, although the proverb might on some occasions be wisely spoken by an artist to a cobbler, it could never be wisely spoken by a cobbler to an artist.[18]   (34.474)

Ruskin abbreviates his punchline, buries its singularity in a truism, and sacrifices its power to the reader's familiarity with Latin. But through the liberating circuit of retrospect, he comes to the point after all. In this book I have taken his rare word that he is an "artist," and held him tenaciously to it.

The result is at some moments a reading against his will, but it is a reading that follows from the language in which he expressed his will in writing, with which he responded to the world that was not himself, by which he directed the movements of an audience in his time and in ours.

CHAPTER 7

THE GENDER OF INVENTION
(1871–84)

In previous chapters we have seen how the figure of a girl or a woman can help Ruskin wield his own power as a writer. This process emerges more fully in biographical or autobiographical passages in which he attempts to show how authority derives itself – does not just constitute but derives itself, provides its own history and genealogy. For Ruskin's history of his authority not only puts females in their place, but puts him in it too.

. . .

Nowhere are Ruskin's relations to authority more various than in *Fors Clavigera*, the ninety-six "Letters" he addressed "To the Workmen and Labourers of Great Britain" between 1871 and 1884. He says, for example, that most of *Fors Clavigera* is "written with absolute seriousness and literalness of meaning" (28.650); also that he cannot take off "the Harlequin's mask for a moment" (28.513). About the authority he assumes outside of the three massive volumes of *Fors*, Ruskin originates a comprehensive design for living in St. George's Company – yet declares (in a Letter he inscribes with the lines "My mind to me a kingdom is" [28.13 n.1]) that the laws are essentially "those of Florence in the fourteenth century" (28.23): "I do not enter into any debates," he says, "nor advance any opinions . . . I should be ashamed if there were anything in *Fors* which had not been said before, – and that a thousand times . . . – there is nothing in it . . . but common truths, as clear to honest mankind as their daily sunrise . . ." (28.107). Honest mankind nonetheless requires the direction of a Master whose "authority over them must correspond precisely . . . to that of a Roman Dictator . . ." (28.649). In this letter Ruskin considers himself to "have powers fitted for this task" (28.648); two years earlier those powers seem to matter less than that "For my own part, I entirely hate the whole business; I dislike having either power or responsibility . . . I don't want to talk, nor to write, nor to advise or direct anybody" (28.22). Between these two letters – and before, and after – Ruskin writes with such breathtaking mastery of his incapacity to master, that what seems "thrust and compelled" on him – " – utterly against my will, utterly to my distress, utterly, in many things, to my shame" – is not authority over the tiny St. George's Company but rather his enormous power and ambition as a writer (28.425–26). It is not the incredulous reader but Ruskin who first, and most obstinately, demands, "Who am I, that [I] should challenge *you* – do you ask?" (28.147). This is where autobiography comes in – not that it has not already, under cover. Part of what is left behind when the same passages are adapted in *Praeterita* is the range of reasons why they were written in the first place. Ruskin writes about himself, he says – and my list follows Ruskin's own ordering, in the main – because he is "weak" and cannot help it (autobiography is a "course of self-applause taken medicinally") (28.270–71); because his feelings are strong and his readers should know why (27.167); because a book cannot be rightly read unless its reader's mind and thoughts are at "one with its author's" (27.459); because all great men know themselves better than anyone else can, and sooner or later let their hearts be seen "deep, and . . . true" (27.598); because Ruskin's own Fors (that is Chance, or Fortune) will help readers understand their own (28.106– 07); because the description not only of what but especially of how Ruskin learned justifies his teaching his readers now (28.271, 348–49); because, in sum, his education is an education for other people (28.392). In fact Ruskin derives a great deal of his authority in *Fors Clavigera* – including that with which he authoritatively denies his authority – from his autobiography.

But, as I said, this begins under cover. It is Sir Walter Scott whose life is first made to explain Ruskin's opinions (27.564) and to show his readers "how to rule their own lives" (27.606). What Ruskin is working towards is the scrutiny, which comes four years later, of the "enchanted Design" of the "great classic masters," achieved, as Scott achieves it, with a "heavenly involuntariness" that is necessarily "an assertion of moral law" (29.265–66). This is the same moral law that prompts Ruskin to say that he is not writing a biography of Scott but merely assembling – and (he acknowledges parenthetically) commenting on – bits from Lockhart. Even without knowing the unpublished manu-script in which Ruskin authorizes his writing about Scott with the information that they bear a family resemblance to each other (29.539), anyone who knows Ruskin's life will recognize that in Fors he defines Scott's history in relation to his own.[1] In fact the famous description in Praeterita of his bible reading with his mother (which he calls "the one *essential* part of all my education" [35.43]) first appeared twelve years earlier in Fors, where it emerges from an account of Scott's education, and an argument that it is his female relatives who ought to teach a boy to read: the "most essential of all questions" to be asked about a man is – in Ruskin's words – "What *patience* had his mother or sister with him?" (27.616).[2] But patience in following Ruskin's account of the experience of reading will eventually lead a reader away from his celebration of his following his mother's lead, and towards the consequences of his following his own.

This process is initiated two years after the death of Margaret Ruskin in his September 1873 Letter of Fors, when he turns from the education of Scott, or any man, to an explanation of his own "power" to "say what I want to say."

He derives, over the course of a long paragraph, his "power" as a writer and speaker from his mother's having made him a good reader. But he puts a crucial emphasis on her having instructed his ear rather than what matters to him still more, his eye or hand, a crucial emphasis on her teaching him to sound the sense of a biblical chapter rather than to make visible his own meanings through a series of markings on his own paper. Whereas in *Praeterita* – that "dutiful offering at the grave of parents" (35.12) – his "deliberate effort" to recall his sessions with his mother directly follows his recognition of the benefits of her coercion, in *Fors* this "deliberate effort" is necessitated by the counterforce of his self-sufficiency:

Well, my own impression about this power [of saying what I want to say], such as it may be, is that it was born with me, or gradually gained by my own study. It is only by deliberate effort that I recall the long morning hours of toil, as regular as sunrise, – toil on both sides equal, – by which, year after year, my mother forced me to learn all the Scotch paraphrases by heart, and ever so many chapters of the Bible besides . . . allowing not so much as a syllable to be missed or misplaced; while every sentence was required to be said over and over again till she was satisfied with the accent of it. I recollect a struggle between us of about three weeks, concerning the accent of the "of" in the lines

> "Shall any following spring revive
> The ashes of the urn?"

I insisting, partly in childish obstinacy, and partly in true instinct for rhythm, (being wholly careless on the subject both of urns and their contents), on reciting it, "The ashes *of* the urn." It was not, I say, till after three weeks' labour, that my mother got the accent laid upon the ashes, to her mind. But had it taken three years, she would have done it, having once undertaken to do it.   (27.616–17)

The paragraph issues in certainty that his mother was right, but the act of disobedience in its midst is given weight by its being at least "partly" an act of obedience to the "true instinct" of his own, rather than his mother's, ear.

The self-affirmation here is lightened by the child's being "careless" of what he could not fully understand. The "struggle" between Ruskin and his mother has a different issue when he returns a year and a half later to events that must actually have preceded this. His description of learning to read in his March 1875 Letter of *Fors* is very precise on the point of his memorizing not only the sequence of sounds but also the visible pattern of words on the page:

. . . the mode of my introduction to literature appears to me questionable, and I am not prepared to carry it out in . . . [the schools I propose] without much modification. I absolutely declined to learn to read by syllables; but would get an entire sentence by heart with great facility, and point with accuracy to every word in the page as I repeated it. As, however, when the words were once displaced, I had no more to say, my mother gave up, for the time, the endeavour to teach me to read, hoping only that I might consent, in process of years, to adopt the popular system of syllabic study. But I went on, to amuse myself, in my own way, learnt whole words at a time, as I did patterns; and at five years old was sending for my "second volumes" to the circulating library.

This effort to learn the words in their collective aspect, was assisted by my real admiration of the look of printed type, which I began to copy for my pleasure, as other children draw dogs and horses. (28.274)

The word "aspect" draws attention to his responding to words less as representations of sound, or signifiers of ideas, than as visible objects, pictures. Like the reading which accumulates what he calls its "flow" by following the "flow" of what is read (29.539), writing assembles its own "aspect" in dutifully retracing the aspect of what was previously written. The self-questioning with which he began the passage has come to coexist with "resolute self-complacency." Like the verbal–visual hybrids we encountered in the previous chapter, the "aspect" of his writing in Fors can look both ways at once. Ruskin promises that he will "have much to say on some other occasion" about "the advantage, in many respects, of learning to write and read . . . in the above pictorial manner" (28.275).[3] That writing, which he says he taught himself, precedes reading in this sentence anticipates Ruskin's explicit conviction that children learn best what they teach themselves. Nine years later, he argues that

nothing could be more conducive to the progress of general scholarship and taste than that the first natural instincts of clever children for the imitation or, often, the invention of picture writing, should be guided and stimulated by perfect models in their own kind.   (29.507)

Here, only paragraphs before he announces he is closing Fors so that he can write the autobiography of his uninventiveness, Ruskin is admiring the "invention" of a manner of writing which he brilliantly mastered in his childhood, and which he considers worthy of use as a model in the education of thousands of other children. When he wants the reader, no less than the children, to understand what he means by "symmetry," "grace," "harmony," he points to picture writing to illustrate that capacity for "composition" which he says he entirely lacked. His disobedient insistence on learning words "in their collective aspect" evolves into an education for the reader of Fors, an education which resolves his double sense of transgression and obedience into a program which implies that his readers must obey their teacher, because he did not.

The absence of any record of his mother's teaching him to write – although she was the only teacher present when he started to send his prodigious poems and letters to the places where his father was traveling on business – may not amount to a distortion of the past. But Ruskin's representation of his mother does register a disturbance about his own unmistakeable inventiveness. For the writing in Fors is significantly shaped not only by his rereading of what he read as a boy – Scott, for instance – but also by his rereading of what he wrote. Part of what is behind the combination of self-assertion and self-denial in Fors is a combination we have seen in his juvenilia – of delight in the "winding way" of his writing as it accumulates on the page, and frustration, often associated with girls and women, with containment of his expansive self-expression. Some forty years later, he readily drops his intention to publish on her birthday his account of his mother's "great power" as a girl, because "Fors . . . has entirely declared herself against that arrangement" (28.169).

The issue is not a simple conflict between figural and literal languages, or between what he calls "Father-Law" and "Mother-Law," or between masculine and feminine principles – to Ruskin, the letter is also a figure, and Fors is always feminine. Nor is the issue a simple conflict between obedience and disobedience. What is centrally in question here is Ruskin's memory of a "disobedience" which is made to issue in his ideas about childhood creativity, and in a vision of that obedience to higher laws which is the defining characteristic of the compositions of Scott and Turner. That the power of Fors is different from, independent of, moral law allows him both to complain that his book is "irregular," "desultory," "fragmentary" – and to commend its being irregular in order to accommodate autobiography (28.101), its being desultory because it is "absolutely" – as he puts it – under the command of Fors (27.553), its being fragmentary as are the pieces of glass which gather into a mosaic (27.669). Ruskin's descriptions of Scott's "enchanted Design" come in the midst of Letters which set out the "involuntariness" of his own. Although he says that Fors never supersedes the moral law, it is his fear that there might be an exception in his case which makes him insist that his involuntariness is not always heavenly, and that his sympathy with Scott (and Tintoretto and Turner) is as a child's – not a peer's – with its "father or mother" (29.539). Father or mother: Ruskin is saying that he can respond to great artists – all of them men – as to a mother. It is worth thinking about why.

The reasons begin to emerge when we go back to his definition, all in capital letters, of an artist: "A PERSON WHO HAS SUBMITTED TO A LAW WHICH IT WAS PAINFUL TO OBEY, THAT HE MAY BESTOW A DELIGHT WHICH IT IS GRACIOUS TO BESTOW" (28.441). This sounds a lot like some of Ruskin's descriptions in Fors of his own life's work. It also (apart from the pronouns) sounds like the work that he sets for girls.

While the writing in Fors is accumulating the authority that comes of its being a "Design," Ruskin introduces a nine-year-old named Agnes, examines her reading, and – in the next Letter of Fors, written in his old nursery on the day after his birthday – considers her future experience with books in relation to what he has just recounted of his own. It is only when he returns to Agnes's cottage nine years later (although Agnes has gone into service now, she has been readily replaced in the cottage by another little girl named Jane Anne) that Ruskin finally explains the "advantages" of his having learned to write in what he had described so long ago as a "pictorial manner" (28.275). The two earlier Letters, in which the authoritarian Ruskin adjudicates upon what Agnes and her like ought and ought not to read, both begin with Ruskin's laments about the "desultory character of Fors," which depends upon the same phenomenon in himself. He has, he says, no more authority over the shape his book will take than a wind- and flood-swept birch tree can have over the eventual arrangement of its boughs (28.254). Now the point is not that Ruskin is willfully contradictory about his authorial control, but that he carefully derives his authority over Agnes from his denial of having any authority over himself – from his having been absolutely obedient not to his mother, but to forces he could not resist as a boy, including the force exerted over him by the look of print on a page. It is the difference between these orders of obedience that lets Ruskin not only draw out a description of what should be read, but also object that he does not care whether children learn to read at all. Writing is "a quack's drug for memorandum, leaving the memory idle." He translated this bit from Plato's parable of Theuth near the beginning of Fors and quotes it again at the end, in case the drugged reader has forgotten (27.294–95; 29.483).[4]

So the conflict is even more complicated, but issues in analogous cross-purposes, when it comes to Ruskin's giving practical lessons in handwriting. He first offers as a model a facsimile of a Greek sentence that begins with an illuminated letter "A." While copying this instance of "pure writing; not painting or drawing," the reader is instructed that "the best writing for practical purposes is that which most resembles print, connected only, for speed, by the current line" (28.495), and that beautiful writing can be produced only by the hand that is "in the true and virtuous sense, free; that is to say, able to move in any direction it is ordered" (28.494). Writing is "ordered" both by the aspect of print and by the impulse of the person who writes. Ruskin's moralization throughout Fors of the implications of handwriting recalls his argument in The Stones of Venice and elsewhere that all handwork expresses the moral state of those who produce it.

Ruskin's analysis of handwriting is the most fundamental deconstruction of this idea in any of his books. For writing is the work of Ruskin's own hand, and the exfoliation of his self-knowledge substantiates the view that handwriting does not simply register the moral condition of the subject and the self; it also has the "aspect" of them.

The bond between the composition of one's words and one's subject is made graphic in Ruskin's next lesson on the writing of the letter "B." Noting that the model "A" instances no "spring or evidence of nervous force in the hand," Ruskin promises (but never delivers) a "B" from the Northern Schools that has so much "spring and power" that the reader cannot hope to imitate it all at once, but must be prepared "by copying a mere incipient fragment or flourish" (28.524). What Ruskin does present is the outline of a shell – insisting that "This line has been drawn for you" not by himself but with "wholly consistent energy" by a snail. The "free hand" required to draw this line will thus be retracing not only a portion of a Gothic letter "B" but also, simultaneously, a picture of a living thing: in Ruskin's case, the hand has traced the living thing itself. Or rather, no longer a living thing but the visible creation and record of one – for the line incarnates and memorializes the "strong procession and growth" of the animal (28.525). Ruskin's idea looks back to the lesson he learned from shells in 1848 – that a "leading line" inscribes form in the flux of its own creation, that history is legible in an image (see above, pp. 120–22) – and ahead to the next four Letters of Fors Clavigera, in which Ruskin's fascination with the snail's record of growth, with the implications of the form of its shell, returns amidst discussions of many other historical subjects, including himself. So that the most interesting implication of the fact that Greek writers "illuminate[d] the letter into the picture" after the Egyptians had "los[t] the picture in the letter"

(28.568) is that the public history of writing is recapitulated in Ruskin's own. His guiding his student's hand as it follows the form, or picture, of its subject is the most basic, and ultimate, demonstration of an identity between what he variously called his "winding way" or "serpentine mode" of composition, and the composition of his favorite subjects. This identity was formed when Ruskin first fused letters and pictures, words and things, in his childhood. Making the flourishes he presented to his father helped Ruskin "understand," decades later, "that the word 'flourish' itself, as applied to writing, means the springing of its lines into floral exuberance, – therefore, strong procession and growth, which must be in a spiral line, for the stems of plants are always spirals" (28.525).

The problem is that the shape of this writing expresses not only the beauty of organic form and the obedience that issues from perfect freedom, but also the danger implicit in self-assertion. Like the quintessential Gothic in *The Stones of Venice* – "subtle and flexible like a fiery serpent, but ever attentive to the voice of the charmer" (10.212) – even the very best handwriting records a sinister association. "In the Psalter of S. Louis itself, half of its letters are twisted snakes" (19.365). Now in *Fors Clavigera* Ruskin takes as his model student the least serpentine being he can imagine, a nice little girl.[5] It is not his own astonishingly precocious childhood work which he elects to reprint in *Fors*, but the rudimentary "picture writing" of his six- or seven-year-old cousin Lily Severn, whose "way of teaching [herself] to draw and write – (and no teaching is so good for [her] as [her] own . . .)" is "harmon[ious]" with "the earliest types of beautiful national writing," with their "enigma[tic] . . . ornamentation" and their underlying confidence in an Adamic bond between name and thing, sign and design (29.507–09) [Illus. 14]. Ruskin's praise and dispraise depend upon a distinction between different kinds of handwriting. Displayed (by Ruskin's editors) in a two-page facsimile, Sir Walter Scott's hand is said to express the great moral character of his life and art (29.263–66). The instances of "incurably desultory" handwriting which Ruskin facsimiles for his lesson in *Fors* are, as we have seen, his own: "distinct evidence . . . of the . . . character which has brought on me the curse of Reuben, 'Unstable as water, thou shalt not excel'" (28.275). Once again, his authority as a teacher develops from his having allegedly been a disobedient student. What Ruskin wants his reader to see is that his early writing prefigured what he dashed off the other day in 1875; yet when one turns from the exasperated denigration of his handwriting in *Fors* to his boyhood manuscripts, one finds instead feats of manual control, vestiges of the days when Ruskin proudly asserted that his pen was his "tool," and he himself a "workman" (RFL, 173).

From the authority that comes of this story of his learning, Margaret Ruskin both is and is not segregated. For he wants to punish his mother, and he wants to perpetuate her as a model in his training of the young girls who domesticate art and protect him from the direr implications of his ambition. Outrage against or compassion for Ruskin's sexism and pedophilia have obscured the fact that his response to children is an often fruitful return to the creativity in himself which he felt compelled to punish or deny. It matters that he chose to reencounter this creativity in the shape of a girl, that his associations of writing with the father and of listening with the mother give way to the inventiveness of girls like Agnes and Jane Anne and Lily Severn. He makes a related choice when he says in *The Laws of Fésole* (1877–78) that "ALL GREAT ART IS PRAISE" (15.351), then in "Of Queens' Gardens" that a woman's "great function is Praise" (18.122). He goes on to say that a girl, unlike a boy, grows as a flower does – "she must take her own . . . form and way" (18.131); he says the same thing of himself in Fors. In the middle of the book, Ruskin links his claim that he has "never disobeyed" his mother and has "honoured all women with solemn worship" to his decision to praise artists rather than be one. And he links both to the charge made by a reviewer that he writes with "'effeminate sentimentality.'" Over the course of this Letter these "effeminate" "sentiments" evolve into "ecstas[ies]" such as those experienced by St. Francis, or by Ruskin when he thought Rose La Touche might love him. Ruskin is not simply recirculating public censure here: as his editors point out, it was he, and not a reviewer, who introduced the adjective "effeminate" into the discussion. By the Letter's end Ruskin has implied that he is not effeminate *enough*, that his wavering between what he calls "good and evil" is "the reason my voice has an uncertain sound" (28.81–89).[6]

In *Fors Clavigera* the sounds of childish petulance or peevishness or flirtatiousness come within – not instead of – the voice of authority. For generally speaking, Ruskin's childlike or childish passages are not uncertain departures or regressions from his role as teacher, but rather reenactments of what certainly stands behind it. This combination of certainty and wavering is never more perceptible than in the piercingly ironic Letter of *Fors* written a few days after the death of Rose La Touche and titled "Platted Thorns." He begins by postponing "the history of my own early submissions to external Force" until he can "fasten down a main principle about doing good work": "The wise man knows his master . . . always some creature larger than himself – some law holier than his own . . . but in order to its discovery, the obedience must be begun first, to the best one knows. Obey *something*; and you will have a chance some day of finding out what is best to obey" (28.342–43). This "being premised," Ruskin returns to the scene of his bible readings with his mother, and to the garden in which, unlike "that of Eden . . . *all* the fruit was forbidden" (28.345). Yet he ultimately agrees with his mother that he was "'too much indulged.'" Ruskin makes a serio-comical connection between the defects of his upbringing, which include his having "had nothing to love," and his failure to endear himself to "any one of three beautiful young ladies who were crushing and rending my heart" just the afternoon before (28.350–53). But it is in a much more complexly mixed humor that his training and his love of girls are connected when he turns to the education and martyrdom of Lady Jane Grey, whom he positions at the crossing of her parents' harsh will and her own literary instincts. On the surface of it, the "extreme severity" of her education is clearly differentiated from Ruskin's, and is clearly celebrated as the source of an obedience which was "the literally crowning and guiding Mercy of her life." But there are enigmas buried within the bold Tudor lettering of the passage Ruskin reprints from *The Scholemaster*, as there are enigmas in the picture writing of the seven-year-old Lily Severn. It is temptingly implied (by the man whose consumption of fruit had once been "carefull[y] restrict[ed]") that tasting the full meaning of Lady Jane Grey's story is like tasting the apple of the Tree of Knowledge of Good and Evil. Although they are as yet only "little Eve and Adam," a bitter conflict must surely ensue when they grow older, and must surely lie in wait for the reader to whom Ruskin holds out the apple. But he so manages his narrative that his own "rightly" filial submissiveness will seem to survive the knowledge that the daughter's honored parents treated her with cruel "selfishness," and the knowledge that the obedience which had been his own "blessing[ ]" too was also accompanied by the "calamit[y]" of the parents' "ceaseless authority." By the end of his Letter the son who wrote about his "blessings" and "calamities" with "thorns in my fingers" has become both "kindly [Roger] Ascham" and the dutiful young pupil: he is at once teacher and taught, the author of Fors Clavigera and a "Princess[ ] of Heaven" who bears "the platted thorn upon the brow, and rooted thorn around the feet" (28.349–57; and see above, pp. 153–55).

. . .

The girls who people Ruskin's later works offer not only a saving grace to an aging man but also a larger scope to his familiar view that childhood is the period of greatest wonder, promise, and happiness – a view that controls both his assessment of individual lives and his reading of the life cycle of the physical world, of nations, cultures, and the arts. In Aratra Pentelici (1872), for instance, the production of energetic sculpture is taken as a sign that a race is in its childhood, for the making of these shapes derives from children's making believe. Ruskin's description of the unstoppable drive towards mimesis, towards "life-shaping," is at once a history of children and of art. Genesis is identified with invention. It is also – in passages which readers have not paused to dispute – identified with girls. The impulse of an eleven-year-old "little lady" to make cats and mice of pastry dough provides Ruskin with the only "true account" of the "irresistible human instinct" for making sculpture or coloring with paint. This girl is no mere freak in her exercise of a "zoo-plastic" drive that is essentially masculine. In fact it is female predilections which give Ruskin a language for the "spirit of sculpture": in the retrospect of a more "manly" future, "all this sculpturing and painting of ours may be looked back upon . . . as a kind of doll-making" (20.220–22).

A few pages later, conventional gender alignments are restored, as it is Ruskin's recollection of his own boyhood which substantiates his view that the imagination of children is neither their waning connection to an invisible life they knew before birth, nor the incipient torment of adult nostalgia. "Confined" to one position, possessed of a few objects, the child makes what it will out of what is physically "*there*" (20.249–50). Yet in describing how the child does his making, Ruskin again departs from other people's conventions, and complicates his own pictures of children – his former self included – who look entirely content to remain where they are. The famous child confined at Herne Hill in *Fors Clavigera* (1875), and the generic one inside a walled garden in *The Seven Lamps of Architecture* (1849), were allegedly freed by their obedience; Ruskin posited such "Freedom" within "wholesome restraint" as the only hope for the art of England (8.259). But in *The Art of England* (1883), there is a lecture called "Fairy Land" in which the child's imagination is associated with escape; what is more, the escape is specifically from parents, and it is a girl who shows the way. Ruskin takes as a text the moment in *Hard Times* when "Louise [sic] and her brother" (who is not dignified with a name) venture to peep at the horse-riding. Their flight from parental discipline remains in mind a page later, when the "exercise of the inventive and believing power" is said to be as necessary to the child's survival as are its legs: it is "forced to develop its power of invention, as a bird its feathers of flight." Ruskin includes several brief, ungendered references to children's preferring toys which are not too realistic, which do not deprive them of the opportunity to imagine a plaything into life. Yet when he enunciates his conclusion that "A man can't always *do* what he likes, but he can always *fancy* what he likes," his model is a six- or seven-year-old girl.

My little – ever-so-many-times-grand – cousin, Lily, took a bit of stick with a round knob at the end of it for her doll one day; – nursed it through any number of illnesses with the most tender solicitude; and, on the deeply-important occasion of its having a new night-gown made for it, bent down her mother's head to receive the confidential and timid whisper – "Mamma, perhaps it had better have no sleeves, because, as Bibsey has no arms, she mightn't like it."

The adult masculine imagination is once again epitomized by a young female; the form on which she seizes might nowadays be described a phallic, but she takes it as another little girl.

These movements from one age and gender to another are related to a translation that appears in Ruskin's most important comment in this passage: rather than spelling out in English the relation between imaginative flight and the forces that keep children put, he rushes in an aside that "the besoin de croire . . . precedes the besoin d'aimer" (33.328–30). Actually, Lily's need to believe is very close to her need to love; but Ruskin is less interested in the daughter's impulse to mother than he is in the fact that it is not to her own mother that Lily first turns. What Ruskin approaches here is his believing in his own imagination first, rather than in his parents or in their imagination of him. But when his account comes too close to home, Ruskin must resort to French, and to the example of a daughter, not of a son – just as, in Arrows of the Chace, he puts his directest claim to being an artist in the shape of a Latin proverb. Like his shifts in age and gender, these linguistic translations are flights of, and from, his own imagination. This situation will show more clearly if compared to another in his more familiar writing. In The Stones of Venice (1853), the survival of genius is endangered not by the child's inalienable nature but by the knowledge that gains on him as he grows older, even knowledge of the "good" kind which, "like the crusader's chain mail . . . throws itself into folds with the body, yet . . . is rarely so forged as that the clasps and rivets do not gall us" (11.66). In The Art of England, on the contrary, the adult who would save himself is turning away not simply from externally imposed constraints, but from (as well as towards) the survival of his childhood in his adult creative life. Against this survival, Ruskin's nostalgia for childhood is a powerful defense.

It is also the avatar of another offense – of a new career as an offender against norms that his parents held dear. This is announced, with retrospective ambivalence, by the image of the child who did not

painfully wish, what I was never permitted for an instant to hope, or even imagine, the possession of such things as one saw in toy-shops. I had a bunch of keys to play with, as long as I was capable only of pleasure in what glittered and jingled; as I grew older, I had a cart, and a ball; and when I was five or six years old, two boxes of well-cut wooden bricks. With these modest, but, I still think, entirely sufficient possessions, and being always summarily whipped if I cried, did not do as I was bid, or tumbled on the stairs, I soon attained serene and secure methods of life and motion; and could pass my days contentedly in tracing the squares and comparing the colours of my carpet; – examining the knots in the wood of the floor, or counting the bricks in the opposite houses; with rapturous intervals of excitement during the filling of the water-cart, through its leathern pipe, from the dripping iron post at the pavement edge; or the still more admirable proceedings of the turncock, when he turned and turned till a fountain sprang up in the middle of the street. But the carpet, and what patterns I could find in bed-covers, dresses, or wall-papers to be examined, were my chief resources, and my attention to the particulars in these was soon so accurate, that when at three and a half I was taken to have my portrait painted by Mr. Northcote, I had not been ten minutes alone with him before I asked him why there were holes in his carpet. The portrait in question represents a very pretty child with yellow hair, dressed in a white frock like a girl, with a broad light-blue sash and blue shoes to match; the feet of the child wholesomely large in proportion to its body; and the shoes still more wholesomely large in proportion to the feet.

(35.20–21; the painting is reproduced as the frontispiece of this book)

The child painted here is of course the creature of an adult who knows very well what his preoccupations will turn out to be, and positions his own frame accordingly. But seeing the frame depends upon the realization that this passage did not appear first in *Praeterita*, the book which deliberately excludes what Ruskin said he had "no pleasure in reviewing" (35.11), but ten years earlier, in the teemingly inclusive *Fors Clavigera* (Letter 51, 9 February 1875, 28.272–73). Mindful of his birthday the day before (and that Rose La Touche was surely dying), Ruskin presents a continuity that was the issue of an entire life: a continuity between rigorous obedience (which, though allegedly no deprivation, requires for its display that he deprive himself of things which we now know he had), intense gratification (which, though accounted freely and innocently available, is taken in forms and objects that mimic the sexuality he denies), and an appearance of girlishness (which, though subject to Ruskin's bemusement, and appearing only when he is representing a representation framed by somebody else, is essential to his confidence in reprinting this passage in the book he called "a dutiful offering at the grave of parents" [35.12]). In his carefully matured design, Ruskin's longing issues not in a daughter or son (those predictable manifestations of desire indulged), but in the reappearance of his own childhood – which is itself the herald of footsteps taken towards political action. For with the serio-comical image of the large shoes, Ruskin simultaneously points to his inalienable masculinity, to its having room to grow in, and to that measured movement within wholesomely fixed bounds which is at once his aesthetic and political ideal.

The implication that he has not overstepped should be read

in relation to another passage from *Fors Clavigera*, which he had written just one year before:

One day last November, at Oxford, as I was going in at the private door of the University galleries, to give a lecture on the Fine Arts in Florence, I was hindered for a moment by a nice little girl, whipping a top on the pavement. She was a *very* nice little girl; and rejoiced wholly in her whip, and top; but could not inflict the reviving chastisement with all the activity that was in her, because she had on a large and dilapidated pair of woman's shoes, which projected the full length of her own little foot behind it and before . . . There were some worthy people at my lecture, and I think the lecture was one of my best . . . But all the time I was speaking, I knew that nothing spoken about art, either by myself or other people, could be of the least use to anybody there. For their primary business, and mine, was with art in Oxford, now; not with art in Florence, then; and art in Oxford now was absolutely dependent on our power of solving the question – which I knew that my audience would not even allow to be proposed for solution – "Why have our little girls large shoes?"   (Letter 37, 1 January 1874, 28.13–14)

The particulars about her whip and her potentially punishing vitality set this little girl off from the "whipped" and nearly toyless Ruskin of Letter 51, as well as from Ruskin's description of himself (in the next paragraph of Letter 37) as a child jumping up and down his nursery stairs, secure in the knowledge that his responsibility for his behavior exists within God's foreknowledge of how many steps he can reach (and, presumably, of God's foreknowledge of whether he will tumble and be punished by his parents, God's surrogates, as in Letter 51). Yet the little girl whose activity is inhibited by the un"wholesomely large" cast-offs of a woman, is crucial to the air of strict obedience with which Ruskin makes his audacious turn from teaching about art, to teaching that he alone will take responsibility for laying out rules for the governance of both parents and children in England.

. . .

The maze of gender crossings and definitions that extends through Ruskin's youth is vital to an understanding of his shifting orientations as an adult. Although there have been valuable critical studies of his attitudes towards gender and sexuality,[7] no sustained attention has yet been paid to their covert, circuitous, and decisive effect on his development as a writer, and on his sense of himself as an artist. Once again, a cycle which seems unreproducibly eccentric turns out to matter in the development of other Victorian writers. The genesis of Ruskin's compositional theory and practice points not only to the will of the Victorian sage to express his own inventiveness but also to his will to deflect attention from it, to disguise and even to punish it. For all the groundbreaking work that has been done about developmental history and the avoidance of creativity in nineteenth-century women, more needs to be said about a comparable avoidance in men – especially in men such as Carlyle and Arnold, who have had an enormous influence on both male and female readers. The case of Ruskin suggests that the denial of self and of literary power – which is so assimilable to the ideal of Keats or of Hazlitt that the artist ought to disappear in his art, or to George Eliot's warnings against self-indulgence, or to the privileging of the unobserved observer in the optics of Lyell and Darwin[8] – needs to be investigated in terms of men's identification with the condition of the feminine, including the stricture that they only translate or trace what others were able to create.[9] Because he was a literary artist, a sage, and a scientist, Ruskin's work suggests how gender roles and sexual experience can bring the disciplines together, concealing as well as revealing what they may have in common.

But a feminist drawn by Ruskin's self-effacement must still contend with his rejection of any woman intent upon his gender and sexuality, and with his rejection of the actual lives of those girls through whose appearance he covers his mastery. Then too, what Ruskin is driven to redress is his very will to creation; and he redresses it in a garb so artful, that no female who puts it on will ever grow up to make art. Yet it would be a mistake to turn away when Ruskin assumes the air of a girl. For if we watch what goes on in his writing, we will get ideas about how, out of an image of artlessness, art is eventually rendered.

CHAPTER 8

THE INVENTION OF GENESIS
(1885–89)

The images of development which Ruskin produced near the end of his career offer the most concentrated answer to the question with which I started this book: what is the relationship between the genesis of invention and the authority of the artist as an adult? In misrepresenting both the past and the present, Ruskin's invention of his own genesis nonetheless involves his first experiences as a writer in what he eventually achieved.

Nine months after he observed the instability of his writing and his character (28.275), forty-two years after he observed that he "roll[s] on like a ball" (RFL, 274), Ruskin says that he can write *Fors Clavigera* only

> as a kind of play . . . by letting myself follow any thread of thought or point of inquiry that chances to occur first, and writing as the thoughts come, – whatever their disorder; all their connection and cooperation being dependent on the real harmony of my purpose, and the consistency of the ascertainable facts, which are the only ones I teach . . . (28.461)

The title of the work itself emblematizes the nexus of values implied or asserted in his writing about writing. Among its other meanings, "Fors" is both the fate that acts upon him from without, and the forces within that work themselves out in his life. In every moment, *Fors* bears the form of those forces in action. It is not simply that Fors will lead to form, but that it already, inherently, has a form, no matter how formless it may seem. The Fors, or force, of the writing reveals a pattern of order in the welter of data, for the interval between flow and form is only the time within which growth and force do their work, the time it takes for them to show

229

themselves as Fors – which is the design of a person's life, the picture of a self and writing as "Unstable as water."

What may seem like the book's waywardness with regard to one set of forces turns out to be its lawfulness with regard to another. Like natural objects and activities constrained to take the shapes or to repeat the patterns that we saw in the first part of this book, or like the children constrained by the powers they obey in the second, Ruskin's writing is, in his account, constrained to assume the forms that it does in Fors. The result is a book at once private and public, intimate and estranged. Fors is Ruskin's own idiosyncratic signature; and it is a design whose emergence he watched as critically as if it were the creation of somebody else.

It is crucial to Ruskin's sense of well-being that what he watches is handwork, that the work "grows under my hands" (28.461):

for us of the old race – few of us now left, – children who reverence our fathers, and are ashamed of ourselves; . . . yet knowing ourselves to be of the same blood, and . . . the same passions, with the ancient masters of humanity; – . . . it is impossible for us, except in the labour of our hands, not to go mad.   (28.207)

But this "labour" must be far enough beyond his mastery to remind him that he is not "Turner . . . Gainsborough . . . Prout," and to remind him that he is the possessor of "that total want of imagination and invention which makes me so impartial and so accurate a writer on subjects of political economy" (28.211–12, 205). Only under these circumstances will handwork protect him from the "miser[y]" of wanting to be an artist or the "isolation" of being one, and from the punishment of those who usurp the dominion of "Doge . . . Pope . . . Lord of the Sun and Moon" (the celestial bodies to which he likened his father and mother in Letter 54). "Manual labour" will keep him patiently in his place, much as it "has kept the honest country people patient in

their task of maintaining the rascals who live in towns"
(28.211, 206, 212, 350). Here as elsewhere, Ruskin uses his
sense of his limitations in drawing to control his still more
uncomfortable sense of his boundlessness as a writer. His
failure to be prodigious in the one medium is made to evince
the triviality of his success in the other. But this strategy is
undermined by his consciousness that writing has visual
antecedents and a visible existence. It is always a physical
exercise to the very young Ruskin; to the old man looking
back on him, writing is manual labor of the most inclusive
kind, bringing personal, social, cultural, and economic
history into view all at once. To make an absolute separation
between Ruskin as a writer and Ruskin as an artist is to
obscure the inseparability of his verbal and visual designs,
and to obscure the inventiveness that is hidden as well as
expressed by his movements back and forth between them.

This inventiveness receives its culminating denial and
display in Praeterita (1885–89),[1] an autobiography in which,
as in Fors Clavigera, Ruskin seeks to show that his teaching has
been justified by the learning which it encodes: "How I
learned the things I taught is the major, and properly, only
question regarded in this history" (35.368). It is because he
revises the versions that appeared in Fors and elsewhere that
this history "has taken, as I wrote, the nobler aspect of a
dutiful offering at the grave of parents" (35.12). Nowhere is
this changing aspect caught more vividly or succinctly than in
"Fontainebleau," the chapter that comes at the center of the
book, and that is centrally about Ruskin's discovery of the
laws of composition during the spring before he began Modern
Painters. The trail of footnotes provided by Cook and
Wedderburn, and the previous records of some of the events
(see above, pp. 169–70, and below, n.3), suggest that
Ruskin's revisions tend to create a more "dutiful" context for
two assertions in particular: that in his sketches of 1842,

"Nature herself was composing with" Turner; and that in his own attempts, Ruskin proved, once again, that "I can no more write a story than compose a picture" (35.310, 304). The connection latent between these two discoveries first emerges just after he recalls his recognition that Turner's "sketches were straight impressions from nature, – not artificial designs" (35.310). While thinking this over on a road near his house, Ruskin has a foretaste of what he will describe as a momentous experience.

... one day on the road to Norwood, I noticed a bit of ivy round a thorn stem, which seemed, even to my critical judgment, not ill "composed"; and proceeded to make a light and shade pencil study of it in my grey paper pocket-book, carefully, as if it had been a bit of sculpture, liking it more and more as I drew. When it was done, I saw that I had virtually lost all my time since I was twelve years old, because no one had ever told me to draw what was really there!

(35.311)

Ruskin's self-reproach that he "was neither so crushed nor so elated by the discovery as I ought to have been" deflects attention from the way his discovery elevates him above his teachers (who forced him to regard nature in terms of previous paintings and principles),[2] and above his father (who was absent when he should have been at home securing a supreme Turner landscape, who had left his son too dependent to take the matter into his own hands, but whose fault is borne by his son in the Praeterita version of the story).[3]

The full force of what has happened is postponed until a few paragraphs (and a month or so) later, when Ruskin finds himself "in an extremely languid and woe-begone condition" in a cart-road at Fontainebleau. As so often in Praeterita, Ruskin arrests that presumably moving thing, himself, and creates a comically deflated variation on his boyhood theme of movement and fixity.[4] But this self-immobilization is also a serious reminder of his early sense of being set most meaningfully in motion by animation that exists outside of himself. And when his passage from sleeplessness to lover-like arousal is interrupted by quotations from John Evelyn, the impression is only intensified that it is not his own imagination by which he is presently moved. The pieces of the account cohere all the more complexly for the detours he sets in their way.

> ... getting into a cart-road among some young trees, where there was nothing to see but the blue sky through thin branches, [I] lay down on the bank by the roadside to see if I could sleep. But I couldn't, and the branches against the blue sky began to interest me, motionless as the branches of a tree of Jesse on a painted window.
>
> Feeling gradually somewhat livelier ... I took out my book, and began to draw a little aspen tree, on the other side of the cart-road, carefully ...
>
> Languidly, but not idly, I began to draw it; and as I drew, the languor passed away: the beautiful lines insisted on being traced, – without weariness. More and more beautiful they became, as each rose out of the rest, and took its place in the air. With wonder increasing every instant, I saw that they "composed" themselves, by finer laws than any known of men. At last, the tree was there, and everything that I had thought before about trees, nowhere ... The woods, which I had only looked on as wilderness, fulfilled I then saw, in their beauty, the same laws which guided the clouds, divided the light, and balanced the wave. "He hath made everything beautiful, in his time," became for me thenceforward the interpretation of the bond between the human mind and all visible things ...   (35.313–15)

Ruskin's critics have been interestingly attentive to the differences between this account and what does or does not appear in his diary of 1842. But what is still more interesting for the study of Ruskin as an artist is the fact that he derives the law he declares from the movements of his own hand. It is entirely characteristic of his prose that in the course of putting his own compositional capacities "nowhere," Ruskin composes one of the most powerful narratives in all his work – a narrative that shows how one can learn what one most inalienably and importantly understands from the process of composition itself. That his writing is based on his past verbal as well as visual achievements is concealed not simply by the inclusion of sentences from Evelyn but also by the exclusion of what had appeared in their place in Ruskin's first draft, a magnificent passage (later removed to an earlier chapter, "The Col de la Faucille" [35.158–68; and see above, pp. 78–80]) whose composition was itself based upon the composition of his 1835 diary and verses.[5]

Nor does Ruskin acknowledge that the image of the tree is his own, that it records the movements of his own mind. Yet the translation from tree to image bespeaks his own language of relationships as surely as does Turner's transposition of a tree in the earth into an image on paper (see above, p. 99, and n.33). Ruskin's picture of a tree is in fact a picture of the laws of composition, a picture of relations between mind and its objects. The picture is a statement about, not a mere imitation of, two things at once: about how a tree is composed, and about how an artist composes. Both statements express order as a visual record of movement, change. This order is an abstraction from the growth of his own compositions, verbal or pictorial, through time – it is the comprehensive grasp of form as an inscription of flux.

The drawing of the tree is not there in *Praeterita*. Instead there is an account of a tree that completes the genealogy affirmed when Ruskin likened the seventeen-year development of *Modern Painters* to the changes "of a tree – not of a cloud"(7.9), and extended in the image of a wind- and flood-swept "birch-tree," that has no more control over the arrangement of its boughs than Ruskin does over the shape of *Fors* (28.254) – a genealogy whose roots reach silently back to the aspen which bears "the melancholy expression of fragility, faintness, and inconstancy" in Modern Painters III (5.237); to the aspen which becomes the "subject of comparison" between six epochal "schools" of painting in Modern Painters IV (6.97–102); to the aspen which evinces obedience to "the gentle law of respect and room for each other" in Modern Painters V (7.41–42); and to the aspen which reveals (like Ruskin) "an expression of anger as well as of fear and distress" in The Storm-Cloud of the Nineteenth Century (34.34). In Praeterita the account of the "young" aspen becomes evidence that "nature" has broken through the "heavy," "languid" dullness induced explicitly by the schooling of the young Ruskin, and implicitly by parenting that was at once "too formal and too luxurious" (35.313, 46). Yet for all his exaltation of the natural, Ruskin is interested in the aspen (as he was in the ivy he drew "as if it had been . . . sculpture") because it is composed as an artifact is composed, because it looks like something "painted." Where there is no Turner to bear responsibility, Ruskin comes to nature as if it already looked like an artifact.

Against the vision of his elders, Ruskin sets not nature but a representation of it – a representation which involves him in a competition that could bear as bitter a fruit as the tree forbidden to Adam. When he wrote about fathers in "Living Waves," it was in sorrowful anger, not in fear of those who "prick the poison of the asp" into their sons, and "sicken their eyes with blindness to all the true joys, the true aims, and the true praises of science and literature" (26.329). But he senses danger for the son who gains his sight in Praeterita. This is one of the reasons for his affirmations of order in apparent disorderliness, for his reliance on metaphors of organic form, for his recurrent assertions that "I was without power of design" (35.120). But none of this is enough. By the end of the chapter, father, mother, and son are all removed from what Ruskin regards as the "Eden" of their home – the home they shared before the achievement of *Modern Painters*, the home to which he returned alone to write the preface of *Praeterita*. Not only parental but also filial ambition is punished in this removal; for "in this hour of all our weaknesses," Ruskin succumbed to his "temptation" to occupy a scene where he might make an artifice. His original idea of building a canal was only realized twenty years later in "water-works, on the model of Fontainebleau" – the place where he both experienced and denied the power of his invention (35.317–18).[6]

It is the punishable implication of invention, of a competition with the father, that Ruskin seeks to displace by introducing the tree of Jesse – another inscription of genealogy which composes moving development into "motionless" pattern, which turns an impulse springing from the loins into the constancy of art. Like the figure of Jesse painted in windows of Gothic cathedrals not very far away, Ruskin's figure of his former self is lying down upon the ground in Fontainebleau. His bearing his own increase without an act of possession, without the loss of virginity, recalls a connection made in *The Ethics of the Dust* between the image of Jesse and the words "virtue," "virgin," "vir" (man), "vis" (force, potency), and "'virga' – a 'rod'" (18.301). The connection is still more telling in *The Queen of the Air*:

Virgil . . . became the fountain-head of all the best literary power connected with the love of vegetative nature among civilized races of men. . . . But the first syllable of the name of Virgil has relation also to another group of words, of which the English ones, virtue, and virgin, bring down the force to modern days. It is a group containing mainly the idea of "spring," or increase of life in vegetation – the rising of the new branch of the tree out of the bud, and of the new leaf out of the ground. It involves, secondarily, the idea of greenness and of strength, but primarily, that of living increase of a new rod from a stock, stem, or root; ("There shall come forth a rod out of the stem of Jesse;") . . .   (19.336)

As in his letter and essay of the early 1840s which pronounce upon the death of trees in Eden (see above, pp. 170–77), time may be sadness, sexuality may be fear; but Ruskin can so frame a composition as to contain vitality and exclude what is bound to die. The asp may lurk in Ruskin's words about the aspen that opened his eyes, but the root of Jesse is there to identify his composition, and his ideas of composition, with God's design for his own true son.

In disguising the role of the will, the chapter called "Fontainebleau" ironically demonstrates the artist's will to compose himself, to grant himself composure. It takes art to redeem the impulse to make art. At the very moment when a pattern materializes out of Ruskin's own mental and physical movements, he devotes all his force to showing that the pattern certifies a force beyond his own. But if it required years of revisions to work out the will that authorizes form in *Praeterita*, the person behind the moment of inspiration is not lost as a tree becomes a drawing, and a drawing becomes print on the page. The development of the prodigiously creative boy (who found his invention in seeing what was already there) and of the self-rejecting "word painter" (who prided himself on finding that great artists tell the same truths that he saw) are both present in Ruskin's late "picture writing." For Ruskin found ways of writing which bring together all of the parts of his being, producing a saving vision of commonwealth while putting him at odds with some of the most important educational and formal conventions he inherited, whether from the masters in each of his disciplines or from the parents before whom his interdisciplinary flights first began. Not in spite of his denials but as a consequence of them, Ruskin wrote what is certainly one of the most inventive autobiographies of the nineteenth century. Not only in spite of the conflicts among his desires but also because of them, Ruskin teaches us as much as anyone can about how the will to design at once bears upon, and is borne upon by, the design of the world that is not oneself.

NOTES

INTRODUCTION

1 Introduced by George Levine and William Madden as "the initial case for Victorian prose as an art form" (xxi), *The Art of Victorian Prose* (New York: Oxford University Press, 1968) opens with an essay detailing the development of the case by the Victorians themselves (Travis R. Merritt, "Taste, Opinion, and Theory in the Rise of Victorian Prose Stylism," 3–38).

2 *The Complete Works of John Ruskin* (Library Edition), ed. E. T. Cook and Alexander Wedderburn, 39 vols. (London: George Allen, 1903–12). Unless otherwise indicated, all parenthetical references are to this edition, and are given by volume and page number.

3 *The Diaries of John Ruskin*, ed. Joan Evans and John Howard Whitehouse, 3 vols. (Oxford: Clarendon Press, 1958), 1.255 (29–30 December 1844). Hereafter cited in the text as *Diaries*.

4 See Landow's introduction (xxxvi–xliv) and LuAnn Walther's "The Invention of Childhood in Victorian Autobiography" (64–83) in *Approaches to Victorian Autobiography*, ed. George P. Landow (Athens, Ohio: Ohio University Press, 1979).

5 See, e.g., "Time. Blank Verse" (2.258–59).

6 See, e.g., Ruskin's letter of 13 February 1829. For the father's delight in his son's precocity, and ambivalence about its being swallowed up into the genius of an adult, see his letters of 6 November 1829 and 24 February 1832 (*The Ruskin Family Letters: The Correspondence of John James Ruskin, His Wife, and Their Son, John, 1801–1843*, ed. Van Akin Burd, 2 vols. [Ithaca: Cornell University Press, 1973], 174–75, 209–10, 264–66. Hereafter cited in the text as RFL).

PART ONE: LOOKING AHEAD

1 Partly based on the treatment of his first writings in *Praeterita*, the biographical introductions and notes to volumes 1 and 2 of the

Library Edition (which includes W. G. Collingwood's 1891 edition of *Poems*) have created another almost inevitable context within which they have been read. Subsequent biographies have referred to Ruskin's early writings but none more fully than Derrick Leon's *Ruskin: The Great Victorian* (London: Routledge & Kegan Paul, 1949), John Dixon Hunt's *The Wider Sea: A Life of John Ruskin* (London: J. M. Dent, 1982), and Tim Hilton's *John Ruskin: The Early Years, 1819–1859* (New Haven: Yale University Press, 1985). Other books and articles that discuss his juvenilia will be cited below as they become pertinent.

1 INTERRELATIONS (1823–29)

1 Ruskin's precocity was repeatedly remarked by his parents and their associates, including some who were in a good position to judge his talent. See, e.g., RFL, 98, 180, 209–10; and 1.xxxvii. For more recent observations, see Michael Brooks, "Love and Possession in a Victorian Household: The Example of the Ruskins" in *The Victorian Family: Structure and Stresses*, ed. Anthony S. Wohl (New York: St. Martin's Press, 1978), 93; and Jeffrey L. Spear, *Dreams of an English Eden: Ruskin and His Tradition in Social Criticism* (New York: Columbia University Press, 1984), 19. To compare Ruskin's juvenilia to that of other children and adolescents who would become famous, see, e.g., *First Lines: Poems Written in Youth, from Herbert to Heaney*, ed. Jon Stallworthy (Oxford: Oxford University Press, 1988); and *Seeds in the Wind: Juvenilia from W. B. Yeats to Ted Hughes*, ed. Neville Braybrooke (London: Hutchinson, 1989).

2 Ruskin did not attend school until he was fourteen and did not receive instruction from anyone other than his parents until he was ten. In 1829 the Reverend Edward Andrews, an Evangelical Congregationalist, became his first tutor (see Hilton, *John Ruskin*, 15, 19–22); by 1831 he had begun to study mathematics with John Rowbotham and to receive drawing lessons from Charles Runciman (see RFL, 261 n.11 and 13). The fullest discussion of Ruskin's training and development as a visual artist is Paul H.

Walton, *The Drawings of John Ruskin* (Oxford: Clarendon Press, 1972).

3 Ruskin's drawing of "harrys new road" fills p. 48 of *Harry and Lucy, Concluded*; the text with which it is surrounded in *Praeterita* is on pp. 93–96 of *Harry and Lucy, Concluded*.

4 Quoted by permission of the Beinecke Rare Book and Manuscript Library, Yale University, from "John Ruskin's 'Harry and Lucy, Poems, etc.,'"97–100. In *Praeterita*, Ruskin calls the six poems written in this notebook between September or October 1826 and January 1827, "The earliest dated efforts I can find, indicating incipient motion of brain-molecules" (35.52), and he quotes the first two lines of "the Steam-engine" (35.56). The entire poem is quoted with revisions in 2.254–55 n.3.

5 The originality of Ruskin's accomplishment seems even more impressive when the poem is set alongside the descriptions of the industrial north of England – of foundries, steam engines, and a journey by steamship – in Maria Edgeworth's *Harry and Lucy Concluded; Being the Last Part of Early Lessons*, 3 vols. (Boston: Monroe & Francis, 1825), 2.41–43 ff.

6 Elizabeth K. Helsinger discusses the "traveler's progressive perception" in Ruskin's writings of the 1830s in terms of the late eighteenth- and early nineteenth-century landscape art and literature which he studied (*Ruskin and the Art of the Beholder* [Cambridge, Mass.: Harvard University Press, 1982], 67–110).

7 See especially *Modern Painters* II (1846) and the studies of composition in *The Elements of Drawing* (1857) and *Modern Painters* V (1860).

8 Quoted by permission of the Beinecke Rare Book and Manuscript Library, Yale University, from "John Ruskin's 'Harry and Lucy, Poems, etc.'" (unpaginated).

9 Quoted by permission of the Beinecke Rare Book and Manuscript Library, Yale University, from "John Ruskin's 'Harry and Lucy, Poems, etc.'" (unpaginated). The text is heavily punctuated in *The Queen of the Air*, but somewhat differently from in 2.262.

10 On the dating of the poem by Ruskin's editors, see *A Tour to the Lakes in Cumberland: John Ruskin's Diary for 1830*, ed. James S. Dearden,

with an introduction by Van Akin Burd (Aldershot: Scolar Press, 1990), 20 n.20. Brian Maidment points to differences between the published and manuscript versions as evidence of the first of what would be many interventions by Ruskin's father, who arranged for the publication of this poem and may also have revised it ("'Only Print' – Ruskin and the Publishers," *Durham University Journal* 63 [1971], 196–97). My quotations of "On Skiddaw and Derwent Water" are from the MS fair copy.

11 Cf. Hunt, "Ut *pictura poesis*, the picturesque, and John Ruskin," *Modern Language Notes* 93 (1978), 811–14 and *The Wider Sea*, 40–41.

2 LAWS OF MOTION (1829–33)

1 All of Ruskin's letters quoted in "Laws of Motion" are addressed to his father. The passages in this sentence are from letters of 10 March 1829, 13 February 1829, 21 March 1831 (RFL, 191, 175, 252).

2 Ruskin would have been aware of Hood and Byron as precedents; but if the subject is conventional, what Ruskin makes of it is not.

3 The tour Ruskin envisions for the coming summer would "be expensive" partly because his father paid him a penny for every twenty lines of verse he wrote. The rhymes he refers to writing in the beginning of this passage are part of his *Iteriad; or Three Weeks Among the Lakes*, a 2310-line account in verse of the tour that Ruskin, his parents, and his cousin made of the Lake District in the summer of 1830.

4 Cf. Ruskin's later assessment of the allegedly unpremeditated "writing to the moment" of Byron, who might be considered one of the models of Ruskin's epistolary (and verse) style (1.445–46).

5 See William Hogarth, *The Analysis of Beauty* (1735) and J. D. Harding, *Principles and Practices of Art* (1845), both of which are cited in George P. Landow, *The Aesthetic and Critical Theories of John Ruskin* (Princeton: Princeton University Press, 1971), 119; Helsinger, *Ruskin and the Art of the Beholder*, 74, 81–83; and David Sonstroem, "Prophet and Peripatetic in *Modern Painters* III and IV," in *Studies in*

Ruskin: *Essays in Honor of Van Akin Burd*, ed. Robert E. Rhodes and Del Ivan Janik (Athens, Ohio: Ohio University Press, 1982), 104–05. See also E. H. Gombrich's revision of Hogarth in his observations on the inevitable causal connection between "the wavy line" and the impression of "motion" (*The Sense of Order: A Study in the Psychology of Decorative Art* [Ithaca: Cornell University Press, 1984], 137).

6 "[N]o great artist *ever* can draw a straight line," Ruskin notes in 1856 (*Diaries*, 521).

7 See RFL, 187; and Hunt, *The Wider Sea*, 32. Although his father tells Ruskin that "Our Letters may be strictly *Confidential*" (RFL, 236), it is clear from Margaret Ruskin's postscripts that she continues to read at least some of her son's letters: see, e.g., RFL, 264, 313–14, 325–26.

8 If (as Burd suggests) it was the ode "On His Lyre" that Ruskin had in mind (RFL, 276 n.3), then the reference to Anacreon also points to his preoccupation with his feelings for his father. For the speaker of this ode (which is part of the *Anacreontea*, and not in fact by Anacreon) is bidding "farewell" to the heroics of Agamemnon and Menelaus and Hercules, since his instrument refuses to express anything but love. Ruskin's closeness to and distance from his father will be explored in the second part of this book.

9 On successive pages of this thirty-one page book, each of the twenty-nine characters is introduced in a verse painstakingly written in "print" hand, which is set between two "Coloured Plates," as he calls his drawings. "The Puppet Show" is a work both of invention and imitation: the drawings are influenced by – and in the case of one figure, directly copied from – George Cruikshank's etchings for the stories of Grimm (2.xxxiii). "The Puppet Show" (autograph manuscript, MA 3451) is quoted and reproduced [Illus. 4] by permission of The Pierpont Morgan Library, New York.

10 See, e.g., "[Papa whats time]" and the verse letters to his father of 10 May 1828 and 1 January 1835 (RFL, 150–51, 169, 293).

11 Quotations from Pope's *An Essay on Criticism* are from *Selected Poetry and Prose*, ed. William K. Wimsatt, 2nd ed. (New York: Holt,

Rinehart and Winston, 1972).

12 Cf. "Of Kings' Treasuries" (18.60–61).

13 These lessons would have reinforced those Ruskin had already learned from Maria Edgeworth's *Harry and Lucy Concluded*. See, for example, the passage in which their father says, "'If you reflect on your own mind, I think you will find that to be the case.' Harry drew closer to his father. This was a subject peculiarly interesting to him, as he had lately been so intent upon finding out what he called the workings of his own mind" (3.360). For a detailed account of the character and educational background of each of Ruskin's parents, see Helen Gill Viljoen, *Ruskin's Scottish Heritage: A Prelude* (Urbana: University of Illinois Press, 1956).

14 The amazement expressed by Ruskin's parents at the conversational fluency of his writing might be compared to that expressed by observers of the results of some late twentieth-century developments in children's education: see Bernard Asbell, "Writers' Workshop at Age 5," *The New York Times Magazine* 26 February 1984: 64, 72).

15 Roy Harris, writing in 1986, argues that the location of "the boundary between pictorial and scriptorial signs" is still "contentious," and that "graphic isomorphism," "the natural coincidence – or rather inseparability – of pictorial and scriptorial functions," is still "hard to get to grips with." See *The Origin of Writing* (La Salle, Illinois: Open Court, 1986), 55–56, 126, 130–31, and passim.

16 See George P. Landow, "J. D. Harding and John Ruskin on Nature's Infinite Variety," *The Journal of Aesthetics and Art Criticism* 28 (1970), 369–80; and Gary Wihl, *Ruskin and the Rhetoric of Infallibility* (New Haven: Yale University Press, 1985), passim.

3 DISCIPLINES (1833–35)

1 On Ruskin's approach to the languages of God and of man, see Landow, *The Aesthetic and Critical Theories of John Ruskin*, 241–457; Helsinger, *Ruskin and the Art of the Beholder*, 217–25; and Jeffrey L. Spear, "Ruskin as a Prejudiced Reader," *ELH* 49 (1982), 73–98.

2 *Ruskin's Letters from Venice 1851–1852*, ed. John L. Bradley (New Haven: Yale University Press, 1955), 293. Cf. Jay Fellows on "The Gastronomic Reflexive" in Ruskin's diaries (*The Failing Distance: The Autobiographical Impulse in John Ruskin* [Baltimore: The Johns Hopkins University Press, 1975], 111–17).

3 See Charles Coulston Gillispie, *Genesis and Geology: A Study in the Relations of Scientific Thought, Natural Theology, and Social Opinion in Great Britain, 1790–1850* (New York: Harper & Row, 1959), 220–21.

4 Cook and Wedderburn have facsimiled a page of Ruskin's "Mineralogical Dictionary," dating it, as do Ruskin's reminiscences, "About 1831" (facing 35.121). He studied both *A System of Mineralogy* (third edition, Edinburgh, 1820), which his father purchased in 1832 (RFL, 260 n.2), and Jameson's *Manual of Mineralogy* (Edinburgh, 1821).

5 The implications of these facts become clearer when one turns to works, like those of the great German geologist and mineralogist, Abraham Werner, which Ruskin said his dictionary was meant to excel (26.97). According to Barbara Maria Stafford, "Werner taught that a significant connection exists between the linguistic science of grammar and the syntactical structure of the earth bodied forth in the lapidary language of minerals" (*Voyage into Substance: Art, Science, Nature, and the Illustrated Travel Account, 1760–1840* [Cambridge, Mass.: The MIT Press, 1984], 301, 536–37 n.34).

6 See Letter 62 of *Fors Clavigera* (28.552). Ruskin's exposure to emblem alphabet books may also have spurred him to make analogies between subject matter and its spelling.

7 Jameson's *System of Mineralogy*, 1.iii. Robert Hewison quotes Jameson to this effect and proposes that he is a source of Ruskin's approach to natural forms in *Modern Painters* (*John Ruskin: The Argument of the Eye* [London: Thames and Hudson, 1976], 21–22). As Jameson was a follower of Werner, it is important to note that although Werner has traditionally been thought to focus on external characters, he in fact believed that minerals should be classified according to their composition. It was Werner who invented the concept of "formation," which was crucial to the development of historical geology. Because Jameson modified,

and Lyell misrepresented, Werner, it is not clear how accurately Ruskin apprehended Werner's achievements. See Rachel Laudan, *From Mineralogy to Geology: The Foundations of a Science, 1650–1830* (Chicago: The University of Chicago Press, 1987), 81–88, 112, 138–39, and passim.

8 Horace Bénedict de Saussure, *Voyages dans les Alpes. Précédés d'un Essai sur l'Histoire Naturelle des environs de Genève* (Neuchatel: Samuel Fauche, 1779), 4 vols.

9 In Saussure's combining natural history with travel narrative Helsinger finds a source of Ruskin's "excursive sight" (67–110), as well as of the format of *The Stones of Venice* I (148–50). But Saussure's remark about the "coup d'oeil" raises a question about the contradistinction Helsinger makes between the "constantly changing . . . perspective" of the excursive beholder, and "the intense, sudden confrontation between an isolated, stationary observer" – usually an artist or writer – "and a single view of overwhelming power" (*Ruskin and the Art of the Beholder*, 68, 63–64).

10 Hunt notes Ruskin's "determination to subject all important matters to various perspectives" in his 1835 diary (*The Wider Sea*, 64–70).

11 *Principles of Geology, Being an Attempt to Explain the Former Changes of the Earth's Surface, by Reference to Causes Now in Operation* (London: James Murray, 1830–33), 3 vols., I.54.

12 See Walton for an account of the effect of Lyell's theory on Ruskin's drawing and writing after 1848, especially in *Modern Painters* IV (*The Drawings of John Ruskin*, 75–81). That Walton emphasizes drawing rather than writing may explain his recognizing the extent of Lyell's influence on Ruskin, although Walton, like many other critics, has not seen how early it begins. See 26.117 and n.1; RFL, 336, 414; *The Winnington Letters*, ed. Van Akin Burd (Cambridge, Mass.: Harvard University Press, 1969), 66.

13 Illus. 11 appears between pp. 80 and 81 of Hunt's *The Wider Sea*, and Illus. 12 appears as the endpaper of *The Ruskin Polygon: Essays on the Imagination of John Ruskin*, ed. John Dixon Hunt and Faith M. Holland (Manchester: Manchester University Press, 1982). In

neither case is Ruskin's appropriation of Lyell mentioned.

14 Gillian Beer, *Darwin's Plots: Evolutionary Narrative in Darwin, George Eliot and Nineteenth-Century Fiction* (London: Routledge & Kegan Paul, 1983), 44–46. See also Stephen Jay Gould, *Time's Arrow, Time's Cycle: Myth and Metaphor in the Discovery of Geological Time* (Cambridge, Mass.: Harvard University Press, 1987), 134–35.

15 My discussion of nineteenth-century geology is based on Gillispie, *Genesis and Geology*, 39–40: and on Mott T. Greene, *Geology in the Nineteenth Century: Changing Views of a Changing World* (Ithaca: Cornell University Press, 1982), especially 25–26, 70–72.

16 See Spear, "'These are the Furies of Phlegethon': Ruskin's Set of Mind and the Creation of *Fors Clavigera*," in *The Ruskin Polygon*, 139–41; and Gillispie, *Genesis and Geology*, 39–40, 129–30, 133–35, 220–21.

17 Greene, *Geology in the Nineteenth Century*, 71–72; and Walton, *The Drawings of John Ruskin*, 78.

18 This characterization is drawn from Gould, who himself draws on Martin J. S. Rudwick (*Time's Arrow, Time's Cycle*, 119–26). See Ruskin's 1875 lecture, "The Three Aeras" (26.117). On the subject of gradation, see the passage previously quoted from *Modern Painters* II (4.89).

19 While I agree with Helsinger that there are differences between the habits of the artist and those of the beholding critic in Ruskin's writing (*Ruskin and the Art of the Beholder*, 63–64), I want to draw more attention to Ruskin's participation in methods and modes that he later says are reserved for artists.

20 Cf. Walton, *The Drawings of John Ruskin*, 79–80. See Michael Baxandall on "The Problem of Linearity" for the critic of art who must necessarily use linear verbal language in dealing with the essentially non-linear art of painting ("The Language of Art History," *New Literary History* 10 [1978–79], 459–60). On the tradition of equating painting and language – which was already old when Ruskin was young – see Landow, "J. D. Harding and John Ruskin on Nature's Infinite Variety," 377.

21 *Iteriad, or Three Weeks Among the Lakes by John Ruskin*, ed. James S. Dearden (Newcastle upon Tyne: Frank Graham, 1969), 28–29, 33–34. Subsequent citations from this edition will be given

parenthetically in the text. See also the stage direction after the char driver speaks in "The Ascent of the St. Bernard" (1.509).

22 Walton, *The Drawings of John Ruskin*, 18–19.

23 Walton, *The Drawings of John Ruskin*, 23, 27–28.

24 *On the Theory of Painting; to which is added an Index of Mixed Tints, and an Introduction to Painting in Water-Colours, with Precepts*, second edition, enlarged (London: J. L. Cox, 1835), 34–35, 52–53. Citations from this treatise will be given parenthetically in the text.

25 See George Berkeley, *An Essay Towards a New Theory of Vision* (1709), volume 1 of *The Works of George Berkeley, Bishop of Cloyne*, ed. A. A. Luce and T. E. Jessop (London, 1948), paragraphs 16–28. It has often been observed that Berkeley's argument was not original. Helsinger points out that Berkeley's *New Theory of Vision* influenced Payne Knight, Goethe, and Turner, and compares his argument to Ruskin's conception of visual language (*Ruskin and the Art of the Beholder*, 194–96).

26 Mitchell Feigenbaum is quoted by James Gleick in "Solving the Mathematical Riddle of Chaos," *The New York Times Magazine* 10 June 1984: 72. On Ruskin's relationship to the new science of chaos, see my "The Authorization of Form: Ruskin and the Science of Chaos," in *Chaos and Order: Complex Dynamics in Literature and Science*, ed. N. Katherine Hayles (Chicago: University of Chicago Press, 1991), 149–66.

27 Landow connects several important arguments in *Modern Painters* – for instance that the artist should "bypass ancient models and return to nature herself," and that "the greatest art . . . must have at its center an expressive rather than a mimetic aim . . . that art primarily attempts to reproduce the artist's 'emotional' impression of landscape rather than to duplicate that landscape itself" – to points made before and afterwards in treatises (1834, 1845) by J. D. Harding, with whom Ruskin studied between 1841 and 1843 ("J. D. Harding and John Ruskin on Nature's Infinite Variety"). Walton argues that the 1842 revelation Ruskin describes in *Praeterita* owed a great deal to Harding and to Turner (*The Drawings of John Ruskin*, 48–51).

28 "I determined that the events and sentiments of the journey should be described in a poetic diary in the style of *Don Juan*,

artfully combined with that of *Childe Harold*," he remembers in *Praeterita* (35.152).

29 See *The Prelude: 1799, 1805, 1850*, ed. Jonathan Wordsworth, M. H. Abrams, and Stephen Gill (New York: Norton, 1979); 1805, Book VI, lines 452–56. For different accounts of nineteenth-century approaches to the sublime, compare Helsinger, *Ruskin and the Art of the Beholder*, 111–39, and Paul H. Fry, "The Absent Dead: Wordsworth, Byron, and the Epitaph," *Studies in Romanticism* 17 (1978), 413–33.

30 Ruskin is working towards the position he will take in *The Seven Lamps of Architecture* (8.22)

31 Letter to Dante Gabriel Rossetti, February 1855 (36.189). The act of translation raises important questions about the verbal and syntactical connections Ruskin finds between the English language and the world it can describe. Do Latin or French, for example, include comparable affinities between words and things? Ruskin did not think his way through this question as a boy; and his sense of cultural centrality kept him from worrying about it. The issues do become vexatious for Ruskin later on: see, e.g., 19.308 n., 29.109–10, 34.615–16.

32 See James C. McKusick, *Coleridge's Philosophy of Language* (New Haven: Yale University Press, 1986), 78–85.

33 In *Modern Painters* I and IV, as Landow has remarked, Ruskin shows how painting displays "structures of relationships" – whether among forms, colors, or tones – which repeat the proportions, though not the scale or intensity, of "the visual structures of the natural world." These "proportionate relationships" are the "basic element of vocabulary" in Turner's "visual language." Art's capacity to create systems of proportionate relationships parallel to those of nature is what "allows the artist to make statements of visual fact" ("J. D. Harding and John Ruskin on Nature's Infinite Variety," 377–78).

4 LEADING LINES (1830–36)

1 Cf. Martin Price, "The Picturesque Moment" in *From Sensibility to Romanticism: Essays Presented to Frederic A. Pottle*, ed. Frederick W.

Hilles and Harold Bloom (New York: Oxford University Press, 1965), 259–92.

2 Both Patricia M. Ball and Elizabeth K. Helsinger offer accounts of the relationship between Ruskin's poetry and his romantic models. Compare, for example, Ball's argument that in Ruskin's poems of the early 1840s "there is none of Coleridge's confidence in the destined union between subject and object, no instantaneous conversion of the 'external real' into the inner world . . . He transfers attention from the scene to the observer not by the fluent handling of imaginative relationship, but by rhetorical emotion and platitudinous moral statement" (*The Science of Aspects: The Changing Role of Fact in the Work of Coleridge, Ruskin, and Hopkins* [London: The Athlone Press, 1971], 49), to Helsinger's view that, in the 1830s, Ruskin's poems "did not attempt the structures of mental action or the meditative passages of Wordsworth's poems, but even at eleven he recognized these as essential to the genre . . . Visual and emotional responses are seldom fused in Ruskin's version of Byron's excursive styles. Buildings and monuments receive increased attention, but Ruskin's account is still predominantly concerned with the description of natural scenery" (*Ruskin and the Art of the Beholder*, 78–79).

3 Ruskin's sources probably include the nursery rhymes he loved, and later discussed in *Fors Clavigera* and in the preface to *Dame Wiggins of Lee*, which he edited and added several verses to in 1885 (28.260–61, 2.518-26).

4 See, for example, Harold Bloom's now classic characterization of Ruskin's "searching criticism of Romanticism from within" (introduction to *The Literary Criticism of John Ruskin* [New York: Anchor Books, 1965], ix–xxvii).

5 See especially Helsinger's analysis (*Ruskin and the Art of the Beholder*, 41–66).

6 See my "Byron's 'one word': The Language of Self-Expression in *Childe Harold* III," *Studies in Romanticism* 20 (1981), 363–82.

7 Linda H. Peterson draws attention to Ruskin's list of "essential qualities" when she traces the influence of Byron on the "stance" and "structure" of *Praeterita* (*Victorian Autobiography: The*

Tradition of Self-Interpretation [New Haven: Yale University Press, 1986], 72–76).

8 *Iteriad*, ed. Dearden, 72 n.61, 76 n.384. See also Ruskin's prose account in *A Tour to the Lakes in Cumberland*, 42–43, 77 n.81.

9 *The Prose Works of William Wordsworth*, ed. W. J. B. Owen and Jane Worthington Smyser, 3 vols. (Oxford: Clarendon Press, 1974), 2.345.

10 Quoted from volume 2 of William Wordsworth, *The Poems*, ed. John O. Hayden (Harmondsworth: Penguin, 1977).

11 Cf. Ruskin's 1835 diary, in which an Alpine valley "had been taken great pains with by nature and she is a good landscape gardener" (*Diaries*, 63).

12 See 15.91. Among other authorities on art who used the term "leading lines" was John Varley, who preceded Copley Fielding as President of the Society of Painters in Water-Colours, and whose *Treatise on the Principles of Landscape Design with General Observations and Instructions to Young Artists* (London: 1815) had a significant influence on Ruskin. See Varley's "Explanation of Plate M"; and Walton, *The Drawings of John Ruskin*, 18–21, 23, 35, 48–50, 96–97.

13 Ruskin's insight may have been influenced by his direct and indirect exposure to Coleridge's ideas about organic form. See the posthumous publication in *Fraser's Magazine* for 1835 of "Monologues by the Late Samuel Taylor Coleridge, Esq. No. 1: Life," quoted by Philip C. Ritterbush in "Organic Form: Aesthetics and Objectivity in the Study of Form in the Life Sciences," in *Organic Form: The Life of an Idea*, ed. G. S. Rousseau (London: Routledge & Kegan Paul, 1972), 34, 42.

14 Stanzas I–XIII, quoted from volume 2 of *Lord Byron: The Complete Poetical Works*, ed. Jerome J. McGann (Oxford: The Clarendon Press, 1980).

15 Quoted from Samuel Rogers, *Italy, A Poem* (London: Edward Moxon, 1838), 45. For the influence of this book on Ruskin's early works, see Jeffrey L. Spear, "Ruskin's Italy," *Browning Institute Studies* 12 (1984), 73–81.

16 John D. Rosenberg has said that "All of Ruskin's writings on nature are an amplification" of this sentence ("The Geopoetry of John Ruskin," *Etudes Anglaises* [January–March 1969], 46).

17 Ruskin's responsiveness to "gradation" not only looks back to his study of drawing and of Lyellian geology but also ahead to Darwin, whose relationship to Ruskin I will touch on when I turn to *The Seven Lamps of Architecture* in chapter 5.

PART TWO: LOOKING BACK
5 SEPARATIONS (1829–49)

1 *A Tour to the Lakes in Cumberland*, 104–06.

2 See Viljoen, *Ruskin's Scottish Heritage*, for an analytical account of this history.

3 Quoted from "John Ruskin, *Poems*" with permission of the Princeton University Library.

4 See *Women Writers and Poetic Identity: Dorothy Wordsworth, Emily Brontë, and Emily Dickinson* (Princeton: Princeton University Press, 1980) and especially *Bearing the Word: Language and Female Experience in Nineteenth-Century Women's Writing* (Chicago: University of Chicago Press, 1986).

5 Among many witnesses of this situation one of the most knowledgeable must be Dorothy DeLay, the teacher of the violin prodigies Itzhak Perlman, Schlomo Mintz, Cho-Liang Lin, Nadia Salerno-Sonnenberg, Midori, and numerous others: "I think all cases of precocity, above and beyond genetic inheritance, have to do with a close relationship with a parent who feels with the child . . . How much of the desire to play came from Midori and how much of it came from her mother I don't even know" (K. Robert Schwartz, "Glissando," in *The New York Times Magazine* 24 March 1991: 32).

6 *Praeterita* reports that Ruskin's father and Adèle's would have been "perfectly ready" to see their children marry in due course if there were liking between them, but that Ruskin's mother "looked upon the idea of my marrying a Roman Catholic" as "monstrous" and "too preposterous to be even guarded against." Yet she did not give "any serious check" to Ruskin's feeling; and two chapters later he says that had Adèle been what she was not – "perfectly beautiful and amiable" and fond of Ruskin – "I suppose then my mother would have been

overcome" (35.181, 229).

7 Detailed analysis of this relationship in romantic writing began relatively recently. See William Keach, *Shelley's Style* (London: Methuen, 1984), 42–117, and my "Byron's 'one word.'"

8 "Preface to *Prometheus Unbound*," in *Shelley's Poetry and Prose*, ed. Donald H. Reiman and Sharon B. Powers (New York: Norton, 1977), 133. Subsequent quotations of P. B. Shelley are from this edition.

9 The loose translation of Aeschylus (E. D. A. Morshead, 1901) is given by Cook and Wedderburn. Ruskin's epigraph is in the original Greek. See Keach, *Shelley's Style*, 69–70.

10 Cf. Karen Swann, "Harassing the Muse," in *Romanticism and Feminism*, ed. Anne K. Mellor (Bloomington: Indiana University Press, 1988), 90–92.

11 See Paul L. Sawyer, *Ruskin's Poetic Argument: The Design of the Major Works* (Ithaca: Cornell University Press, 1985), 23–24.

12 Cf. Helena Michie's observation in *The Flesh Made Word: Female Figures and Women's Bodies* (New York: Oxford University Press, 1987): "A long philosophical tradition from Locke to Derrida . . . links women with metaphor and rhetoric, with language and textuality itself . . . An equally long and complex tradition . . . identifies woman with the body and the physical, as opposed to language and the intellectual" (7–8).

13 Consider Ruskin's response to the invitation to visit which he received from James Hogg, "the Ettrick Shepherd": although honored to be invited, and tempted by the prospect of his beloved Scotland, he says (and repeats it later in the same paragraph), "I cannot at this period make up my mind to leave my parents, even for a short time. Hitherto I have scarcely left them for a day, and I wish to be with them as much as possible, till it is necessary for me to go to the university" (1.xxviii). Ruskin is writing in 1834, three years before he went to Oxford.

14 Pertinent research into these subjects includes Eve Kosofsky Sedgwick, *Between Men: English Literature and Male Homosocial Desire* (New York: Columbia University Press, 1985); Catherine Gallagher, "George Eliot and *Daniel Deronda*: The Prostitute and the Jewish Question," in *Sex, Politics, and Science in the Nineteenth-Century*

Novel, ed. Ruth Bernard Yeazell (Baltimore: The Johns Hopkins University Press, 1986), 39–62; Marlon B. Ross, "Romantic Quest and Conquest: Troping Masculine Power in the Crisis of Poetic Identity," in *Romanticism and Feminism*, 35–36; Sonia Hofkosh, "The Writer's Ravishment: Women and the Romantic Author – The Example of Byron," in *Romanticism and Feminism*, 93–114; Carol T. Christ, "'The Hero as Man of Letters': Masculinity and Victorian Nonfiction Prose," in *Victorian Sages and Cultural Discourse: Renegotiating Gender and Power*, ed. Thaïs E. Morgan (New Brunswick: Rutgers University Press, 1990), 19–31; Bradford K. Mudge, "The Man with Two Brains: Gothic Novels, Popular Culture, Literary History," *PMLA* 107 (1992), 92–104.

15 See 2.xix–xx; Maidment, "'Only Print,'" 196–200; Hilton, *John Ruskin*, 29–30.

16 Ruskin reports in *The Stones of Venice* (9.452) and *Praeterita* "his habit of keeping a skull on his chimney-piece, and looking at it before he went to sleep" (35.498).

17 See Hilton, *John Ruskin*, 37–40.

18 See Christ, "'The Hero as Man of Letters.'"

19 On the anticipation of Ruskin's theory of the pathetic fallacy in the romantic aesthetics of his "Essay on Literature" and other prose pieces between 1836 and 1840, see Harold I. Shapiro, "The Poetry of Architecture: Ruskin's Preparation for *Modern Painters*," *Renaissance and Modern Studies* 15 (1971), 70–84. See also Hunt, "*Ut pictura poesis*," 808; and *The Wider Sea*, 92–93.

20 See Hilton, *John Ruskin*, 37–38.

21 See Richard L. Stein on Ruskin's attempts in *The Poetry of Architecture* to segregate architecture from social, economic, historical, and scientific – especially biological – facts (*Victoria's Year: English Literature and Culture, 1837–1838* [New York: Oxford University Press, 1987], 194–211).

22 See George L. Hersey, *High Victorian Gothic: A Study in Associationism* (Baltimore: The Johns Hopkins University Press, 1972), 23–34, 48–60; Patrick Conner, *Savage Ruskin* (London: Macmillan Press, 1979), 4–15, Michael W. Brooks, *John Ruskin and Victorian Architecture* (New Brunswick: Rutgers University Press, 1987), 7–9.

23 See U. C. Knoepflmacher, "Resisting Growth through Fairy Tale in Ruskin's *The King of the Golden River*," in *Children's Literature* 13 (New Haven: Yale University Press, 1985), 3–30.

24 On Ruskin's views of reproduction in the natural world, see Frederick Kirchoff, "A Science against Sciences: Ruskin's Floral Mythology," in *Nature and the Victorian Imagination*, ed. U. C. Knoepflmacher and G. B. Tennyson (Berkeley: University of California Press, 1977), 246–58. On Ruskin's revulsion from sexual intercourse and conception, see Richard Ellmann, "Overtures to 'Salome,'" in *Golden Codgers: Biographical Speculations* (New York: Oxford University Press, 1973), 39–59.

25 Compare the argument of Eve Kosofsky Sedgwick that in the Gothic a barrier is typically imposed between two things that are connected and that can only be rejoined by violence or magic (*The Coherence of Gothic Conventions* [New York: Methuen, 1986], 12–13).

26 See, e.g., E. T. Cook, 2.xix, xxvii–xxix; W. G. Collingwood, 2.42 n.1; Ball, *The Science of Aspects*, 48–51, 55–56, 75; Wendell Stacy Johnson, "Memory, Landscape, Love: John Ruskin's Poetry and Poetic Criticism," *Victorian Poetry* 19 (1981), 20; Tim Hilton, "Great Issues in the South London Suburbs," TLS 28 December 1990–3 January 1991: 1401.

27 *Ruskin in Italy: Letters to his Parents, 1845*, ed. Harold I. Shapiro (Oxford: Clarendon Press, 1972), 142 n.2.

28 *Ruskin in Italy*, 142–43.

29 For a discussion of the implications of "manliness" in *The Stones of Venice*, see David Sonstroem, "John Ruskin and the Nature of Manliness," *Victorian Newsletter* 40 (1971), 14–17.

30 See the facsimile of the first edition, ed. Ernst Mayr (Cambridge, Mass.: Harvard University Press, 1964), 186–90. C. Stephen Finley offers a comprehensive argument about the Victorian response to Darwinism in "Ruskin, Darwin, and the Crisis of Natural Form," *Cahiers Victoriens & Edouardiens* 25 (1987), 7–24.

6 UNLAWFUL MOTIONS (1843–80)

1 Cf. 10.199. See Dinah Birch on Ruskin's attitudes towards his classical studies at Oxford in *Ruskin's Myths* (Oxford: Clarendon Press, 1988), 4–27.

2 Rpt. in *Ruskin: The Critical Heritage*, ed. J. L. Bradley (London: Routledge & Kegan Paul, 1984), 100. For a survey of critical responses to Ruskin as a verbal artist during his lifetime, and of Ruskin's response to reviewers, see my review of this volume ("Ruskinism," *Essays in Criticism* 35 [1985], 173–79).

3 See Wihl, *Ruskin and the Rhetoric of Infallibility*, 179–81; and David R. Ellison, *The Reading of Proust* (Baltimore: The Johns Hopkins University Press, 1984), 59–60.

4 See Spear, "Ruskin as a Prejudiced Reader," 73–98. Ruskin's insistence on "accuracy" in reading (18.64–65) anticipates his descriptions of his mother's procedure in their daily bible sessions when he was a boy (*Fors Clavigera*, 27.616–17; *Praeterita*, 35.40–43). On Ruskin's attitudes towards language and contemporary philology, see also Michael Sprinker, "Ruskin on the Imagination," *Studies in Romanticism* 18 (1979), 115–39; Helsinger, *Ruskin and the Art of the Beholder*, 256–67; Sawyer, *Ruskin's Poetic Argument*, 139–40, 234–41; Wihl, *Ruskin and the Rhetoric of Infallibility*, passim; Robert Casillo, "Parasitism and Capital Punishment in Ruskin's Fors Clavigera," *Victorian Studies* 29 (1986), 556–60; Birch, *Ruskin's Myths*, 107–13; Linda M. Austin, *The Practical Ruskin: Economics and Audience in the Late Work* (Baltimore: The Johns Hopkins University Press, 1991), 106–30. On the critical implications of nineteenth-century language theory and philology, see Linda Dowling, *Language and Decadence in the Victorian Fin de Siècle* (Princeton: Princeton University Press, 1986), 1–103.

5 The connections are striking to a passage in the third of Wordsworth's "Essays upon Epitaphs," which Ruskin could not have read until it was published in 1876 (*The Prose Works of William Wordsworth*, 2.84–85).

6 Hilton, *John Ruskin*, 205.

7 To a close friend who ventured it as a term of approbation in 1874, Ruskin retorted that "It is the chief provocation of my life

to be called a 'word painter' instead of a thinker" (37.136). "My vanity is never more wounded than in being called a fine writer, meaning – that nobody need mind what I say" (22.302), he declared in an 1872 lecture at Oxford. See Merritt on the "almost simultaneous" establishment and undermining of Victorian prose stylism in the 1880s and '90s ("Taste, Opinion, and Theory in the Rise of Victorian Prose Stylism," 21–34). His citation of an 1857 piece in *Fraser's* which "approvingly . . . define[d] the coming ideal" might be suggestively set alongside R. H. Wilenski's declaration that after 1859, Ruskin "detested his reputation as a fine writer." Wilenski seconds this opinion of his later prose, attributing the failure of Ruskin's art first to his indulgence of "his social conscience and his manic impulse to preach," and ultimately to his mental illness (*John Ruskin: An Introduction to Further Study of his Life and Work* [London: Faber & Faber, 1933], 357–68).

8 Cf. Wihl's argument that, in "The Mystery of Life and its Arts," "The literary imagination is by definition deceptive" (*Ruskin and the Rhetoric of Infallibility*, 129–32).

9 Compare the description in *Praeterita* of the fresco of the conversion of St. Ranieri in the Campo Santo of Pisa:

> . . . he is playing, evidently with happiest skill, on a kind of zithern-harp . . . to the dance of four sweet Pisan maids . . . And one with graver face, and wearing a purple robe, approaches him . . . it meant that his joyful life in that kind was to be ended. And he obeys her, and follows, into a nobler life.   (35.354–55)

In her study of *Praeterita*, Heather Henderson argues that "Saint Ranieri thus serves as an image or type for Ruskin himself, whose own conversion would mark his transition from artist to prophet" (*The Victorian Self: Autobiography and Biblical Narrative* [Ithaca: Cornell University Press, 1989], 94). I agree, but would emphasize the new departures in and into verbal art spurred by this "transition," especially in "The Mystery of Life and its Arts." See also the 1845 letters in which Ruskin crows to his father about the merits of his drawing after the original, and laments that "St Ranieri's conduct, breaking off in the middle of his conquest to go and be a saint, [is] ungentlemanly in the extreme, and so thinks the proud little puss with the golden hair" (*Ruskin in Italy*, 72–75). The drawing survives, but in *Praeterita* Ruskin tellingly says he destroyed his "coloured sketch of the whole group . . . in shame of its faults, all but the purple-robed warning figure; and that is lost, and the fresco itself now lost also, all mouldering and ruined" (35.355).

10 Delivered in Dublin on 13 May 1868, Ruskin's lecture was first published in 1871. Pater's "Conclusion" was originally part of his anonymous review, "Poems by William Morris," published in October 1868. It was slightly revised for *Studies in the History of the Renaissance* (1873).

11 See, e.g., my "Byron's 'one word'"; Carlyle on symbol and silence in *Sartor Resartus*; and Stephen K. Land, "Wordsworth and the Silent Poet" (*University of Toronto Quarterly* 42 [1973], 157–69).

12 There is of course a great deal of commentary on Ruskin as a reader of the visible and a visualizer of the verbal. But commentary on the script of William Blake and theories about the design of writing and writing as design will also be suggestive to those interested in the relation in Ruskin's work between the scriptorial and the pictorial, the letter and the figure, the meaning and the material form. See, for example, L. S. Vygotsky, *Thought and Language*, ed. and trans. Eugenia Hanfmann and Gertrude Vakar (Cambridge, Mass.: The MIT Press, 1962); Jacques Derrida, "Scribble (writing-power)," trans. Cary Plotkin, *Yale French Studies*, No. 58 (1979), 117–47; Nelson Hilton, *Literal Imagination: Blake's Vision of Words* (Berkeley: University of California Press, 1983); Gombrich, *The Sense of Order*; Harris, *The Origin of Writing*; W. J. T. Mitchell, *Iconology: Image, Text, Ideology* (Chicago: University of Chicago Press, 1986). Helsinger places Ruskin in the tradition of "English double art" which includes Blake, Turner, and Dante Gabriel Rossetti (*Ruskin and the Art of the Beholder*, 1–3, 289–300); and Austin argues that by the 1850s, "Ruskin was reading modern literature . . . as an objective imitation of visual impression" (*The Practical Ruskin*, 113).

13 For a consideration of other phenomena with which Ruskin associates the serpent, including female sexuality and capitalism,

see Marc A. Simpson, "The Dream of the Dragon: Ruskin's Serpent Imagery," in *The Ruskin Polygon*, 21–43. See also Jay Fellows, *Ruskin's Maze: Mastery and Madness in His Art* (Princeton: Princeton University Press, 1981), 198–221; Raymond E. Fitch, *The Poison Sky: Myth and Apocalypse in Ruskin* (Athens: Ohio University Press, 1982), 348–51, 419–21, 569–70; Sawyer, *Ruskin's Poetic Argument*, 282–91.

14 *John Ruskin and Rose La Touche: Her Unpublished Diaries of 1861 and 1867*, ed. Van Akin Burd (Oxford: Clarendon Press, 1979), 116–18, 124–25.

15 *Victorian England: Portrait of an Age* (New York: Oxford University Press, 1971), 112. The book was first published in 1936.

16 *Ruskin's Letters from Venice, 1851–1852*, 293.

17 See Helsinger's account of the development of Ruskin's identity as a critic in *Ruskin and the Art of the Beholder*.

18 Ruskin's words are the more meaningful in that they are actually spoken by an artist to another artist. Anthony Trollope had berated Ruskin for being "as the fiddler in the tale," who abandons his powerful music and suspends the dancing of his audience – one thinks of Ruskin's thinking about St. Ranieri – in order to preach feeble sermons. "To a fiddler so foolishly ambitious, *Ne sutor ultra crepidam* would have been the advice given by all his friends." Trollope's complaint appeared in a signed review of *Sesame and Lilies* (*Fortnightly Review*, July 1865; rpt. in *Ruskin: The Critical Heritage*, 296–300), three years before Ruskin said "I could play you a tune on the harp yet, that you would dance to" in "The Mystery of Life and its Arts" – which was itself added to the *Sesame and Lilies* volume in 1871.

7 THE GENDER OF INVENTION (1871–84)

1 On this relationship see C. Stephen Finley, "Scott, Ruskin, and the Landscape of Autobiography," *Studies in Romanticism* 26 (1987), 549–72.

2 For a view of British educational conventions during the period about which Ruskin writes, see Karen Clarke, "Public and Private Children: Infant Education in the 1820s and 1830s," in *Language*,

Gender and Childhood, ed. Carolyn Steedman, Cathy Urwin, and Valerie Walkerdine (London: Routledge & Kegan Paul, 1985), 74–87.

3 Austin argues that Ruskin's "demand[ ] that language be pictorial, that it yield conventional images only," was his way of "compensat[ing]" for the disappearance "of shared beliefs on which literature relied for its effect and meaning" (*The Practical Ruskin*, 113). Catherine Gallagher considers related motives in George Eliot's *Felix Holt* (*The Industrial Reformation of English Fiction: Social Discourse and Narrative Form, 1832–1867* [Chicago: University of Chicago Press, 1985], 240–43).

4 Drawing on "Plato's Pharmacy" in Jacques Derrida's *Dissemination* (trans. Barbara Johnson [Chicago: University of Chicago Press, 1981], 61–171), Casillo argues that writing is perhaps "Ruskin's most troublesome *pharmakon*": "for Plato (and implicitly for Ruskin) writing is a parricide, cutting itself off from its parent or father, the authoritative voice. It is also cut off from external reality since its referent, a physical image, is replaced by a written sign…" ("Parasitism and Capital Punishment," 556–59). Yet as we have also seen, Ruskin regarded his writing as putting him in the presence of his readers, especially his father.

5 Of course in other moments, in other places, a girl can be "like a snake" (36.291). See also Simpson, "The Dream of the Dragon," 25–32.

6 On the other hand, in an 1863 letter to his father Ruskin complained that "Mama and you . . . fed me effeminately and luxuriously . . . but . . . thwarted me in all the earnest fire of passion and life" (36.461). See Dinah Birch, "Ruskin's 'Womanly Mind,'" *Essays in Criticism* 38 (1988), 308–24; and Dennis Baron on "Effeminate Language" in *Grammar and Gender* (New Haven: Yale University Press, 1986), 62–66.

7 Among early studies that contributed terms to the debate about Ruskin and women are Charles T. Dougherty, "Of Ruskin's Gardens," in *Myth and Symbol: Critical Approaches and Applications*, ed. Bernice Slote (Lincoln: University of Nebraska Press, 1963), 141–51; Kate Millett, "The Debate Over Women: Ruskin Versus Mill," *Victorian Studies* 14 (1970), 63–82; Sonstroem, "John

Ruskin and the Nature of Manliness" and "Millett Versus Ruskin: A Defense of Ruskin's 'Of Queens' Gardens,'" *Victorian Studies* 20 (1977), 283–97. Important recent work on the subject includes "John Ruskin and 'Of Queens' Gardens,'" in *The Woman Question: Society and Literature in Britain and America, 1837–1883*, ed. Elizabeth K. Helsinger, Robin Lauterbach Sheets, and William Veeder, 3 vols. (Chicago: University of Chicago Press, 1983; rpt. 1989), 1.77–102; Spear, *Dreams of an English Eden*, 30–34, 59–60, 167–77; Linda M. Austin, "Ruskin and the Ideal Woman," *South Central Review* 4 (1987), 28–39; Birch, "Ruskin's 'Womanly Mind'"; Deborah Epstein Nord, "Mill and Ruskin on the Woman Question Revisited," in *Teaching Literature: What Is Needed Now*, ed. James Engell and David Perkins (Cambridge, Mass.: Harvard University Press, 1988), 73–83; Paul Sawyer, "Ruskin and the Matriarchal Logos," in *Victorian Sages and Cultural Discourse*, 129–41; Richard Dellamora, *Masculine Desire: The Sexual Politics of Victorian Aestheticism* (Chapel Hill: University of North Carolina Press, 1990), 117–29. See also Claudia Nelson, "Sex and the Single Boy: Ideals of Manliness and Sexuality in Victorian Literature for Boys," *Victorian Studies* 32 (1989), 525–50.

8 George Levine locates in the autobiographies of Mill, Darwin, and Trollope patterns of self-deprecation and "casual and relatively unrhetorical styles" which he associates with the contemporary ascendency of empirical science ("Science and Victorian Autobiography: The Arrogance of Humility," MLA Convention, San Francisco, 29 December 1987). See also George Levine, "Dying to Know," *The Victorian Newsletter* 79 (1991), 1–4; Martin J. S. Rudwick, *The Great Devonian Controversy: The Shaping of Scientific Knowledge among Gentlemanly Specialists* (Chicago: University of Chicago Press, 1985), 7; and Stephen Jay Gould, *Time's Arrow, Time's Cycle*, 66–67, 143.

9 On the association of woman with the self-suppressing act of translation, see Homans, *Bearing the Word*, 31, 177–78, 208–12, 217–20, 270; Lori Chamberlain, "Gender and the Metaphorics of Translation," *Signs* 13 (1988), 454–72; Christ, "'The Hero as Man of Letters,'" 25.

8 THE INVENTION OF GENESIS (1885–89)

1 In addition to titles mentioned in subsequent notes, helpful commentary on *Praeterita* includes Timothy Peltason, "Ruskin's Finale: Vision and Imagination in *Praeterita*," *ELH* 57 (1990), 665–84; Henderson, *The Victorian Self*, 65–115; David C. Hanson, "Ruskin's *Praeterita* and Landscape in Evangelical Children's Education," *Nineteenth-Century Literature* 44 (1989), 45–66; Linda M. Austin, "*Praeterita* In the Act of Rebellion," *MLQ* 48 (1987), 42–58; Peterson, *Victorian Autobiography*, 60–90; William Arrowsmith, "Ruskin's Fireflies," in *The Ruskin Polygon*, 198–235; Claudette Kemper Columbus, "Ruskin's *Praeterita* as Thanatography," in *Approaches to Victorian Autobiography*, 109–27.

2 Cf. Hewison, *John Ruskin: The Argument of the Eye*, 40–42; George P. Landow, "Ruskin, Holman Hunt, and Going to Nature to See for Oneself," in *Studies in Ruskin*, 67–70, 82; Susan A. Walsh, "Ruskin's *Praeterita* and the Mediated Self," *Victorians Institute Journal* 19 (1991), 51–55, 67–68. See also Chapter 3 n.27, above.

3 The various accounts of his desire for Turner's pictures suggest an ambivalence about his father, and an effort to control it, that were literally maddening to Ruskin. See 13.475–89, 513–19; 36.125–26, 134–35; and *The Brantwood Diary of John Ruskin*, ed. Helen Gill Viljoen (New Haven: Yale University Press, 1971), 61–79, 105, 134.

4 For an approach different from the one I have taken to motion and motionlessness, see Pierre Fontaney, "Ruskin and Paradise Regained," *Victorian Studies* 12 (1969), 347–56. And see Elizabeth K. Helsinger on the "spiral movement" of *Praeterita* in "Ruskin and the Poets: Alterations in Autobiography," *Modern Philology* 74 (1976), 142–70.

5 Ruskin's first draft of these materials was written in his *Diary* (vol. 3, 138–200) for 22 June–14 July 1885, now in the Beinecke Rare Book and Manuscript Library, Yale University.

6 My own emphasis is different from but (given Ruskin's ambivalence) not inconsistent with George Landow's account of the subordination of art to nature in "Fontainebleau" (*Ruskin* [Oxford: Oxford University Press, 1985], 79–82), and Paul Sawyer's

argument that these "water-works" are also redemptive (*Ruskin's Poetic Argument*, 322–24). See also C. Stephen Finley, "Ruskin and Mimic Engineering," *Nineteenth-Century Literature* 44 (1989), 213–14.

INDEX

"Account of a Tour on the
Continent," 95–97, 114–16,
147
Acland, Henry, 84, 90, 154, 189
"[Adèle, On]," 144
"Adèle, By Moonlight, On," 144
Aeschylus, 148–49
"Agonia," 159–60, 170
Anacreon, 50, 55, 102
Antigone, 72
Aratra Pentelici, 221–22
Architectural Magazine, 83, 166
Architecture, Ruskin on, 68, 93,
117, 150–51, 177–86,
188–89, 197–98, 205
Arnold, Matthew, 227
Arrows of the Chace, 204–06, 223
Art
as produced involuntarily and
in silence, 192–93, 196,
200, 209, 214
as involved in recollections of
juvenilia, 1–3, 9–10, 93,
127–28, 229–38
see also Childhood, Composition,
Form, Gender and Sexuality,
Invention, Language, Writing
Art of England, The, 222–24
"Ascent of the St. Bernard, The,"
68–69, 87–88
Ascham, Roger, 220–21
"Avalanche, The," 133

"[Bed-Time]," 138–39
Berkeley, George, 90
Bible, 174, 195–96
Ruskin's childhood reading of,
17, 63, 209–11, 220, 256
n.4
and science, 74, 81, 172–73,
189
see also Genesis; Jesse; Reuben;
Ruskin, John (bearing of
religion on)
Blackwood's Magazine, 7–8
Brown, W. L., 157–58
Browning, Elizabeth Barrett, 12
Browning, Robert, 12
Bulwer-Lytton, Edward, 15,
162
Byron, George Gordon, Lord, 3,
14, 17, 23, 97, 99, 101,
104–05, 107–08, 110–12,
123, 125, 142, 148, 149,
163, 171, 174–75, 196,
201, 242 n.4

Carlyle, Thomas, 29, 189, 196,
227
Chaos, the science of, see Science
"Charitie," 169
Childhood
the beginnings of creativity in,
1–5, 17–18, 33–34, 35,
138–39, 141–42, 194–96,

Childhood (cont.)
212–13, 217–28, 237, Illus.
14
see also Gender and Sexuality;
Ruskin, John (Drawing and
Designing)
Child prodigies
as separating from mentors,
135–36, 143–44, 153–54,
177, 237–38, 253 n.13
as becoming adults with public
careers, 2–3, 9, 144, 237,
240 n.1
"Christ Church, Oxford," 156
Chronicles of St. Bernard, 69–71,
123–26
see also Velasquez, The Novice
Clarke, James, 113
Clayton, Edward, 156–57,
171–73
Coleridge, Samuel Taylor, 89, 99,
148, 161, 174–75, 202, 251
n.13
Community/Communion, and
the individual, 163–64,
165–69, 170–86, 207–09,
237–38
Composition
difficulty of beginning, 35–36,
37–38, 46, 55–56, 112,
141–42
difficulty of ending, 55–62, 64,
112, 141–42, Illus. 7
modes of in relation to Ruskin's
early education in science,
72–84, 118; in art, 84–93,
114, 118, 121–22, 231–34;

in literature, 93–102,
103–12, 133, 136, 142,
187–88, 194, 208–21,
233–34
process of, as inexplicable, 16,
200
Ruskin's retrospect on
discovering laws of, 231–38
metaphors or figures of curves,
curvature, 22–24, 44–46,
75, 88, 121, 122, Illus. 1, 2,
3; flaming lines, flamboyant,
183–86, 188; gradation, 45,
82–83, 84, 125, 126–27,
178–79, 182–83, 185–86;
"leading lines," 120–22,
127, 185, 216; serpent,
"serpentine mode," 44,
61–62, 106, 109, 147–48,
165, 196–200, 217, 235,
237; spiral lines, 65, 217,
262 n.4; "winding way,"
38–39, 41, 44–45, 54, 61,
106, 107–08, 118, 123,
127, 147, 196–97, 213,
217
see also Form, Gender and
Sexuality, Invention,
Language, Subject, Writing
Cook, E. T., 231
Cruikshank, George, 59
"Crystal-Hunter, The," 146–47

Dale, Thomas, 163
Dante, 192
Darwin, Charles, 179, 180,
182–83, 184, 185, 227

"Despair," 133
Deucalion, 183
   "Living Waves," 198–200, 235
Dickens, Charles, 222
Domecq, Adèle-Clotilde, 14,
      144–47, 150, 153, 155–58,
      159–60, 163, 165, 166,
      169, 170, 173, 175–76,
      177, 183
Dublin University Magazine, 188

Early Geology, 80, Illus. 11, 12
Edgeworth, Maria, 23, 241 n.5,
      244 n.13
Edinburgh Review, The, 88
Elements of Drawing, The, 20, 87,
      121, 127, 176, 200
Eliot, George, 227
"Enquiries on the Causes of the
      Colour of the Water of the
      Rhine," 74
"Essay on Literature," 13–15,
      162–64, 198
"Essay on the Relative Dignity of
      the Studies of Painting and
      Music," 164–65
Ethics of the Dust, The, 185–86, 195,
      236
Evelyn, John, 233, 234
"Evening in Company – May
      18," 144–45

"Facts and Considerations on the
      Strata of Mont Blanc . . . ,"
      75
"Farewell," 147–48
Feigenbaum, Mitchell, 91

Feminine, Ruskin's identification
      with the condition of the, see
      Gender and Sexuality
Feminist perspectives on Ruskin,
      15, 155, 213, 227–28
   see also Gender and Sexuality
Fielding, Copley, 84–85, 87, 88
Fielding, T. H., 88–90
"Flamboyant Architecture of the
      Valley of the Somme, The,"
      183–86, 188–89
Forbes, James, 101
Form, Formal design, 118–27,
      142–43, 147, 177–86,
      188–89, 199, 213–18, 258
      n.12
   the authorization of, 127–28,
      182, 215, 229–38
   see also Composition, Writing
Fors Clavigera, 7, 111, 121, 122,
      142, 154, 169, 199–200,
      207–21, 222, 224–27,
      229–31, 234–35
Friar's Crag, 42–43, 108–10,
      165

Gainsborough, Thomas, 230
Gender and Sexuality, 7–8, 14,
      138–86, 194–95, 197–200,
      201, 203, 207–28, 236–37
   see also Genre(s)
Genesis
   as beginning of Ruskin's
      invention, 2, 123, 221, 229
   as source of biblical references
      to Tree of Knowledge,
      Adam, and serpent, 172–73,

Genesis (cont.)
196–97, 199, 220, 235,
236, 237
Genre(s)
Ruskin's crossing of, 13–15,
41–42, 68–70, 95, 159–60,
160–62, 174–75, 201
in relation to gender and
sexuality, 140–42, 150,
154–55, 160–63, 174–77
Geological Society, 104
"Gipsies, The," 156
"Glenfarg," 30–32, 33, 42
"Glen of Glenfarg," 32
Gothic, the, in nature and art,
115–18, 123–26, 133–34,
136, 150–55, 161, 173,
177–86, 188–89, 196–98,
205–06, 216, 217, 236, 255
n.25
Gray, Euphemia Chalmers (Mrs.
John Ruskin, later Lady John
E. Millais), 180
Gray, Thomas, 47, 136
Grey, Lady Jane, 154, 220–21

Harding, J. D., 44, 87, 248 n.27
Harrison, W. H., 145–46, 158–59
Harry and Lucy, Concluded, 22–24,
27, 59, Illus. 1, 2
Hazlitt, William, 227
Heber, Bishop Reginald, 38–39,
40
Herodotus, 156, 158, 174
"Highland Music," 30
"hill of kinnoul, The," 30, 33, 86
Hogarth, William, 44

Homans, Margaret, 141
Homer, 99

Invention, 34, 122–23, 127, 143,
162, 221–24, 236–38
Ruskin's attitudes towards his
own, 2, 5–7, 9–10, 14–15,
15–16, 17, 36, 37–38, 43,
86, 93, 111–12, 127–28,
131, 170–71, 174–77,
187–206, 207–28, 229–38
expressed and denied by other
nineteenth-century writers,
227
revealed and concealed by
interacting creative and
critical methods, 15–16,
174, 201–06, 227, 230–32
Byron's having "scarcely any,"
175
"artifice of" in Milton, 192
see also Art, Childhood, Gender
and Sexuality
Iteriad; or Three Weeks Among the Lakes,
44–45, 86, 103–04,
106–08, 109–10, 112–14,
139–41, 146, 155, 165, 242
n.3, Illus. 6, 7

Jameson, Robert, 73–74, 80
Jesse, tree of, 233, 236–37
Johnson, Samuel, 101
"Journal of a Tour through France
to Chamouni," 75, 79,
96–98, 99–101, 104–05,
116–17
Joyce, Jeremiah, 23

Kata Phusin (Ruskin's nom de plume), 166, 168
Keats, John, 227
King of the Golden River, The, 169–70
"Kings' Treasuries, Of," 101–02, 189–91

Language
    acquisition of, 3, 66–67, 121, 138–39, 141–43, 187–88, 209–24
    laws of, role of obedience and restraint in, 45, 49–55, 67, 71, 122, 176–77, 210–15, 217–21, 225, 230
    as connecting nature, human life, and artifacts, 70, 71, 72–74, 80–81, 84–85, 89, 93, 99, 103, 104, 122–23, 137, 144–45, 150–52, 172, 187, 188–89, 197–200, 211, 215–18, 230, 232–35
    as visual and verbal, pictorial and scriptorial, 45, 63–66, 73–74, 80–81, 142, 196–200, 210–18, 220, 230–31, 234
    as audible, aural, 19, 26, 30–31, 47–48, 62–64, 66, 74, 196, 210–11, 218, 219
    as material, words and things, 25–26, 58, 62, 63–66, 71, 73–74, 84–85, 99, 188–91, 194, 196–200, 210–18, 220, 249 n.31, Illus. 4, 5, 6, 7, 14
    as signifying, words and
        thoughts, 48, 63, 187–92, 194, 210, 211, 213, 217
    as Adamic, 172, 188–91, 217
    picture writing, 211–18, 220, 237–38, 258 n.12
    as expressive rather than mimetic, 66–67, 122–23, 187, 248 n.27
    as translation, 39, 69–70, 72–74, 77–78, 99, 101–02, 122–23, 205, 223, 227, 234
    alterations in Ruskin's attitudes towards in adulthood, 66, 187–206
    as duplicitous, sinister, unlawful, 188–91, 197–200, 217–18
    political and economic implications of, 203–05, 230–31
    see also Composition, Gender and Sexuality, Invention, Writing
"Last Smile, The," 144
La Touche, Maria, 198
La Touche, Rose, 154, 191, 195, 198, 219–21, 225
Laws of Fésole, The, 218
"Leoni," 146, 153–54, 155, 175, 191
Locke, John, 63
Lockhart, John Gibson, 209
Loudon, J. C., 120
"Love," 133
Lyell, Sir Charles, 80–83, 99, 182–83, 227, Illus. 8, 9, 10

Magazine of Natural History, 70, 99, 120

Malthus, Thomas, 173

Manliness, Masculine authority, *see* Gender and Sexuality

Marcolini, 151–56, 161, 175, 191

Mazzini, Giuseppe, 202

"Memory," 149

Mill, John Stuart, 12

Milton, John, 142, 174, 192

"Mineralogical Dictionary," 73–74

"Mirror, The," 145–46

Modern Painters, 66, 79, 87, 99, 128, 200, 231, 234, 236, 248 n.27

Modern Painters I, 3, 5–9, 15, 37–38, 84, 90–91, 187, 190, 203–04

Modern Painters II, 29, 45, 176, 196–97

Modern Painters III, 12, 14, 15, 17, 35, 42–43, 93–94, 97, 98, 101, 108–09, 188, 235

Modern Painters IV, 10, 12–13, 17, 75–76, 80, 81–82, 121–22, 128, 187–88, 235

Modern Painters V, 34, 123, 126, 127, 176, 203, 235

"Readings in *Modern Painters*," 203–05

"[Moment's Falter, A]," 144–45

Müller, F. Max, 190

Murillo, 7

"Mystery of Life and its Arts, The," 191–96, 259 n.18

"Name, The," 145, 149

"[Nature Untenanted]," 147, 148

Northcote, James, 224–25, frontispiece

Norton, Charles Eliot, 28

"Observations on the Causes which Occasion the Variation of Temperature between Spring and River Water," 120

"Oh dear the feminine gender," 139

Oxford University, 70, 134, 144, 156, 157, 158, 159–60, 169, 173, 203, 226

"Papa whats time," 32

Pater, Walter, 193–94

Pathetic fallacy, 35, 67, 157–58, 188

Plato, 215

"Poesie, To," 59–60

Poetry of Architecture, The, 165–68, 183

Pope, Alexander, 60–62, 99, 101, 142

Praeterita, 6, 9–10, 12, 14, 17–18, 19, 21, 22–23, 29–30, 36, 39, 68, 73, 77–79, 86–87, 92–93, 95, 101, 103, 104, 108, 111–12, 118, 128, 129, 136, 142, 145, 146, 147, 148, 154–55, 156, 161, 162–63, 164, 167, 168, 171, 174, 175–76, 183, 184, 185, 200, 201–2,

204, 209–10, 212, 224–25,
231, 236, 238, 257–58 n.9,
Illus. 1; "The Col de la
Faucille," 77–80, 234;
"Fontainebleau," 93, 171,
231–38
Proserpina, 129–31, 138, 160
Proust, Marcel, 11, 138
Prout, Samuel, 87, 230
"Puppet Show, The," 58–59,
Illus. 4

Queen of the Air, The, 31–32, 122,
125, 197–98, 236–37
"Queens' Gardens, Of," 218–19
Quintilian, 89

"Remembrance," 144
"Reply to 'Blackwood's' Criticism
of Turner, A," 6–8, 14,
161–62, 163–64, 171
Reuben, Ruskin's identification
with the curse of, 200, 218
"Revenge," 133
Reynolds, Sir Joshua, 5
Richardson, Mary, 36, 45, 49, 51,
52, 138–39
Richardson, Samuel, 169–70
Roberts, David, 87
Rogers, Samuel, 95, 125
Romanticism
Ruskin's relation to, 13–14, 94,
103–12, 140–42, 146,
148–51, 155–56, 170–71,
174–75, 176
reflexivity and self-projection,
6–7, 14, 70–71, 104,

110–12, 145, 148–50,
151–52, 156–58, 162, 164,
170–71, 185, 188–89
reverie, 96–99, 114, 147
see also Byron, Coleridge,
Gothic, Hazlitt, Keats, Scott,
Shelley, Wordsworth
Rousseau, Jean-Jacques, 3
Rowbotham, John, 50, 240 n.2
Runciman, Charles, 36–37,
85–87, 114, 240 n.2
Ruskin, John
precocity, 11–12, 17, 19–20,
24, 239 n.6, 240 n.1
representations of his own age,
5-6, 11, 201, 205, 223–28
artistic development in relation
to mother and father, see
Margaret Ruskin, John James
Ruskin
artistic development in relation
to gender and sexuality, see
Gender and Sexuality
first tutors of, 240–41 n.2, see
also Rowbotham, Runciman
early education in science, art,
literature, see Composition
judgments of poetry and
decision to give up writing
it, 13–15, 60, 107–08,
140–41, 162, 174–77, 202
bearing of religion on the
writing of, 27, 32, 38, 70,
71, 74, 81, 93–94, 95, 98,
123, 129–30, 136, 169–70,
174, 189, 195–200, 233,
235–37, see also Bible

Ruskin, John (cont.)
  as "word painter," 191, 237,
    256–57 n.7
  comic and serio-comic modes
    of, 103–04, 107, 110–12,
    175, 220, 225, 232–33
  identification with girls and
    young women, 153–55,
    201, 207, 214, 217–28, see
    also, Gender and Sexuality
  madness of, 230, 262 n.3
  WORKS, see individual titles
  DRAWING AND DESIGNING OF,
    22–24, 30, 36–37, 44,
    64–65, 68, 84–87, 90,
    201–02, 203, 230–38; harrys
    new road, 22–23, Illus. 1;
    harrys river, 23–24, Illus. 2; My
    First tree! from nature, 20, 24,
    Illus. 3; "The Puppet Show,"
    58–59, Illus. 4; 1828 letter
    to his father, 64, Illus. 5;
    Iteriad, title and finis pages,
    64, Illus. 6, 7; Early Geology,
    80, Illus. 11, 12; Traceries from
    Caen, Bayeux, Rouen, and Beauvais,
    181, Illus. 13
Ruskin, John James, 7, 20, 21,
    45, 47–50, 52–54, 55,
    64–66, 110–11, 133–44,
    149, 154, 155–60, 169–70,
    171, 173–77, 185, 190–91,
    199–200, 204, 213, 217,
    218, 223–27, 230, 232,
    235, 236, 237–38, 243 n.7,
    243 n.8, 260 n.4, 260 n.6,
    262 n.3

Ruskin, Margaret, 19, 21–22, 45,
    48, 49, 51, 57, 62–64, 66,
    110, 134–36, 138–44, 160,
    175–77, 185, 191, 204,
    209–15, 218–21, 223–27,
    230, 235, 236, 237–38, 243
    n.7, 256 n.4

St. George's Company, 207–08
Saussure, Horace Bénedict de,
    76–80, 84, 97, 99
Science/Natural history, 71–73,
    87, 90, 92, 118, 227
  mineralogical and geological,
    68, 69, 73–84, 88, 90–92,
    150, 177–78, 182–83, 199
  biological (reproductive),
    170–73
  evolutionary, 179, 180,
    182–83, 184, 185
  of chaos, 15, 91, 248 n.26
"scotland, on," 28, 86
Scott, Sir Walter, 3, 17, 93, 142,
    162, 185, 201, 209, 213,
    214, 218
"Scythian Banquet Song, A,"
    158–59, 176
"Scythian Guest, The," 158
Serpent, Serpentine, see
    Composition (metaphors or
    figures of)
Seven Lamps of Architecture, The, 67,
    79, 177–86, 188, 222, Illus. 13
Severn, Lily, 217, 218, 220,
    222–23, Illus. 14
Shakespeare, William, 161, 163,
    202

Hamlet, 47–48, 136, 164

King Lear, 154

Much Ado About Nothing, 49

Romeo and Juliet, 161

Shelley, Percy Bysshe, 3, 6, 71, 98, 104, 111, 145, 148–49, 151, 153, 161, 171, 174–75

"Shipwreck, The," 133–34, 137

"Skiddaw and Derwent Water, On," 32–33

Smith, Adam, 63, 90

"Song," 147

"Spring," 28

"Steam-engine, the," 24–28, 51

Stones of Venice, The, 20, 71, 79, 115–16, 117, 118, 126, 167, 182–83, 184, 196–97, 215, 217, 223–24

Storm-Cloud of the Nineteenth Century, The, 235

Subject (matter)

want of a, 35–38, 46, 53–54, 58, 122, 142

excess of, 43–44, 49, 51–54, 57, 131, 137, 138, 141–43, 149, 213

see also Composition

"Tears of Psammenitus, The," 156–58

Tennyson, Alfred Lord, 12, 189

Tintoretto, 214

Tooke, John Horne, 63

"To What Properties in Nature is it Owing that the Stones in Buildings . . . Become Indurated . . . ?," 74–75

Trench, R. C., 190

Turner, Joseph Mallord William, 54, 75–76, 87, 90–91, 95, 118, 203, 213, 214, 230, 232, 234, 235

Ruskin's first defense of, 6–8, 161–62

art of as female love object, 7

Two Paths, The, 189

Unto this Last, 203–04

Velasquez, The Novice, 123–26, 150–51, 153, 155

see also Chronicles of St. Bernard

Virgil, 236

"Wales," 28–30

"Was There Death Before Adam Fell, In Other Parts of Creation?," 172–73, 237

Water-Colour Society, 84, 87, 88

Wedderburn, Alexander, 204–05, 231

West, Thomas, 113

Withers, Charlotte, 164

Wordsworth, William, 3, 17, 29, 93, 98, 104, 108, 109, 111, 113, 141, 174–75, 193, 194, 196, 256 n.5

Ruskin's differences from in the treatment of childhood, 4–6, 11–12

Ruskin's differences from in defining the poetic process, 14

Writing
  distinctions between creative
    and critical, fiction and non-
    fiction, 2, 123, 145–46,
    203, 230–31, 233–34,
    237–38
  as physical act and object,
    handwriting, 63–66, 73–74,
    84–85, 121, 122, 184,
    196–98, 200, 210–18, 220,
    230–31, 233–34, Illus. 4, 5,
6, 7
  picture writing, *see* Language
  Ruskin's criticism of his own,
    see Invention
  Fors or force of, 229–30
  history of Egyptian and Greek,
    216–17
  see also Art, Composition,
    Language, Subject

Young, G. M., 202